Constituency Representation in Congress

Congressional representation requires that legislators be aware of the interests of constituents in their districts and behave in ways that reflect the wishes of their constituents. But of the many constituents in their districts, who do legislators in Washington actually see, and who goes unseen? Moreover, how do these perceptions of constituents shape legislative behavior? This book answers these fundamental questions by developing a theory of legislative perception that leverages insights from cognitive psychology. Legislators are shown to see only a few constituents in their district on a given policy, namely those who donate to their campaigns and contact the legislative office, and fail to see many other relevant constituents. Legislators are also subsequently more likely to act on behalf of the constituents they see, while important constituents not seen by legislators are rarely represented in the policy-making process. Overall, legislators' views of constituents are limited and flawed, and even well-meaning legislators cannot represent their constituents if they do not accurately see who is in their district.

Kristina C. Miler is currently Assistant Professor of Political Science at the University of Illinois. She received her Ph.D. from the University of Michigan. Her research has been published in the *Journal of Politics, Legislative Studies Quarterly,* and *Political Psychology.* She has received funding from the National Science Foundation and the Dirksen Congressional Center, among other sources.

For Todd

Constituency Representation in Congress

The View from Capitol Hill

KRISTINA C. MILER
University of Illinois

CAMBRIDGE
UNIVERSITY PRESS

CAMBRIDGE
UNIVERSITY PRESS

32 Avenue of the Americas, New York NY 10013-2473, USA

Cambridge University Press is part of the University of Cambridge.

It furthers the University's mission by disseminating knowledge in the pursuit of
education, learning and research at the highest international levels of excellence.

www.cambridge.org
Information on this title: www.cambridge.org/9781107677005

First published 2010
First paperback edition 2013

A catalogue record for this publication is available from the British Library

Library of Congress Cataloguing in Publication data
Miler, Kristina C., 1974–
    Constituency representation in Congress : the view from Capitol Hill /
    Kristina C. Miler.
        p.   cm.
    Includes bibliographical references and index.
    ISBN 978-0-521-76540-4 (hardback)
    1. United States. Congress – Constituent communication.   2. Representative
    government and representation – United States.   I. Title.
JK1131.M55 2010
324.73'074–dc22   2010033396

ISBN 978-0-521-76540-4 Hardback
ISBN 978-1-107-67700-5 Paperback

Contents

Acknowledgments

There are numerous people to thank, since this book has benefited from the advice and friendship of many.

A large debt is due to the members of my dissertation committee at the University of Michigan, where this project began. Rick Hall, Ken Kollman, Don Kinder, and Norbert Schwarz provided invaluable feedback from the very beginning of the endeavor. Their different perspectives pushed me to examine the question of legislative perceptions from multiple angles, and the book is undoubtedly better for their suggestions. I am especially thankful to Rick Hall, who has worn the many hats of mentor, enthusiast, editor, and friend. I have benefited greatly from his help in learning the craft of elite interviewing, his comments on later additions to the manuscript, and his unflagging enthusiasm for the project.

This project also bears the imprint of a number of other people who contributed to this book in direct and indirect ways. Ron Rapoport and Larry Evans have provided advice, encouragement, and friendship in the years since I first sat in their classrooms, and I am grateful to them for their support. Matt Beckmann deserves many thanks for his friendship and thoughtful feedback on the project from the on-the-ground research on Capitol Hill to the final drafts. While at the University of Michigan, I also benefited from the helpful suggestions of many, including Scott Allard, Adam Berinsky, Doug Dion, John Jackson, Susan Moffitt, Irfan Noorudin, and Nick Winter. I thank my colleagues at the University of Illinois, in particular Scott Althaus, Bill Bernhard, Brian Gaines, and Pete Nardulli, who offered valuable feedback on this project in its later stages. I especially thank Jim Kuklinski, who read the entire manuscript, and Tracy Sulkin, who shared data, advice, and a sympathetic ear along the way of turning this project into a book. Lastly, thanks are due to a number of colleagues at other institutions, in particular Jeff Berry, Richard Fenno, David Rohde, and Chuck Shipan, who also provided helpful feedback on the project.

In addition, I appreciate the helpful assistance of numerous staff members at the University of Michigan and the University of Illinois: Margarita Ham, Lili Kivisto, Michelle Spornhauer, Brenda Stamm, and Delinda Swanson. I also benefited from financial support provided by the National Science Foundation (under Grant Number 0213959), the Gerald R. Ford Fellowship Program, the University of Michigan, the University of Illinois, and the Cline Center for Democracy. I also thank Lew Bateman, Anne Lovering Rounds, Emily Spangler, and the reviewers at Cambridge University Press for their excellent assistance.

This project would not have been possible without the cooperation of the many legislators and legislative staff members in the U.S. House of Representatives who agreed to participate in the research. Although their identities remain confidential, their impact on this project is immeasurable. I am grateful for their willingness to grant interviews as well as for their insights and candor. My time spent on Capitol Hill researching this book was stimulating and rewarding due in large part to the people with whom I spent my days talking. It is my hope that the book reads true to them.

Thanks are also due to a wonderful circle of friends, including many with Michigan ties, whose contributions to this project have been indirect but invaluable. I also thank the Deucher-Rubin family – J. D., Max, Christine, and Steve – for providing levity and good humor. And Phoebe Avery, Cameron Ishaq, Laura Cohn, and Peter Spiegel have my thanks for making Washington, D.C., a home away from home.

I thank my parents, Veronica and Josef Miler, for their unwavering support. They instilled an interest in politics, a belief in equality, and a sense that the right path is often not the straight and well-traveled one. I also thank Michelle, Joe, Katie, and Alison Miler for keeping me grounded in the world of things not involving political science. My grandparents, Evelyn Bruman, Sylva Milerova, and Josef Miler, taught me by example about perseverance, dedication, and being true to oneself; these are lessons for which I am deeply grateful. I also thank my second family, Norma and Gary Allee, and Teresa, Paul, Mara, Max, and Alexandra Bridwell, for their encouragement and support.

Lastly, I thank my husband Todd for his enthusiasm, patience, and support. Anything I write here only scratches the surface of my appreciation for all the conversations about this project from the earliest stages to the very last edits. Not only has it been far more enjoyable as a result, but the book is better for his advice and tireless effort. It is certainly true that together the happiness has been doubled and the difficulties halved. I dedicate this book to him.

The Unanswered Question of Legislative Perceptions

In his influential study of House members in their districts, Richard Fenno asked: "What does the representative see when he or she goes home to look at the represented?" He then followed this question by asking about the effects of a legislator's view of his district: "How does what he or she sees affect his or her representational activity? What can we learn, from this perspective, about the nature, the quality, and the problem of representation in this country?"[1] Although Fenno posed these questions from the district vantage point and explored the ways in which members interact with constituents when they are in the district, he also called attention to the importance of considering how members see their constituents from Washington, D.C. Legislators spend the majority of their time in Washington, where they make countless decisions about what actions to take or not to take, and they do this with their constituents "in mind." As a result, the questions Fenno posed when examining legislators in their districts can be restated in terms of legislators in Washington: When a representative considers how to best represent the interests of his district in the policy-making process, who does he see back in the district? Furthermore, how does his view of the district influence his representational activity? This book argues that legislative perceptions of constituents are at the heart of the answers to these questions.

The congressional literature has devoted much attention to issues of constituency representation. As part of this tradition, an earlier generation of scholars highlighted the importance of legislative

---

[1] Fenno (1978, 233).

perceptions by calling attention to legislators' general image of the district (Dexter 1957), their beliefs about the "state of nature" in their district (Fiorina 1974), and their stylized characterizations of the district (e.g., Fenno 1978; Kingdon 1967; Miller and Stokes 1963). These scholars argued that understanding how legislators and their staff see the district is essential to understanding legislators' voting decisions, their political priorities, and their campaign strategies.

However, as the congressional literature expanded, attention to legislative perception surprisingly did not. Instead, the literature began to focus largely on explaining congressional representation in terms of responsiveness to the median district preference. As Jewell (1983, 321) writes: "there is an intermediate variable – the legislator's perception of constituency opinion – that assumes so much importance in policy responsiveness that it should be dealt with squarely; in fact, it is a logical place to begin." Or as Fenno (2006, 11) says when looking back on his experiences traveling with legislators:

> The insight I drew from my experiences was this: that the constituency an elected representative represents is, to an important degree, the constituency in the mind's eye of the representative. In the study of representation, therefore, *perception matters a lot*. From this view, a "constituency" becomes more complex than a set of census statistics – more even than the data in the pioneering *Almanac of American Politics*. A constituency is, to an important degree, what the elected representative thinks it is.

As he did thirty years ago, Fenno reminds us of the central challenge facing students of representation. To consider any question about congressional representation, we first need to identify what is in "the mind's eye" of the representative when he legislates, and to explain why he sees what he does. However, there is little guidance about how to proceed in this important area of inquiry. This book takes up the challenge of seeing the district as the legislator does by proposing a theory of legislative perception rooted in the cognitive processes by which individuals use information to assess the world around them and then examining the impact of these perceptions on how Members of Congress represent their constituents.

Perception, therefore, refers to how legislators see their districts. This definition is consistent with both the psychology literature and congressional scholars' references to legislators' mental pictures of their districts. Legislative perceptions of constituents are *not* conscious decisions about how to act, but rather they reflect legislators' views of who comprises the constituency with respect to specific policy issues. Put differently, perceptions of the district are what legislators see in their mind's eyes when they look at their districts. These perceptions, however, are neither a perfect nor a representative reflection of the constituents actually in their districts. Moreover, the cognitive processes that structure how legislative perceptions of constituents are formed are not politically neutral. Rather, perceptions have the effect of systematically biasing which constituents are seen – and which are not seen – by legislators as they attend to policy on Capitol Hill. These flawed perceptions affect legislative behavior because legislators are more likely to act on behalf of those constituents they perceive in the district.

How legislators perceive the constituents in their district has both normative and substantive implications for constituency representation in Congress. First, legislative perceptions can be evaluated in terms of the normative ideals about representative democracy, which suggest that legislators should at least be aware of the constituents they represent. As John Stuart Mill (1861) espoused, the representative should "make present" in the legislative body the range of constituency views and interests evident among the citizens. Evidence that certain constituents are systematically less likely to be seen by legislators than others makes Mill's admonition hard to implement for basic reasons that he did not anticipate. Simply put, a representative's democratic intentions may not be enough to ensure constituency representation. If the cognitive mechanisms of representation create distortions and biases, then legislators will fall short of this democratic ideal without noticing it. Second, the importance of legislative perceptions also can be assessed in light of their impact on legislative activity on Capitol Hill. Flawed perceptions of the constituency may affect the daily decisions legislators and their staff make about what positions to take and how to allocate their time and energy in the policy-making process on behalf of their district.

Two important policy issues, health policy and natural resources policy, are the substantive focus of the empirical investigation of legislative perceptions of their constituents. Both of these issues are prominent in the contemporary national political dialogue, and Congress has played an important role in shaping them. Health policy and natural resources policy also encompass a range of specific issues including high-profile federal programs like Medicare, contentious proposals like oil exploration on protected lands in Alaska, and technical programs like physician payment formulas or scientific standards for clean air. These policy areas make up a significant part of the congressional agenda, raising issues on which legislators frequently must act on behalf of their constituents. By examining legislative perceptions and constituency representation in the context of these two important areas, this study both sheds light on two of the major policy issues of the day and also situates legislative perceptions in the real world of Capitol Hill. In sum, understanding legislators' perceptions of their constituents may change both our positive theories of legislative behavior and our normative assessments of the quality of political representation afforded citizens.

TWO PRIMARY QUESTIONS

The first of two key questions addressed throughout this book is: What factors affect how legislators perceive their districts? With approximately 700,000 citizens in each U.S. House district and a wide-ranging congressional agenda, it is unrealistic to expect legislative offices to see the interests of all constituent on every issue taken up on Capitol Hill. Furthermore, the cognitive psychology literature tells us that it is unrealistic to expect legislative offices to see a neutral or representative subset of all the constituents in the district. The development of an information-based theory of legislative perception, therefore, provides a foundation from which to examine why legislators systematically perceive some constituents over others.

The second question goes to the policy-relevant consequences of the cognitive processes identified: How do perceptions of their districts shape legislators' behavior on Capitol Hill? We need to know which constituents legislators see – and which they fail to see – in order to explain their behavior. The overarching concern is that flawed perceptions affect legislators' decisions about the actions they take in Congress in the name of their constituents. There are numerous ways in which legislators act on behalf of their districts, and this book focuses on bill sponsorship, participation, and voting. The biases in legislative perceptions of their constituents shape these behaviors in ways that cannot be explained solely by party politics, institutional structure, or electoral calculations. Rather, rational choice approaches should incorporate complementary insights from psychological approaches to sufficiently account for legislators' actions. The systematic impact of legislative perceptions on legislative behavior provides evidence that biases in perception become biases in representation. Overall, these two questions constitute the core focus of this book and provide a proverbial "roadmap" of the theoretical discussions and empirical analyses to follow.

Explaining Legislative Perceptions: The Accessibility Heuristic

To answer the first question of who is seen by legislators when they look at their districts, the theory of legislative perception developed here focuses on how individuals use information when assessing the interests of constituents in the district. As a general matter, the congressional environment is characterized by time pressure, multiple sources of information, and competing expectations, all of which lead legislators to act in a boundedly rational manner, or as "cognitive misers" to use Simon's (1985) phrase, in order to fulfill their responsibilities (e.g., Bianco 1994; Fiorina 1974; Jones 2001; Kingdon 1989; R. Smith 1984). Just as individuals use cognitive shortcuts, or heuristics, to simplify their environment when using information and making decisions, legislators are subject to the same cognitive limitations and employ efficiency-gaining shortcuts (see Jones 1994; Jones and Baumgartner 2005; Kingdon 1977; Matthews and Stimson 1975).

This book argues that the use of cognitive heuristics informs constituency representation in politically consequential ways. In order to make decisions that reflect their constituents, legislators and their staff must first assess the interests of their constituency. Legislators do not conduct exhaustive information searches about constituents in the district when making these judgments, nor do they approximate a process of random sampling to infer what constituents want. Rather, legislators and their staff rely on the information that comes to mind most easily. This notion of information accessibility is rooted in the cognitive psychology literature where scholars long have examined individuals' propensity to conduct truncated information searches and to rely on accessible information when making judgments (e.g., Higgins et al. 1977; Markus and Zajonc 1985; Tversky and Kahneman 1973, 1974). Reliance on accessible information is generally considered to be an efficient adaptation to complex environments such as Capitol Hill, but scholars also note that it can result in flawed and biased assessments if certain types of information are systematically more (or less) accessible than others (e.g., Kahneman and Tversky 1973; Nisbett and Ross 1980).

This perceptual framework is adapted from the psychology literature to the congressional context and is used to examine the likelihood that a legislative office will see specified constituents in the district. The data provide strong evidence that information about constituents that is more accessible shapes legislative perceptions of the district. On the other hand, when information is systematically less accessible, legislators are less likely to perceive those constituents, and the result is an incomplete and biased view of the district. The impact of the accessibility heuristic on Capitol Hill is illustrated by the finding that information about sub-constituencies who have more resources or who are more active in contacting the legislative office is more accessible than information about other relevant constituents. As a result, resource-rich and active constituents are significantly more likely to shape legislative perceptions of the district.

In short, legislators and their staff do not see all, or even a large percentage, of the relevant constituents to whom the issue at hand is important. This ultimately can lead to many constituents' interests going unrepresented. The incompleteness of perceptions is especially striking when one considers that legislators' awareness of the relevant interests in the district is a very low threshold for constituency representation. The criteria for providing representation here is not whether legislators take costly political action, but rather whether legislators can identify that certain issues are relevant to certain constituents.

That resource-rich constituents are more likely to be perceived by legislators is democratically discouraging because it reveals that some constituents are favored over others when it comes to being represented by their elected legislator. The evidence here suggests that when resource-rich constituents expend their financial resources, they gain "mental access" to their legislator. This notion of mental access draws on the fact that contributions increase the accessibility of information about constituents, and more accessible information is more influential when legislators consider the interests of their district. Mental access provides a prominent place in legislators' image of the district they represent. An important implication, then, is that money influences congressional representation in a more subtle, and arguably more insidious, way than often assumed in conventional stories of vote buying in Congress. Moreover, the notion of mental access helps to reconcile the popular belief that money matters in congressional politics with the mixed evidence in the political science literature of such influence (e.g., Grenzke 1989; Hall and Wayman 1990; Wawro 2001; Wright 1985, 1996).

The finding that active constituents are more likely to be perceived by legislators can be assessed in light of the competing interpretations of the role of citizen-initiated contact. On the one hand, this finding appears normatively less troublesome than the finding concerning resource-rich constituents. A representative democratic political system requires that constituents participate in their government, and constituents who are active are simply fulfilling their civic responsibility. As a result, information heuristics that advantage constituents who participate, and disadvantage those who do not, seem consistent with democratic norms. Accordingly, the fact that control of the congressional-constituency relationship is located, at least in part, in the hands of constituents is desirable. On the other hand, the fact that active constituents are favored in congressional representation raises significant normative concerns if the literature on bias in citizen participation is taken into account. Concluding that active constituents should be more prominent in legislators' perceptions of their district ignores the host of undemocratic barriers to participation in American politics, including inequalities in political resources and political mobilization (e.g., Kollman 1998; Rosenstone and Hansen 1993; Schattschneider 1960; Verba, Schlozman, and Brady 1995). If some constituents are systematically less likely to participate by contacting their legislator, then the relationship between constituent activity and legislative perception of constituents in the district is plagued by an underlying bias that weakens constituency representation. In fact, the bias of mobilization raises normative concerns that are arguably similar to those raised when considering the influence of money on legislative perceptions.

Explaining Legislative Behavior: The Effects of Perceptions

The second question focuses on the impact of legislative perceptions on legislators' actions on behalf of their constituents. Legislators are sent to Congress by the voters to represent their interests, and legislators consistently call attention to the need to represent their constituents in Washington. This is evident in the advice they receive when beginning their careers and first confront the challenges of representing their constituency. One House member interviewed recounts the advice his mentor gave him when he first came to Capitol Hill concerning the importance of acting on behalf of the constituents in the district: "He said to remember that no one else represents your district. ... They elected you. You're their voice."[2] Another House member highlights similar advice he received from a trusted advisor to focus on taking actions for the district, or as he put it, "you're in the representation business."[3] These comments underscore the importance of constituency representation to

---

[2] Personal interview with author.
[3] Personal interview with author.

Members of Congress, as well as hint at the challenges of representing multiple constituency interests within a district.

Scholars, too, recognize the incentives that drive constituency representation and incorporate them in their theories of legislative behavior. As Mayhew (1974) famously argues, Members of Congress have good reason to be attentive to the interests of their constituents because of the strong electoral connection. Mayhew's logic has had a powerful effect on the study of legislative behavior and has led congressional scholars to conclude that "constituents matter." In recent scholarship, political scientists reach this conclusion largely by relying on theories of legislative behavior informed by traditions in economics and spend little time looking to psychology for explanations (but see Jones 1994, 2001; Jones and Baumgartner 2005; Kathlene 1994). This book takes the psychology of representation seriously in order to explore a distinct and important mechanism by which "constituents matter" for legislative activity – perceptions.

This is not to say, however, that rational choice explanations for legislative behavior are dismissed, but rather that strategic behavior is considered alongside cognitive psychology-based arguments, including in the analyses presented in Chapters 5, 6, and 7. The inclusion of both psychological and rational choice theories highlights the possibilities to bridge these distinct approaches (see also Bianco 1998; Kinder 1993; Quattrone and Tversky 1988; Turner 2000). As scholars have noted, a psychological approach is valuable to political scientists when used "to supplement (rather than supplant) explanations at other levels,"[4] since "being integrated with cognitive science"[5] can improve upon the plausibility of pure rational choice theory. A key implication of this research is that legislators' perceptions of their district set the stage for later strategic decisions that rational legislators make. Consequently, attention to perceptions is logically consistent with rational choice models of legislative behavior. Psychological and rational choice approaches to legislative behavior are not mutually exclusive, and ignoring either approach leads to an incomplete understanding of legislative behavior.

As Fenno (2006, 205) writes, "the politicians' perception of the constituency is crucial" for understanding different types of legislative behavior. Legislators' decisions in Washington about how to represent constituents in the district are determined by the constituents they see,

---

[4] Kanwisher (1989, 673).
[5] Turner (2000, 279).

and do not see, in their district. One venue in which perceptions can affect legislative behavior is participation in the committee and floor debate of a bill. Before legislation can come before the House for a floor vote, legislators can participate in the committee markup, committee hearings, and floor debate by asking questions and making statements to express the interests and concerns of their constituents (Evans 1991b; Hall 1987, 1996). Participation in the policy debate allows a legislator to demonstrate to his constituents that he is aware of their interest in the issue and provides tangible evidence of constituency representation. It also affects whether he will influence legislation in tangible ways that promote their interests (Hall 1992).

However, legislators do not participate on behalf of all interested constituents in their districts. Legislators are more likely to participate on behalf of constituents whom they see when they look at their districts and are unlikely to voice the interests of those relevant constituents they do not see. This relationship between perception and participation persists even when alternate explanations are taken into account, including institutional, electoral, and partisan considerations. Which constituents legislators perceive in the district, therefore, directly affects how legislators participate in the policy-making process by stifling the concerns of unseen constituents and amplifying the concerns of those constituents with mental access to the legislator.

Legislative perceptions not only clarify which constituents a legislator sees when looking at the district but also capture a legislator's overall image of the district he represents. Perceptions of the district as a whole vary along two important dimensions, completeness and balance, such that some legislators perceive a much more diverse district than other legislators. Variation in these overall district perceptions affects legislative activity, including the introduction of legislation on health policy and natural resources policy, as well as the votes cast on these issues. Introducing bills requires an investment of a legislator's time and resources, but it also demonstrates a legislator's attentiveness to issues of interest to constituents (e.g., Fenno 1973; Hall 1996; Schiller 1995; Sulkin 2005). Legislators who perceive a more complete district – that is, who see a greater number of relevant constituents in their district – sponsor more legislation in these two policy areas than those who do not. Additionally, legislators who see constituents on both sides of the policy debate in their district are more likely to introduce legislation on that issue. This finding is consistent with the psychology-based theory of representation put forth here but is counterintuitive when viewed through the lens of an incentive-based logic (e.g., Arnold 1990; Fiorina 1974; Hall 1996). Legislators who see competing constituency interests might be expected to be less active in order to avoid alienating part of their district, but in fact, these legislators sponsor more legislation than their colleagues. In short, legislators do not shy away from the challenge of representing a complex district.

Legislative perceptions of the totality of the district also affect legislators' votes. Voting records are visible and heavily studied summaries of the actions a legislator takes on behalf of his constituents on Capitol Hill. The collection of votes a legislator casts on health or natural resources legislation, therefore, should reflect the collection of constituency interests a legislator perceives in his district on those issues. But conventional theories do not tell us how legislators will navigate votes when representing a diverse constituency. In fact, legislators who perceive a balanced district with constituents on both sides of the issue have a more moderate voting record than their colleagues who see constituents on only one side of the policy debate. This is especially striking when considering that the moderating effect of a balanced district perception exists even when controlling for the potential effects of party, institution, and electoral politics. When looking at issue-specific roll-call voting records, then, legislators are quite responsive to their districts as they perceive them, not simply how the political scientist measures them.

Taken as a whole, this book provides unique evidence of the relationship between legislative perceptions and legislative behavior. Legislators are responsive to the district they see and act in ways that represent their perception of constituency interests. On the one hand, this is good news for constituency representation in Congress. The adage that "constituents matter" for legislative behavior can be rephrased as "perceived constituents matter." On the other hand, legislative perceptions are flawed and favor active and resource-rich subconstituencies at the expense of equally relevant subconstituencies who lack these political and monetary resources. Moreover, these biases are amplified through legislators' actions. Legislators are more likely to see the subset of advantaged constituents in the district and their actions reflect this perception. This is not to say that legislators consciously choose to act on behalf of active and resource-rich subconstituencies. Rather, legislators act in good faith on behalf of the district they see, but the district they see is a misperception of the collection of relevant constituent interests in their district. Consequently, inequalities make their way into congressional representation not through outright favoritism or unethical dealings, but through a much more subtle, and nefarious, path – legislators' perceptions of the constituents they represent. This research, therefore, suggests that scholars cannot neglect legislative perceptions if the goal of congressional research is to explain legislative behavior completely and accurately.

CONTRIBUTIONS OF THE STUDY

These findings concerning the nature of legislative perceptions and their impact on legislative behavior constitute the core contributions of the book. However, this study also makes several broader contributions to the study of congressional representation. These additional contributions arise because the central questions raised in this book are arrived at by conceptualizing congressional representation in a particular way.

The first feature of the study that contributes to the broader congressional literature is the focus on the cognitive processes employed by legislators and their staff when representing constituents on Capitol Hill. The arguments and evidence presented here demonstrate the need for a psychology of representation. Fenno's (2006) call to return to legislative perceptions coincides with the increasing use of political psychology in studies of citizen behavior in American politics in both the academic and popular presses (e.g., Lakoff 2008; Westen 2007). The growth of the political psychology subfield reflects political scientists' increasing interest in unpacking the proverbial "black box" of human behavior. While the vast majority of this literature focuses on citizens, the cognitive psychology literature also can illuminate the way that legislative elites make decisions in the policy process (see Jones 1994, 2001; Jones and Baumgartner 2005). By drawing upon the cognitive psychology tradition and theories of information processing, this book provides a unique access point to unlocking the puzzle of constituency representation. The emphasis on understanding the microfoundations of legislative perception and behavior are consistent with the rational choice tradition in the congressional literature, as well as the interdisciplinary tradition in political science more broadly. However, rather than turning to economic theory to inform the conceptualization of constituency representation, this book draws on psychological theory to gain insight into legislative perceptions of constituents and the implications of these perceptions for congressional representation. Focusing on how individuals process and use information moves beyond the simplified, yet unrealistic, assumptions of classic rational choice models to provide a more realistic model of how legislative elites make judgments. Issues of strategic behavior are no doubt an important part of the story of legislative behavior, yet they are reconsidered using this new framework in the empirical analyses that follow.

The second contribution to the broader congressional literature is the dyadic conceptualization of congressional representation. The extant literature generally speaks of the representative relationship as existing between a legislator and a district, but this specification assumes that legislators represent a single district entity.[6] The district is commonly conceived of as the district's median voter, although it is sometimes specified as the interests of the legislator's supporters or co-partisans (e.g., Hurley and Hill 2003; Wright 1989). At the early stages of research, such simplifications are reasonable, if not necessary, given the complexity of congressional representation. But their continued use limits our ability to account for the considerable variation in constituents' interests within the district, and consequently can only roughly approximate constituency representation as practiced on Capitol Hill. In contrast, the district as envisioned here contains a number of subconstituencies, or informal groups of constituents with shared interests in a given issue, which may or may not get heard. The structure of the representative relationship therefore occurs between legislative office-*subconstituency* dyads, or pairings. Legislators represent multiple subconstituencies within their districts on any given issue and therefore can have multiple representative relationships. This dyadic model of congressional representation better captures the challenges of constituency representation and allows scholars to theorize and empirically examine questions about *which* constituents are represented in Congress.

The third contribution of this study lies in its illustration of the advantages of using multiple methodological approaches when studying the U.S. Congress. Using a combination of quantitative and qualitative analyses, this book addresses questions about legislative perceptions that were raised decades ago yet remain unanswered. The analytical insights in the following chapters are based on in-depth interviews conducted with legislative staff members in eighty-one offices in the U.S. House of Representatives during the 107th Congress (2001–2002). In

---

[6] In addition, some scholars focus on macro-level representation wherein the representative relationship exists between the chamber (or Congress) as a whole and the national population (see Adler and Lapinski 2006; Erikson, MacKuen, and Stimson 2002; Page and Shapiro 1983).

addition, personal interviews conducted with a half-dozen U.S. House Members confirm the accounts provided by staff members and provide additional personal insights into the challenges of constituency representation. These interviews are the source of unique data used in the statistical analyses and in illustrative cases. Qualitative and quantitative approaches are also combined in the examination of the content of legislative participation on behalf of constituents on health policy and natural resources policy. In addition, multiple data sources are used throughout the book, and information drawn from primary sources and secondary sources, including congressional transcripts, the *Congressional Record*, Federal Election Commission records, and U.S. Census reports complement the interview-based data. The combination of in-depth personal interviews, detailed studies of important policy areas, and careful statistical analyses provide numerous illustrations of the impact of legislative perceptions on constituency representation.

OVERVIEW OF THE BOOK

This book bridges the classic congressional focus on constituency representation with innovations from the psychology literature to develop a new theory of legislative perception rooted in theories of information. Furthermore, the book examines the nature of legislative perceptions, establishes why legislators see the district as they do, and provides careful and thorough evidence that these perceptions affect legislative behavior in the U.S. House of Representatives. The bias in congressional representation is *not* the result of conventional exchange theory or political corruption; rather it reflects the limitations of legislative perceptions and the challenges of representing a complex constituency.

The book takes up the two core questions of constituency representation and unfolds in the following fashion. Chapter 2 examines constituency representation, both as the object of considerable scholarly attention and as a conceptual challenge. The discussion of the tradition of studying constituency representation in Congress is punctuated by revisions to the conventional notion of this relationship. In particular, a theory of dyadic subconstituency representation is advanced, which focuses on the series of relationships between a legislative office and the multiple subconstituencies in the representative's district. Chapter 3 develops a theory of legislative perception rooted in cognitive psychology and the theory of information accessibility. Key hypotheses drawn from the psychology literature are reinterpreted in the context of legislative perceptions of constituents and the implications for constituency representation are considered. Chapter 4 moves from a theoretical discussion of constituency representation and legislative perception to examining these ideas on Capitol Hill. The health policy and natural resources policy context of the 107th Congress (2001–2002) is discussed, including the specific bills that serve as the basis of analyses in subsequent chapters. This chapter also introduces the rich data used in the analyses, describing the structured, personal interviews conducted with eighty-one legislative offices in the U.S. House of Representatives (additional detail is provided in the appendix) and the measurement of perception in these interviews. Chapter 5 focuses on understanding which constituents legislators perceive in their district. Using hypotheses derived from the information-based theory of legislative perception discussed in Chapter 3, legislative perceptions are analyzed for each of the specific bills identified in the preceding chapter.

The next chapters consider the impact of these perceptions on legislative behavior. Chapter 6 takes legislative perceptions as the explanatory variable of primary interest and examines the impact of perceptions on legislators' participation in the policy debate. The data on participation are collected from committee (and subcommittee) markup and hearings as well as floor debate, and the key variables are discussed in further detail. Chapter 7 steps back from the focus on specific sub-constituents and examines how perceptions of the district as a whole affect patterns of legislative behavior. Two dimensions of variation in district perception – completeness and balance – are conceptualized and measured across health and natural resources policy. The effect of legislators' district perceptions on legislators' activity at the early stages (bill introductions) and the later stages (roll-call voting patterns) of the policy-making process are examined. Finally, Chapter 8 concludes with a summary discussion of the importance of legislative perceptions for constituency representation. Additionally, the implications of this book for political science research, as well as for the practice of constituency representation on Capitol Hill, are discussed.

2

A Dyadic Theory of Subconstituency Representation

Despite widespread agreement on the importance of constituency representation in Congress, what representation looks like in practice is highly problematic. A number of issues complicate scholars' inquiries and make it challenging to recreate the reality of Capitol Hill in models of congressional behavior. The most notable of these issues is the question of who is being represented by a Member of Congress. In its most simplified form, representation is assumed to be the match between a single district interest and the actions taken by a legislator. However, this parsimonious notion of representation falls short of capturing the reality of congressional districts or the challenges of constituency representation. Concerns with summary measures of "the district" have been raised at least as far back as Fiorina (1974), and this chapter builds on the argument that legislators do not represent a single constituency, but rather multiple subconstituencies within their district. As a result, there is not one representative relationship between a legislator and his district, but rather a collection of representative relationships within a district that scholars must examine in order to understand constituency representation in Congress.

Toward this goal, this chapter develops a new theory of congressional representation that reflects this more complex notion of the representative relationship. This dyadic theory of subconstituency representation focuses on the relationship between legislators and the multiple subconstituencies in their district who are relevant to a specific policy issue. In doing so, the dyadic theory of subconstituency representation addresses the central issue of which constituents are represented, as well as the corollary issue of who does the representing. Who legislators represent on

Capitol Hill is a question rooted in the complexities of the congressional district and the limitations of legislative perceptions of their district. When legislators consider the interests of their district, they do not see a uniform district, nor do they see every single constituent. Rather, they see groups of constituents – or subconstituencies – with shared interests in the issue at hand. This theory of subconstituency representation also requires a reconsideration of who is responsible for representing constituents in Washington. Close observers of Congress contend that the effective agent of representation is not the legislator, but the legislator's larger organization, or what Salisbury and Shepsle (1981) call the "legislative enterprise." This legislative enterprise includes not only the legislator, but also the professional staff members who carry out much of the everyday work of representation and policy making in Washington. This dyadic theory of subconstituency representation, therefore, moves the study of constituency representation closer to the ways in which representation is practiced on Capitol Hill.

THE FOLLY OF THE UNITARY CONSTITUENCY

How does a legislator serve as the voice of hundreds of thousands of constituents in his district? Democratic theorists have long commented on the difficulty of understanding how an individual legislator can represent the varied interests of all the district's constituents. Hobbes notes that it is "the *unity* of the represener, not the *unity* of the represented" that transforms a collection of constituents into a district.[1] In his essay on the complexity of representation in democratically elected legislatures, Mill (1861) laments the fact that elected representatives reflect the choice of only a subset of citizens, thereby leaving numerous constituents either unrepresented or misrepresented in government.[2] In her famous exposition of the concept of representation, Pitkin also highlights the theoretical challenges of representing the full collection of constituents in a district. She argues that instructing representatives to act "as if their constituent were acting themselves" is dubious when legislators are representing a constituency, not "a single principal" (Pitkin 1967, 145). Pitkin points out that this directive provides little guidance to legislators and is best described as "a questionable slogan."[3]

[1] Hobbes quoted in Pitkin (1967, 30, emphasis in the original).
[2] In particular, see J. S. Mill (1861, Chapter 7).
[3] Pitkin (1967, 145).

But even Pitkin and Mill theorize about constituency representation as if a constituency is something that can be reduced to some unity, some average, or some summary characterization. Many contemporary scholars do the same and examine congressional representation as if it were possible to capture the constituency with one tidy measure. Indeed, the challenges faced by legislators trying to represent a complex constituency are mirrored in the challenges that political scientists face in measuring the constituency (Goff and Grier 1993). Notorious in this respect are reductionist models that assume the district median voter along a single dimension is a sufficient stand-in for the constituency (e.g., Black 1958; Shotts 2002). The stylization inherent in this type of research can provide formal analytical value; however, it neglects the reality of congressional districts and limits scholars' ability to understand constituency representation as it is practiced. Matthews and Stimson (1975, 30) highlight the discrepancy between scholars' and legislators' image of the district, noting that "where outside observers see simplicity, members, close at hand, see complexity." As a result, this stylized approach is foregone here and instead the chapter begins to move in the opposite direction.

Miller and Stokes (1963) provide an important point of departure for thinking about how much of the complexity should be retained in theories of representation. Well known in the literature is Miller and Stokes' influential "diamond of representation," which calls attention to the ways that constituents' preferences affect legislators' votes. This parsimonious and insightful model of representation in Congress has served as a template for volumes of research that followed. Miller and Stokes highlight the potential influence of constituents' preferences via two intervening considerations: a legislator's own attitudes and a legislator's perceptions of constituency attitudes. The authors find that both paths play a role in constituency representation by members of the U.S. House of Representatives, although the dominant path of representation varies by policy area. The intuitions of the model and their empirical findings are largely echoed by scholars who reexamine Miller and Stokes's analyses (e.g., Achen 1978; Erikson 1978; Kuklinski and McCrone 1980).

The lasting impact of Miller and Stokes's article is that it inspired many scholars to examine the representative relationships they outlined. However, the overwhelming majority of subsequent studies, formal and empirical, focus on the agreement between constituency preferences and legislator behavior without much attention to a more realistic, and more complicated, concept of constituency. Miller and Stokes use the mean constituency opinion as if legislators represent a population average of the district rather than a collection of subconstituencies. An extensive literature on the congruence between constituency preferences and legislative behavior does the same (e.g., Erikson 1990; Hill and Hurley 1999; Hurley 1982; Page et al. 1984). Similarly, some of the most influential formal analyses of congressional representation (e.g., Denzau, Riker, and Shepsle 1985; Shotts 2002) rely on a single, summary measure of constituency preferences. Most of these studies find that Members of Congress are generally responsive to their constituents (e.g., Converse and Pierce 1986; Fiorina 1974; Jackson 1974; Kingdon 1989). Moreover, most of this research defines constituency representation as the congruence between a legislator's roll-call votes and an indicator of average district preference.[4] This focus on representation as congruence between a single measure of the constituency and legislative voting is common across different measures of constituency preferences, including public opinion, characteristics of the district, and citizens' voting behavior (e.g., Bartels 1991; Erikson and Wright 1990; Holian, Krebs, and Walsh 1997; Jackson and King 1989; Kalt and Zupan 1984).

There is reason to worry, however, that this stylized conceptualization of representation of "the district" is one of empirical or analytical convenience, not a valid reflection of the core elements of congressional practice. As Fenno (1978, 3) writes, "No congressman sees, within his district's boundaries, an undifferentiated glob. And the rest of us should not talk about his relations with this 'constituency' as if he did." Similarly, Fiorina's formal analysis (1974, 31) criticizes scholars' reliance on the geographic definition of the constituency, instead characterizing it as "a collection of groups of voters with the members of each group holding like preferences." Converse and Pierce (1986, 511) further point out that "the representative has multiple constituencies.... This is an aspect of the representation problem which classical theory very nearly ignores." Consequently, the challenge of constituency representation is to make sense of whom legislators represent when the mysterious median voter is not in sight. To do this, the dyadic theory of subconstituency representation focuses on the series of relationships between a legislator and the issue-specific subconstituencies in his district.

---

[4] But see Achen's (1978) reexamination of Miller and Stokes's data that considers the variance of mean constituency opinion and recognizes the underlying distribution of constituency preferences while still employing an aggregate measure of constituency opinion. Also see Eulau and Karps (1977) and Hall (1996) for a discussion of other ways that constituency representation can be approached.

THE REPRESENTATION OF DISAGGREGATED DISTRICTS

This book is far from being the first, or the last, to address constituency representation in the U.S. House of Representatives. The fact that core questions about constituency representation in Congress remain unanswered despite the vast literature testifies to the complexity of the representative relationship. Numerous studies seek to break apart the district along certain lines – electoral, partisan, and racial – in order to study representation at a different level of analysis than the aggregate district. In doing so, these studies lay the groundwork for the dyadic theory of subconstituency representation presented here. Perhaps the most influential step toward disaggregating the district is Fenno's notion of concentric circles (1978). One of Fenno's many contributions to the study of Congress is his argument that legislators conceive of the district as a series of concentric circles rather than "an amorphous mass."[5] These concentric circles denote levels of electoral support for a legislator and reflect legislators' beliefs about constituents' party affiliation, personal loyalty to the legislator, and likelihood of voting. Although Fenno focuses on the importance of electoral considerations in determining the concentric circles, he also acknowledges that electoral support is not the only factor that determines a legislator's sense of his constituency. The clarity and explanatory power of Fenno's concentric circles, therefore, appeal to other scholars who echo his observation that a district is not strictly defined by its legal boundaries.[6]

Following Fenno's lead, other scholars unpack the district along one of three dimensions: voting status, partisanship, and race. The first of these dimensions follows closely from Fenno's concentric circles and divides constituents within a district according to their propensity to vote. Legislators view the district in terms of the constituents who are most likely to vote in upcoming elections as contrasted with those constituents who do not vote (e.g., Griffin and Newman 2005; Kingdon 1967; Kuklinski 1978; Martin 2003; Peltzman 1984). The logic of this distinction lies once again in the electoral incentives of policy responsiveness. Strategic legislators are

---

[5] Bauer, Pool, and Dexter (1963, 419).

[6] Although the focus here is on the different subconstituencies within the legal bounds of a congressional district, other scholars have noted another shortcoming of the strict geographic definition of constituency, namely that it excludes representation of interests outside a legislator's district. This type of collective, or national, representation is beyond the scope of this research, but prominent contributions to the literature include Jackson and King (1989), Reingold (1992), and Weissberg (1978).

more responsive to the interests and preferences of constituents who vote because of the greater potential gains in the next election.

The second dimension along which constituents are separated is party identification. Here, the belief that legislators are more responsive to their own partisans (and perhaps independents) than partisans of the other party motivates the disaggregation of the district. The basis of this distinction is quite similar to that described earlier; strategic legislators derive greater electoral benefit by being responsive to co-partisans and independents. This partisan-based approach to understanding constituency representation is the most common approach to unpacking "the district" (e.g., Bishin 2000; Clausen 1973; Clinton 2006; Fiorina 1974; Hurley and Hill 2003; McCrone and Stone 1986; Shapiro et al. 1990; Wright 1989). Legislators are more responsive to partisan identifiers and independents than constituents affiliated with the opposing party, which makes strategic electoral sense but also suggests that opposing partisans are not equally represented. The popularity of this approach to disaggregating the district is largely due to the literature's focus on the reelection goal, but it also reflects the ease with which partisan distinctions can be made empirically.

A third approach to breaking apart "the district" is to divide constituents along a race/ethnicity dimension. This distinction is generally made in order to assess the extent to which African American and white legislators differ in their responsiveness to African American constituents in the district (e.g., Canon 1999; Cobb and Jenkins 2001; Griffin and Newman 2008; Hall 1996; Hutchings 1998; Tate 2003; Whitby 1997). African American legislators seem to be more responsive to African American constituents than their white colleagues due, in part, to electoral motivations similar to those outlined earlier, but also due to a sense of shared identity. Disaggregating the district by race reveals both that descriptive and substantive representation are connected in important ways, and that congressional representation is not shaped exclusively by strategic considerations.

Taken together, these studies move the study of congressional representation away from the classical notion of "the district," and toward a better understanding of the practice of representation. Across these three distinctions, scholars overwhelmingly conclude that legislators are more responsive to some constituents than others. The dyadic theory of subconstituency representation builds upon this tradition, but instead breaks "the district" into a collection of interest-based, issue-specific subconstituencies.

THE REPRESENTATION OF LEGISLATIVE OFFICE –
SUBCONSTITUENCY DYADS

Fiorina (1974) argues that developing a theory of representation requires scholars to approximate the key features of legislative reality insofar as we can discern them. Given that modern House districts include an average of almost 700,000 constituents, it is reasonable to describe a constituency as "an object of considerable complexity" (Kingdon 1989, 32). If we heed Fiorina's advice, then our theory of constituency representation should take at least some of this complexity into account.

The reality of congressional representation is that "the district" encompasses a number of subconstituencies. These subconstituencies are collections of individual constituents identified by their common interest in a given policy area.[7] Subconstituencies are not synonymous with interest groups, nor are they inevitably organized. Moreover, while constituents within a subconstituency have a shared policy preference, there can be multiple subconstituencies relevant to a given issue and these different subconstituencies do not necessarily have the same preferences on an issue. For example, ethanol subsidies are important to a number of subconstituencies, including farmers, consumers, and automobile manufacturers, but these subconstituencies do not have the same policy preferences. Whereas farmers are primarily concerned with the effects of policy on the profitability of growing corn, consumers prefer policies that address the costs of fuel and food, and automobile manufacturers are concerned with the implications of policy for consumer demand for cars. Additionally, subconstituencies relevant to one issue may not be relevant to another issue. For instance, subconstituencies relevant to Medicare policy may include physicians, seniors, and hospitals such that when a legislator considers the interests of "the district" on health policy, he sees these subconstituencies. However, when that same legislator considers the district's interests on energy policy, the relevant subconstituencies are likely to include utilities, small business owners, and consumers, not physicians and hospitals.

Conceptualizing the district as a collection of interest-based, issue-specific subconstituencies has major implications for constituency representation in Congress. Legislators face the challenging task of representing multiple subconstituencies within their district – who likely have competing interests – and the collection of relevant subconstituencies changes

---

[7] See also Williams (1998) regarding the notion of "communities of interest."

by policy area. The structure of congressional representation, therefore, is dyadic, where "dyadic" refers to the pairings, or dyads, between a legislative office and the multiple, issue-relevant subconstituencies in the district.[8] As Figure 2.1 illustrates in simplified form, a single legislator represents a variety of subconstituencies in the district. When a legislator looks at the district all together, the district resembles Figure 2.1a where a wide range of interests is represented. But for any given issue, the view of the district may be quite different (see Figures 2.1b and 2.1c).

There are many subconstituencies within the district (Figure 2.1a), but not all of these constituents are relevant to every issue that comes before Congress. As a result, when legislators and their staff consider the importance of a specific issue to the district, their view of the district is comprised of the relevant subconstituencies, not all possible subconstituencies. The stylized examples of energy and Medicare policy illustrate that dyadic subconstituency representation varies by issue and includes competing subconstituency preferences. In the case of energy policy (Figure 2.1b), small business owners, consumers, and utilities all have an interest in the policies considered by Congress, but they do not all have the same preferences for what that policy looks like. Similarly, in the case of Medicare policy (Figure 2.1c), physicians, seniors, insurers, and hospitals are all relevant to the issue, but their preferences over the services, costs, and payments under Medicare differ. Overall, Figure 2.1 demonstrates that, in order to understand congressional representation, it is essential to think about what the district looks like from the perspective of the legislative enterprise.

Reconceptualizing congressional representation as dyadic representation, therefore, captures the reality of what Kingdon (1989, 32) refers to as the "mottled collection of many subgroups" in the district. In doing so, this theory presents a picture of the district that better approximates the district that legislators see from Capitol Hill. Furthermore, dyadic constituency representation recasts the classic question of whether a legislator represents their constituency by asking *which* constituents in the district a legislator represents.

Three key features of this theory of dyadic subconstituency representation distinguish it from classical notions of congressional representation: the disaggregation of the district into interest-based subconstituencies, the importance of issue specificity, and the role of legislative enterprises rather

---

[8] Note that this use of "dyadic" is distinct from Weissberg's (1978) use of the term to refer to district representation as compared to collective, or national, representation.

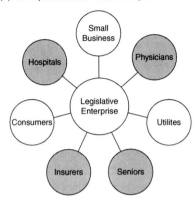

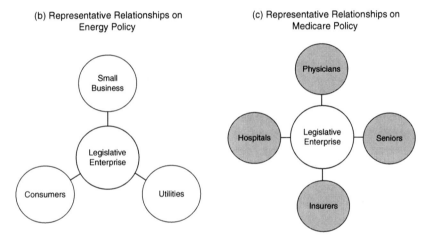

FIGURE 2.1. The Structure of Dyadic Constituency Representation.

than the sole legislator. Each of these aspects is rooted in the congressional literature, but when taken together, they provide a fundamentally different notion of the structure of congressional representation.

Interest-Based Subconstituencies

The first feature of the dyadic theory of subconstituency representation is that constituents in the district can be identified according to their policy interests. Legislators view the district in terms of the constituents that are interested in a given policy (e.g., Adler 2000, 2002; Adler and

Lapinski 1997; Fiorina 1974; Hall 1996; Kau and Rubin 1978; Kingdon 1989; Sullivan et al. 1993). The logic of this method of disaggregating the district lies both in legislators' electoral incentives to represent those constituents with a higher level of interest in an issue and in normative arguments that intense preferences should be represented. Legislators, therefore, are responsive to constituents interested in an issue because it is more likely that those constituents' votes will be shaped by their interest in, and legislators' actions on, the issue.

Previous research, however, tends to examine responsiveness by identifying a single subconstituency in the district that is interested in an issue. This approach assumes that constituency interest in the issue is one-sided and that there is a single dominant district interest for each issue (e.g., Lindsay 1990; Welch and Peters 1983).[9] In contrast, the dyadic theory of subconstituency representation posits that for any given issue there are multiple interested subconstituencies, which do not all share the same preferences on the issue. As an illustration, consider legislative responsiveness to constituency interest in agricultural issues. The conventional approach identifies farmers as the subconstituency to whom legislators are more responsive. However, farmers are not the only relevant constituency. In addition to farmers, other subconstituencies such as lower income constituents affected by food prices, conservationists concerned with land use, alternative fuel industries affected by crop prices, and local manufacturing industries reliant on agricultural business may have an interest in agricultural legislation. The challenge for legislators, therefore, is to represent this complex collection of subconstituencies who share a common interest, but not preference, in the issue.

Issue Specificity

The second feature of the theory of dyadic representation is that congressional representation is issue-specific. Issue specificity is quite closely linked to the use of interest-based subconstituencies, since these subconstituencies exist in a specific issue context. Indeed, there is a long tradition in the congressional literature of examining policy responsiveness in the context of a specific issue area, including civil rights, fiscal policy, and social policy (e.g., Bartels 1991; Evans 2001; Jackson and King 1989; Miller and Stokes 1963; Overby 1991; Wlezien 2004).[10]

---

[9] But see Hall (1996, Chapter 7).
[10] There are notable exceptions to this tradition, including Page and Shapiro (1983) and Stimson, MacKuen, and Erikson (1995).

However, not every constituent is affected by all issues equally, nor does every constituent care about all issues equally (e.g., Arnold 1990; Fenno 1978; Fiorina 1974; Hall 1996; Kingdon 1989; Stone 1979). The implication of this issue specificity is that "the effective constituency for a member of Congress also shifts from one issue to another,"[11] further complicating the task of representation.

The dyadic theory of subconstituency representation highlights issue specificity not only because constituents' interests vary by issue, but also because the design of Congress promotes issue-specific legislative activity. The issue specificity of the congressional policy-making process is reflected in the organization and deliberations of the institution. For instance, the structure of the congressional committee system in the U.S. House reflects the issue-specific nature of legislating and divides the institution according to policy area (e.g., Adler 2002; Bianco 1994; Hardin 1998; Hurwitz, Moiles, and Rohde 2001; King 1997; Krehbiel 1991; Shepsle 1978). Further evidence of issue specificity in Congress is the fact that responsibilities within each legislator's office are delegated according to the relevant issue area (e.g., Romzek and Utter 1997; Whiteman 1995). Each staff member specializes in certain issues and assumes the lead role when that issue is taken up by the legislative office. In these ways, the institutional structure of Capitol Hill focuses legislators' attention on particular issue areas.

Because both constituent interests and the policy-making process are defined by issue area, it follows that legislative representation of constituents also is issue-specific. When a legislator assesses the interests of the district, decides to participate in committee hearings, or casts a vote on the House floor, these actions are taken on specific issues (e.g., Hall 1996; Kingdon 1989). Legislators represent their constituents with respect to policy issues, and empirical examinations of representation need to capture this policy context in order to better approximate the practice of congressional representation.

The Legislative Enterprise

The third feature of the dyadic theory of subconstituency representation addresses the question: Who is doing the representing in congressional representation? Answering this question is necessary in order to understand legislative perceptions of constituents and how these perceptions

[11] Jackson and Kingdon (1992, 808).

affect representation in Congress. The classical notion of congressional representation invokes the legislator as the primary actor. This simplification reflects the dominant tendency in the theoretical literature to focus on a unitary actor, and also facilitates empirical studies of representation by making the representative relationship more tractable. The assertion that legislators are the sole actors responsible for representing constituents' interests on Capitol Hill, however, does not capture the practice of congressional representation. Legislators exist in the context of their legislative office, which includes numerous professional staff members. Salisbury and Shepsle (1981) coin the term "congressman as enterprise" to call attention to the fact that legislators serve as the CEOs of their office, but much of the everyday work in Washington is done by professional staff members. Although the legislator is the most visible member of the legislative enterprise, Salisbury and Shepsle assert that "the core of any congressional enterprise is the personal staff of the member."[12]

Several previous studies of congressional behavior examine the actions of both legislators and their staff members in order to create a more complete picture of activity on Capitol Hill. This tradition begins with an earlier generation of scholars, including Bauer, Pool, and Dexter (1963), Kingdon (1989), Matthews (1960), and Ripley (1969), and continues with more recent work that examines congressional decision making and participation (e.g., Evans 1991a, 2002; Evans 2004; Hall 1996; Hall and Evans 1990; Jacobs et al. 1998). Within a legislative enterprise, legislators remain the central figure in each congressional office, but the term captures the fact that both the legislator and his professional staff are relevant to understanding constituency representation on Capitol Hill. In contrast, focusing exclusively on the legislator ignores the important role that staff members play representing constituents.

The dyadic theory of subconstituency representation posits that legislators and their staff members are jointly responsible for representing the interests of constituents on Capitol Hill. The demands on Members of Congress are too great to realistically assume that a legislator alone is responsible for all of the activity in a modern legislative office. A legislator's staff members contribute to the overall congressional enterprise in many ways (Fox and Hammond 1977). Staff members are often the substantive policy experts in a legislative office and are responsible for working with other congressional offices and congressional committees

---

[12] Salisbury and Shepsle (1981, 560).

on behalf of the legislator. As Hall (1996, 78) notes, "it is not so much the member per se, but the member's enterprise that acts in the legislative deliberations of Congress." Staff members are also the primary link between the legislative office and constituents, as well as between the office and organized interests in the policy community (DeGregorio 1995; Schiller 1995; Whiteman 1995; Wolman and Wolman 1977). In fact, when constituents or interest groups contact a legislator's office, it is generally a staff member who speaks with them and who is responsible for assessing constituency interests in a given policy. Consequently, staff members are an integral part of what scholars are referring to when they invoke the legislator. The use of the "legislative enterprise" makes explicit this reality.

The concept of a legislative enterprise also helps to reconcile how a legislator can pursue his electoral goals, participate in multiple committee venues, offer legislation and amendments, and formulate positions on a range of policy areas without requiring the legislator to possess super-human powers. Staff members expand legislators' capacity to both represent their constituents and engage in policy making. Given this book's focus on constituency representation from the vantage point of legislators on Capitol Hill, it would be foolish to ignore the legislative organization that represents the district in practice. Understanding how constituents are represented in Congress requires looking at the perceptions and actions of the congressional enterprise, not just the legislator.

CONSEQUENCES OF A DYADIC THEORY OF SUBCONSTITUENCY REPRESENTATION

Congressional representation is not a single relationship between a legislator and a summary measure of his district, but it is instead a series of relationships between a legislative enterprise and the collection of subconstituencies in the district relevant to the issue at hand. The theory of dyadic representation is structured by these legislative enterprise–subconstituency pairings, which serve as the unit of analysis for examining congressional representation. Conceptualizing constituency representation in this way has implications for the study of Congress and, specifically, for questions about legislative perception and representation.

One important feature of this conceptualization of constituency representation is that it more accurately reflects the practice of constituency representation on Capitol Hill. Legislative enterprises represent a collection of constituents within their district who share an interest in the issue at hand, not a single district interest. Eulau (1987, 187) captures this when he notes, "That a representative should represent the 'entire' district where he stands for election is another normative prescription defied by real-world impossibility, for the simple reason that the holistic notion of 'entirety' is a philosophical ghost." Indeed, the challenges of constituency representation for legislative enterprises involve identifying the relevant subconstituencies and representing competing constituency interests, not summarizing the interests of the district in a single, aggregate measure.

For congressional scholars, the dyadic theory of subconstituency representation also has implications for how to study congressional representation. Representation does not take place in a vacuum; rather it occurs in the broader context of an issue and the relevant legislative office-subconstituency relationships. Efforts to capture the nested structure of the congressional context will help congressional research to more fully resemble congressional reality. This means features of the legislative enterprise may affect all relationships that an office has with constituents. For instance, whether a legislator is more senior may systematically shape the representative relationships with subconstituencies in the district. Another implication of the dyadic nature of representation is that there may be features of a subconstituency that affect its relationships with all legislative enterprises. For example, whether a subconstituency has traditional partisan ties may systematically shape their relationship with all legislative offices on Capitol Hill. Although analytical convenience dictates that some aggregate measures of the district will continue to be used, a better understanding of what such measures capture – and what they do not – will improve the tractability between theory and practice.

Finally, the dyadic theory of subconstituency representation further highlights the importance of understanding legislative perceptions. This theory calls attention to the complexity of the district and the challenges of constituency representation, both of which render legislative perceptions of the district all the more important. The increased complexity of constituency representation compels scholars to return to Miller and Stokes's (1963) "diamond of representation," which identifies legislative perceptions of constituency interests as one of the central paths by which constituents are represented in the House. When the default conceptualization of constituency representation is whether a legislator casts a vote consistent with the average preference of a stylized district, then legislative perceptions receive little attention because assessing the interest of the district appears to be relatively straightforward. However, when constituency representation is reconceived as dyadic representation of multiple subconstituencies relevant to each issue, then understanding how legislative enterprises perceive their district takes on new significance. Put differently, if the simplifying assumptions about "the district" are relaxed to allow for a more realistic, and more complicated, portrayal of the district as a collection of subconstituencies, then legislative perceptions of the district reclaim a central role in understanding constituency representation in Congress.

3

The Psychology of Constituency Representation

Legislative perceptions of constituents are a fundamental component of political representation because legislators represent the district they see. In order to understand legislative behavior, therefore, it is essential to see the constituency through the eyes of the legislative enterprise. Despite the early consensus on the importance of legislative perceptions (e.g., Dexter 1957; Fenno 1978; Kingdon 1967; Miller and Stokes 1963), political scientists' understanding of how perception affects congressional representation has been limited by the lack of a theory of perception. With no explicit model of the process by which legislative perceptions of the district are formed, questions about which subconstituencies are more or less likely to be perceived by legislative offices – and the impact of these patterns on congressional representation – remain unanswered.

Two important developments offer new insights into the cognitive processes that shape how legislators perceive the constituents in their district. The first of these developments is the growth of research on social cognition in the psychology literature, particularly individuals' use of heuristics, or mental shortcuts, to simplify complex environments. The cognitive psychology literature offers an information-based approach to individuals' perceptions of the world around them that emphasizes how individuals use information, including their reliance on the accessibility heuristic. The second, related, development is the growth of political psychology within the political science discipline, especially research on citizens' use of information in political judgments. Taken together, these advances promise to shed new light on the question of legislative perceptions of their constituents by opening the "black box" of human behavior and allowing scholars to see the district through legislators' eyes.

The term *legislative perception* refers to the collection of constituents that a legislator and his staff see when they look at their district. Put differently, it is a legislative enterprise's impression of the constituents in a legislator's district (Lau 1989). Legislative perceptions of the district are not readily apparent to the congressional observer, nor are they discussed in the corridors of Capitol Hill. Indeed, perceptions are *not* conscious decisions about which constituents to represent or what policy actions to take. Rather, legislative perceptions exist at the preconscious level and represent what legislators and their staff perceive to be "out there" in the districts.[1] As a result, legislators represent their perception of their districts, or to borrow Lippman's (1922) oft-quoted phrase, legislators represent the "pictures in their head" about their districts.

This notion of legislative perception calls to mind the common-sense definition of the term "perception," or how we see the world around us. It also references the sense that this view is subjective and fallible. These connotations of the term *legislative perception* are deliberately retained because they evoke the complexity of constituency representation. However, the importance of perception does not suggest that there is some implicit passivity among legislators. Individuals do not need to be passive for cognitive processes to occur, nor for those cognitive processes to affect their behaviors (Jones 1998). Rather, legislative perceptions that result from preconscious, cognitive processes serve as the mental backdrop against which legislative elites take conscious – and often strategic – actions. The fact that legislative elites are subject to the limitations of human cognitive processing is not incompatible with political scientists' model of legislative elites as rational, strategic actors, but instead reflects scholars' attention to different aspects of human behavior.

The environment on Capitol Hill inhabited by legislators and their staff provides congressional enterprises with an abundance of information about constituents, but legislators and their staff must gather and process this information under intense time pressure due to competing demands on their time. Indeed, the number of legislative duties (including committee meetings, floor votes, and caucus meetings), amount of constituency casework, and time devoted to fund-raising are substantial (see Hall 1996), making it less likely that legislators and their staff engage in comprehensive information processing. Consequently, understanding how legislative enterprises process information is essential

[1] Smith (1998, 403).

to comprehending who legislators see when they look at their district because "reality is funneled through the representative's perceptions."[2] More broadly, how legislators and their staff perceive the constituents in their districts has important implications for constituency representation. Democratic representation as envisioned in the U.S. Congress is rooted in the notion that legislators are the voice of the people who reside in their district; this is the political contract into which elected officials enter with their constituents. If a subconstituency in the district is not seen by a congressional enterprise when considering the district, then it is unlikely that the legislator will represent that subconstituency's interests in the policy-making process.

To understand why congressional offices see some subconstituencies in the district and not others, it is necessary to understand how perceptions are formed and the factors that shape them. As Lodge et al. (1991, 1369) write:

A theory about the mental processes of human actors is necessary to answer many of the questions examined by political scientists. Even studies of institutions such as Congress, the courts, or the presidency require that we understand how the individuals who fill the offices of those institutions make decisions ... political scientists need a theory of how individuals perceive and structure the social world in which they participate as political actors.

Drawing on the cognitive psychology literature, this chapter articulates an information-based theory of legislative perception that calls attention to the importance of how individuals use information to make judgments.

INFORMATION PROCESSING AND HEURISTICS

The cognitive perspective in the psychology literature emphasizes the process by which individuals gather information and use this information to make judgments about the world around them. Markus and Zajonc (1985) define the cognitive approach as focusing on "how social information is gleaned from the environment and then how it is represented, processed, stored, and retrieved for purposes of inference, attribution, judgment and evaluation."[3] Individuals' ability to use information, however, is constrained by their own cognitive limitations as well as by the complexity of the environment. As Jones (1994) notes, "no individual can pay attention to all things of importance at once."[4]

---

[2] Fiorina (1974, 32).
[3] Markus and Zajonc (1985, 141).
[4] Jones (1994, 7).

Consequently, central to our understanding of this process is the notion that individuals do not use all available information, but rather concentrate on a subset of information, which renders the judgment task more manageable (Bodenhausen and Wyer 1987; Wyer and Srull 1989). Noting this tendency, Simon (1957) described humans as "cognitive misers" who exert the minimal amount of cognitive effort necessary to make a satisfactory judgment. Individuals are characterized as selective perceivers with cognitive structures that simplify information and allow "the perceiver to reduce an enormously complex environment to a manageable number of meaningful categories."[5] The miserly nature of individuals in the psychology literature is consistent with political scientists' notion of bounded rationality, which presumes that individuals want to gain an adequate amount of information, but not necessarily complete information, in order to make decisions. A key implication is that individuals do not conduct exhaustive information searches when making judgments, but rather rely on a variety of shortcuts.

The cognitive psychology literature calls attention to these mental shortcuts, or heuristics, that allow individuals to select a subset of information in an efficient and effective manner. One of the most common and most important heuristics is the accessibility heuristic, where individuals rely on the information that is retrieved more quickly and with greater ease than other information.[6] Given the vast amount of information that could be used to inform any given decision, it is "manifestly impossible to attend to all of [it]."[7] As a result, Carlston and Smith (1996, 198) note that "the principle of accessibility is so prominent that it ... has even been labeled a general law of psychology." Similarly, Schwarz et al. (2003, 2) note that "highlighting the role of information accessibility in human judgment has been one of the core contributions of social cognition research."

Classic experimental research on information accessibility shows that the ease with which information is recalled plays an important part in determining individuals' judgments (Tversky and Kahneman 1973, 1974). More accessible information has a greater impact on individuals'

[5] Markus and Zajonc (1985, 143).

[6] Scholars have examined whether more accessible information is recalled due to the ease of retrieval (i.e., the subjective experience of recall) or the content of recall (i.e., the information that is retrieved). Although the literature addresses these different mechanisms underlying information accessibility, in real-world situations accessible content and ease of experience are naturally confounded (see Schwarz 1998; Schwarz et al. 1991; Schwarz and Vaughn 2002).

[7] Shaw and Costanzo (1970, 184).

judgments and subsequent behaviors, and less accessible information is significantly less likely to shape behavior (e.g., Ajzen 1996; Fazio 1990; Fazio and Williams 1986; Higgins et al. 1977). A primary benefit of the accessibility heuristic is that it improves the efficiency of decision making by allowing an individual to focus on certain pieces of information rather than expending unnecessary time gathering all relevant information (e.g., Ajzen 1996; Eagly and Chaiken 1998). It is not difficult to imagine individuals becoming overwhelmed by the enormity of the decision task if it were necessary to evaluate all relevant information for every decision. However, this increased efficiency assumes that a decision reached via heuristics is the same as the decision the individual would have reached had he conducted an exhaustive information search. In order for an individual to benefit from the time and energy saved by heuristics, the subset of information used must be representative of the universe of all relevant information.

Heuristics, however, are not foolproof, and they can result in judgment errors. As Fiedler and Schmid (1995, 296) note, "according to the now prevailing definition, heuristics are rather parsimonious and effortless, but often fallible and logically inadequate, ways of problem solving and information processing." If an individual uses flawed information, his decisions will reflect the limitations and biases of that information. For instance, information based on personal experience is more easily accessible than other types of information, so if an individual's personal experience is unusual, then the accessibility heuristic can result in flawed judgments. In fact, when individuals are asked to estimate the probability of a heart attack, those people who know heart attack victims are likely to overestimate the likelihood of heart attacks more generally (Tversky and Kahneman 1974). When the use of heuristics leads individuals to rely on a subset of information that is systematically biased, then the usual efficiency gains associated with using cognitive shortcuts, such as the accessibility heuristic, will be outweighed by the costs of making poor decisions (e.g., Kahneman and Tversky 1973; Lindzey and Aronson 1985; Nisbett and Ross 1980). In sum, although the accessibility heuristic is potentially helpful, it is imperfect and judgments based on accessible information are not necessarily the best judgments.

HEURISTICS, INFORMATION, AND POLITICAL SCIENCE

The cognitive approach to understanding individual decision making, and the accessibility heuristic in particular, is rooted firmly in the psychology literature but has influenced many political scientists (for reviews see Kuklinski 2001, 2002, and McGraw 2000). In general, the political science literature shares the psychology literature's view of heuristics as an efficient and effective way for citizens to make judgments about policies and candidates in light of the fact that citizens rarely gather full information (e.g., Herstein 1981; Lau and Redlawsk 2006; Lodge, McGraw, and Stroh 1989; Lodge, Stroh, and Wahlke 1990; Zaller 1992). It is believed that citizens do not need full information in order to act as if they had engaged in an exhaustive information search because they can use heuristics to compensate for their low levels of information and make higher-quality decisions about politics than their knowledge levels would suggest. For instance, citizens can use shortcuts based on the race, gender, or party of a candidate to facilitate making decisions about political candidates (e.g., Conover and Feldman 1989; Gilliam and Whitby 2000; Huddy and Terkildsen 1993; Koch 2002; Kuklinski and Hurley 1994; Peffley, Hurwitz, and Sniderman 1997; Rahn 1993; Sanbonmatsu 2002). Citizens also can take cues from better informed citizens or from information provided by political elites when evaluating candidates or policies (e.g., Carmines and Kuklinski 1990; Carmines and Stimson 1989; Lupia 1994; Mondak 1993). In general, then, heuristics allow citizens to approximate better informed decisions about policies and candidates than their knowledge levels would otherwise allow (e.g., Popkin 1991; Sniderman, Brody, and Tetlock 1991).

A significant subset of this research concerns citizens' use of the accessibility heuristic when assessing political candidates (e.g., Conover and Feldman 1986; Huckfeldt et al. 2005; Lau 1989; Lau, Smith, and Fiske 1991). Three types of information are believed to be more accessible to citizens and to influence their assessment of political candidates: partisanship, personal character, and issue positions. There is evidence that information about partisan or ideological beliefs is more readily accessible to voters and consequently is more likely to influence their assessment of political candidates (e.g., DeSart 1995; Huckfeldt et al. 1999). Additionally, some studies find that a candidate's character influences voters' evaluations. In particular, attitudes about candidates' competence and integrity are highly accessible to citizens and have been found to affect their judgments of candidates (Mondak and Huckfeldt 2006). Still other studies argue that the accessibility of information about issues varies across citizens and policies, which helps to explain why some citizens are more likely to base their political decisions on the issues (Goren 1997; Lavine et al. 1996).

Research on framing and its impact on citizens' evaluations of political candidates and issues is another area of research informed by information accessibility. As Iyengar and Kinder's (1987) influential study demonstrates, television news affects the accessibility of information about politics, and consequently affects citizens' political judgments. Media do not impact political priorities and opinions by altering the content of information, but by affecting the way in which citizens use information (e.g., Druckman 2001; Gilliam and Iyengar 2000; Iyengar 1990; Nelson, Clawson, and Oxley 1997). Moving beyond the media, elected political officials also use framing in their campaign advertisements, public statements, and press coverage to make certain information more easily accessible to voters and thereby increase the likelihood that they will use it (e.g., Fenno 1978; Valentino, Hutchings, and White 2002). As Jacobs and Shapiro (2000, 50) note, public statements can be used deliberately by politicians to "influence which attitudes and information individuals retrieve from memory and incorporate into their judgments." Similarly, other political organizations such as parties and interest groups also attempt to make certain information more easily accessible to citizens in hopes of affecting their political decisions (e.g., Jacoby 2000; McKissick 1995).

Given the attention to citizens' use of the accessibility heuristic, it might be expected that the concerns about the limitations of heuristics raised in the psychology literature would be echoed in the political context. However, this is generally not the case. Although some scholars express skepticism that voters' use of heuristics fully compensates for low levels of citizen information (e.g., Bartels 1996; Kuklinski and Hurley 1994; Kuklinski and Quirk 2000), the majority of the political science literature focuses on the benefits of heuristics. To this point, Lau and Redlawsk (2001) criticize the tendency of political scientists to invoke heuristics as a "solution" to the problems of an inattentive, uninformed electorate while ignoring the potential pitfalls of these shortcuts: "heuristics can sometimes introduce serious *bias*, along with cognitive efficiency, into decision-making."[8]

Political Elites and Heuristics

Political science research not only takes a generally positive approach to cognitive heuristics but also focuses on the mass public rather than political elites. Without detracting from the importance of understanding

---

[8] Lau and Redlawsk (2001, 952, emphasis in original). See also Kuklinski et al. (2001).

how citizens use heuristics in their political lives, it is surprising that similar attention has not been paid to how political elites use heuristics when making political judgments. In fact, the relative lack of attention to elites in the political psychology literature has been noted by some scholars as a weakness of the literature (e.g., Lau, Smith, and Fiske 1991; Rahn, Sullivan, and Rudolph 2002). To the extent that political elites are included in existing studies, it is most often as sources of information for citizens, rather than as the decision makers of interest.

However, political elites, including legislators and their staff, face the same cognitive limitations as other individuals, and the Capitol Hill environment provides the conditions (including time pressure and an abundance of information) under which individuals are especially likely to rely on heuristics (Hall 1996; Kingdon 1989). Indeed, scholars refer to "the *fact* of limited-information processing capabilities"[9] in humans and note that elites and experts in general are vulnerable to the same cognitive constraints and biases as citizens (see Tetlock 2005). In fact, psychologists have examined the use of heuristics among professionals who may have stronger incentives than the average citizen (or experiment participant) to engage in costly information processing and have found that these elites use heuristics and exhibit the same patterns of bias and error as non-elites (e.g., Arkes and Hammond 1986; Tversky and Kahneman 1982b; 1983).

Moreover, the implications of political elites' use of information, especially the limitations of reliance on the accessibility heuristic, are substantively and normatively important for policy outcomes and representation. Whereas citizens' use of heuristics affects their individual preferences and votes, legislative enterprises' use of heuristics affects hundreds of thousands of individuals in their district because their judgments and decisions have the cumulative weight of all the constituents for whom they speak. If legislative elites' reliance on shortcuts like the accessibility heuristic leads them to use incomplete or biased information about their constituents, then they are unlikely to make decisions on Capitol Hill that reflect their full constituency.

Some earlier studies speak to political elites' use of information but do so in particular settings or without explicit consideration of the underlying cognitive processes. One area in which political scientists have examined elites' use of heuristics is in foreign policy decision making.[10]

---

[9] McGraw (2000, 814, emphasis added).
[10] For an excellent review of the history of this literature, see Levy (2003).

Foreign policy elites often forego complete information in favor of relying on heuristics, despite the limitations of these shortcuts. In his discussion of foreign policy scholars' recognition of the importance of the early stages of decision making and the role of perception, Taber (1998, 31) notes, "Foreign policy decision makers, like other information processors, must interpret the events that concern them; that is, they must build subjective understandings of world events." Classic studies in this literature include George's (1969) work on the cognitive elements of individuals' "operational codes" or belief systems, Allison's (1971) study of the Cuban Missile Crisis, and Axelrod's (1976) research on elite decision making and cognitive mapping. Of particular relevance here is Jervis's (1976) seminal work on cognitive biases and the dangers of elites' misperception of motivations and consequences of foreign policy action. Jervis challenges the conventional notion among international relations scholars "that decision-makers usually perceive the world quite accurately and that those misperceptions that do occur can only be treated as random accidents," and instead argues that perceptions "diverge from reality in patterns that we can detect and for reasons that we can understand."[11] As Levy (2003, 260) notes, Jervis's 1976 study "was, and still is, the most influential study of the role of misperception in foreign policy and international politics," and it has shaped much of the subsequent research on threat perception and deterrence (e.g., Lebow 1981; Levy 1983; Stein 1985, 1993).

Scholars continue to call attention to the ways in which incomplete and biased information affects foreign policy elites' perceptions of their environment and the subsequent risk of poor judgments (e.g., Hermann 1985; Janis 1982; Kanwisher 1989; Larson 1985; Levy 2003; Mercer 1996). In this literature, the world is a complex place where individuals are constrained by cognitive limitations and therefore employ heuristics, which are "the source of significant errors and biases."[12] Indeed, this literature's attention to the potential costs of heuristics reflects the high stakes of foreign policy elites' decisions, especially during the Cold War. Research on political elites involved in foreign policy decision making, then, is consistent with the work on cognitive processes and the limitations of heuristics in the psychology literature.

Cue taking by legislative elites is a second literature that is informed by theories of how individuals use information and heuristics, but the

---

[11] Jervis (1976, 3).
[12] Levy (2003, 264).

influence of psychology in these studies is largely implicit. Legislators rely on cues from their colleagues (e.g., Kingdon 1977, 1989; Matthews and Stimson 1975) and congressional committees (e.g., Bianco 1997; Krehbiel 1991) when deciding how to cast their votes (see also Sullivan et al. 1993). These studies assert that legislators use cues to reduce the amount of time and energy required to collect sufficient information to make a decision about a legislative proposal. Given the numerous bills introduced in Congress and the multiple sources of information that legislators could consider, cues are believed to increase the efficiency of legislative decision making and voting. This research employs the language of bounded rationality, but does not unpack the cognitive mechanisms underlying legislative cue taking.

Studies of the accuracy of legislators' predictions of district opinion are another example of how psychology has indirectly informed research on elites. The emphasis in these studies is on the match between prediction and outcome rather than the cognitive mechanisms at work in the underlying process. The most influential of these studies is Miller and Stokes's (1963) examination of the degree to which Members of Congress are able to predict whether the majority of the constituents in their district are in favor of, or opposed to, a given policy. Legislators' predictions are compared to survey measures of the mean district opinion to determine their accuracy. Although the initial attention to legislative judgments of constituents' attitudes came from scholars of the U.S. Congress, the study of legislative predictive accuracy took hold primarily in the context of state legislatures.[13] A primary reason for the relocation of these studies to the state level is that statewide ballot measures allow citizens to express their policy preferences through voting behavior. State legislators' ability to predict the outcome, or majority district opinion, of a given referendum in their districts varies across issues, but there is evidence that legislators' expectations are reasonably accurate (Erikson, Luttbeg, and Holloway 1975; Hedlund and Friesema 1972). When faced with the more difficult task of forecasting the percentage of the district vote in support of (or opposition to) referenda, state legislators provide less-accurate predictions of their constituents' preferences (Kuklinski and Elling 1977; McCrone and Kuklinski 1979). Similarly, scholars have examined the accuracy of legislators' predictions of majority constituency opinion in legislatures beyond the United States, notably in Sweden and France. Whereas early studies focused on legislators' ability to accurately judge

---

[13] But see Wolman and Wolman (1977) and Lascher, Kelman, and Kane (1993).

the partisan composition of their district (Kornberg 1966), more recent research examines legislators' ability to accurately predict majority positions in the district, especially among same-party constituents (e.g., Clausen, Holmberg, and deHaven-Smith 1983; Converse and Pierce 1986; Esiasson and Holmberg 1996).

The literature on the accuracy of legislators' predictions makes important inroads into understanding how legislators evaluate constituency opinions and concludes that legislators' expectations of constituency opinion are not always accurate. This finding is notable because these studies generally define constituency preference as the majority opinion in the district, which is a relatively easy target for prediction. However, these studies are largely silent on the cognitive processes underlying whether elected legislators correctly predict citizens' preferences, and highlight the results but not the mechanisms (but see Clausen 1977 and Esiasson and Holmberg 1996).

AN INFORMATION-BASED THEORY OF LEGISLATIVE PERCEPTION

Legislators are believed to make decisions based on "enough" information and to simplify the political world in order to make their responsibilities more manageable. However, the implicit, rather than explicit, use of cognitive psychology means that studies of legislative elites do not address the limitations of heuristics despite the potentially important implications of these cognitive processes for congressional representation and policy making. By focusing on the mechanisms by which cognitive processes shape legislative elites' view of the constituents in their district, this information-based theory of legislative perception sheds new light on core questions about constituency representation raised by earlier congressional scholars.

The ease and efficiency of heuristics are attractive to legislators and their staff who do not have the time to seek out exhaustive information about constituents' interests on every policy issue that comes before the U.S. Congress. Legislators and their staff are responsible for representing approximately 700,000 constituents in a congressional district, and it is unlikely that legislative elites conduct a thorough information search when assessing the interests of the district. In fact, the conditions in which psychologists assert that individuals are cognitive misers – an abundance of information from various sources, time limitations, competing demands on individuals' attention – are exactly the conditions that exist on Capitol Hill (Hall 1996). As Kingdon (1989) writes, "To an exaggerated degree, congressmen face this problem of too many decisions and too little time in which to make them. ... Thus congressmen, fully as much as other decisions-makers, and perhaps much more than many of them, avoid time-consuming information searches."[14] Furthermore, many public policy issues are technically complex and all of these decisions are made under significant time pressure. E. Smith (1984) echoes this sentiment and notes that "the quantity of information required is too large, the time available to attend is too limited, and the calculations required are too complex"[15] for legislative enterprises to make fully researched decisions all the time. As a result, legislative staff are prone to using cognitive heuristics to simplify the tasks of gathering and using information necessary to make decisions about the interests of their constituents. Recent work by Jones (1994, 2001) and Jones and Baumgartner (2005) discusses the constraints on democratic decision making in the U.S. Congress and argues that both cognitive limitations and complex political environments result in a decision-making process that looks quite different from the rational-choice ideal. Since legislators and their staff cannot pay attention to all available information, how they process information should be central to theories of democratic decision making.

The theory of legislative perception developed here emphasizes the accessibility of information about different constituents to explain why legislative enterprises perceive some constituents in their district and not others. Information accessibility has "profound influence"[16] on judgments, including those made by legislators and their staff about their constituents. When a legislative enterprise considers the importance of a policy to the district, information about some subconstituents will come to mind more readily than information about other relevant subconstituencies in the district. As a result, those subconstituents about whom information is more accessible receive more mental attention and assume a more prominent place in the legislator's perception of the district. This task of looking back to the district when evaluating proposed policies is a routine component of congressional representation on Capitol Hill. Staff members are regularly asked by legislators, other legislative staff, and other policy makers to succinctly assess a policy's relevance

---

[14] Kingdon (1989, 228).
[15] E. Smith (1984, 44).
[16] Schwarz et al. (2003, 2).

to constituents in the district. In doing so, staff are likely to rely on the information about constituents that is most accessible.

According to the cognitive psychology literature, legislative staff members' reliance on the accessibility heuristic improves efficiency when considering the policy interests of the district, but it also increases the risk that these judgments will be flawed. If staff members use information about constituents that is incomplete or unrepresentative of all relevant constituency information, then their assessment of the importance of a policy to the district also is likely to be limited and biased. Moreover, a flawed view of the district may lead legislative enterprises to advocate policies that do not reflect the constituents they represent and to systematically privilege a narrow subset of their constituents. Understanding how legislative enterprises use information about their constituents, therefore, contributes to our understanding of constituency representation in Congress. Or as Lodge et al. (1991, 1358) note, "The cognitive message is clear: if we want to understand why people act as they do, we must understand how they picture the world around them."

Determinants of Information Accessibility

In order to examine whether legislators and their staff members rely on information that is systematically biased in favor of some constituents over others, the focus shifts to the factors that affect the accessibility of information. In short, what are the characteristics of information that is more (or less) accessible to legislative staff? Drawing on the psychology literature, four factors are hypothesized to affect the accessibility of information about constituents: frequency of information, familiarity of information, salience of information, and predisposition toward information. Before discussing each of these considerations, it is important to emphasize that individuals do not choose whether or not a piece of information is accessible. Rather, the accessibility heuristic works through a cognitive process that "takes place outside of consciousness, and so we do not even recognize that it is happening" (Turner 2000, 265).

The first factor that affects the accessibility of information is the *frequency* with which it is encountered (e.g., Bodenhausen and Wyer 1987; Carlston and Smith 1996). Information that an individual comes across more frequently is more easily accessible, and therefore more likely to be used when making judgments. The underlying mechanism of this increased accessibility is the repetition that comes from frequent contact with information. As Tversky and Kahneman (1982a, 164) note, "that associative bonds are strengthened by repetition is perhaps the oldest law of memory known to man."

The second factor that affects information accessibility is the *familiarity* of information because more familiar information is more easily accessible. Information can be more familiar to an individual because of past experiences or expertise (Ajzen 1996). The importance of personal history in determining accessibility was championed by Bruner (1957), who argued that each individual's past experiences create a cognitive structure of expectations that affects the accessibility of information. Put differently, information familiar from previous experiences is more easily accessible because it maps onto existing cognitive structures (see also Jones 1998; Lindzey and Aronson 1985; Ross 1977).

The *salience* of information is the third factor that may determine the accessibility of information about constituents. Information is more salient when it is particularly vivid or compelling, and as a result, salient information is more easily accessible and has a greater impact on individuals' judgments (e.g., Krosnick 1989; Reyes, Thompson, and Bower 1980; Taylor and Fiske 1978). For instance, information conveyed during face-to-face interaction is considered to be more accessible than information expressed through mass communications because personal contact renders the information experience more vivid (McGuire 1969). Salient information may be "overvalued" by staff members, which makes it more likely to be recalled (Tversky and Kahneman 1974).

The fourth factor believed to affect the accessibility of information is individuals' *predisposition toward information*. Conventional wisdom suggests that information should be more easily accessible when it is consistent with an individual's attitude or position, although evidence regarding the impact of predisposition on information accessibility is mixed (see Smith 1998). Cognitive dissonance theory emphasizes individuals' desire for consistency and the subsequent avoidance of dissonant information (e.g., Festinger 1957; Heider 1944, 1958). Studies show that individuals are likely to dismiss information that challenges their predispositions and to neglect the possibility that consistent information may be irrelevant or faulty (e.g., Houston and Fazio 1989; Lord, Ross, and Lepper 1979; Markus and Zajonc 1985). Moreover, there is evidence that information processing is biased in favor of information that is congruent with individuals' attitudes (e.g., Eagly and Chaiken 1998; Jones 1998; Sherif and Hovland 1961). Some scholars have found that predisposition does not necessarily determine how individuals use information when making judgments (e.g., Freedman and Sears 1965; Huckfeldt et al.

2000), and there is some evidence that inconsistent information may be more accessible because it contrasts with individuals' preexisting attitudes (e.g., Hastie and Kumar 1979; Higgins and Bargh 1987). Overall, however, information with which an individual is predisposed to agree is expected to be more accessible than other information.

CONCLUSION

It is important to understand which subconstituencies legislative enterprises see when they look at their districts. Are legislative staff members equally likely to see all constituents in their district, or is there a systematic process by which information about some constituents is more likely to shape their view of the district than information about other, equally relevant constituents? In order to answer these questions, this book provides an information-based theory of legislative perceptions that draws on the cognitive psychology literature. Like all individuals, legislators and their staff are likely to prefer to use information shortcuts, such as the accessibility heuristic, that reduce the time and effort spent gathering information rather than conducting exhaustive information searches. As a result, legislative staff members are more likely to recall information about constituents that is more easily accessible. Jervis (1986) illustrates this tendency by likening the use of accessible information to the proverbial drunkard's search for his keys under the streetlight, and notes "people often select information to use because it is readily available, not because it is especially valid."[17]

The gains in efficiency, however, come at a potential price. Accessible information is also likely to be an incomplete – and potentially biased – sample of all information about the district. The consequences of legislative elites' reliance on accessible information, therefore, are significant. If legislative staff members see an incomplete and biased view of the district, their judgments about the interests of their constituents are likely to be flawed as well. Legislative perceptions of the district that are limited and unrepresentative raise normative concerns that legislative elites fall short of a basic, yet fundamental, standard for political representation – legislative elites should at least be aware of the constituents they represent. If certain constituents are not on legislative elites' proverbial "radar screen," then legislators and their staff are unlikely to provide accurate representation on Capitol Hill. Put simply, incomplete

---

[17] Jervis (1986, 330).

and biased perceptions of the district are likely to translate into biases in congressional representation. The next chapter takes up this question by addressing the policy context in which legislators' perceptions of their districts – and the impact of these perceptions on legislative behavior – are examined: health policy and natural resources policy.

4

Subconstituents Relevant to Health Policy and Natural Resources Policy

From their vantage point on Capitol Hill, legislators and their staff are attentive to their responsibility to represent the interests of the constituents back in their district. One Member of Congress highlighted the importance of constituency considerations in Washington, D.C., when he noted, "You always have to think, what's in the best interest of my district? . . . Do you have a sense of where your district is?"[1] However, who in the district is part of a legislative enterprise's "sense of the district" is a question that warrants further investigation.

This chapter takes three essential steps toward answering this question and assessing legislative perceptions of constituents in the district. The first of these is to describe the policy context in which legislators' "sense of the district" is formed. Legislators and their staff members do not represent their constituency in the abstract, but rather they represent their constituency on the issues that come before the U.S. House of Representatives. The focus here is on health care policy and natural resources policy, with attention to four legislative proposals that serve as the basis for the analyses of legislative perceptions of constituents that follow. A discussion of these bills conveys the policy environment in which legislators represent their constituents, and also highlights the dimensions on which these bills differ, thereby increasing the generalizability of the findings.

The selection of these issues also facilitates the second step, which is the identification of the policy-relevant subconstituencies that legislative enterprises realistically can be expected to see when they look at

[1] Personal interview.

46

their district. Distinguishing the relevant subconstituencies is essential to examining legislative perceptions of the district because these subconstituencies are the foundation of the legislative enterprise-subconstituency dyads used in subsequent analyses. The third step is to actually measure which subconstituencies legislative enterprises see when they look at the district. Drawing on measures from the cognitive psychology literature and personal interviews with legislative staff members, structured interviews are used to determine which subconstituencies each legislative office sees when considering health policy, or natural resources policy, in its district.

Having taken these three steps, the chapter then provides a descriptive overview of whom legislative enterprises see in their districts. The data reveal that legislators' perceptions of their districts are far from comprehensive. In the case of both health policy and natural resources policy, legislators and their staff see an average of only one of every three relevant subconstituencies in their district, which means that they fail to see many constituents relevant to the policy at hand. Although normatively disheartening, legislative enterprises' incomplete view of their districts is consistent with the information-based theory of legislative perception. Moreover, these findings suggest that understanding legislators' "sense of the district" is central to constituency representation because the perceived district differs significantly from the objective district. In short, this chapter situates the theories of constituency representation and legislative perception articulated in the previous chapters in the real-world of Washington, D.C., and begins to examine their implications for the practice of constituency representation on Capitol Hill.

THE ISSUE CONTEXT

Scholars interested in constituency representation face the challenge of deciding which policies or bills to include in their analyses of legislative behavior. There are two prominent approaches to this decision: to synthesize individual policies into a single indicator of a legislator's behavior, or to highlight the particulars of a policy and draw lessons from that policy to broader behaviors. The first of these envisions a single ideological dimension along which the vast majority of policies can be aligned and draws heavily on the creation of the NOMINATE dataset by Keith Poole and Howard Rosenthal (Poole and Rosenthal 1985, 1991). In this approach, congressional representation focuses on the congruence between a legislator's cumulative score, which is based on their roll-call votes, and the preferences of the district. The widespread use of NOMINATE has sparked debate within the literature over whether policy making in Congress can be reduced to one dimension (e.g., Clausen 1973; Poole 1981; Poole and Rosenthal 1985, 1991; Wilcox and Clausen 1991).[2] Despite this debate, the creation of a single index of legislative voting histories (and the updating of NOMINATE scores each congress) is one of the most influential contributions to the empirical study of Congress.

It is perhaps not surprising that the second approach prioritizes depth over breadth and emphasizes the importance of the particular policy context. This tradition highlights the complexity of constituency representation and the fact that details of legislative decision making and constituency interests may vary across issues (e.g., Bishin 2000; Clausen 1973; Converse and Pierce 1986; Fiorina 1974; Hall 1996; Jackson and Kingdon 1992; Lascher, Kelman, and Kane 1993). As a result, scholars focus on legislative behavior in a particular issue area such as abortion policy (Brady and Schwartz 1995), environmental policy (Kalt and Zupan 1984), trade policy (Bailey and Brady 1998; Holian, Krebs, and Walsh 1997), defense spending (Bartels 1991), tax policy (Jackson and King 1989), health policy (Evans 2001), social welfare (Barrett and Lomax Cook 1991), and government reforms (Theriault 2005). Evaluating theories in the context of specific issues offers the advantage of more fully capturing the political context in which legislative behavior occurs, yet these studies must also address questions of whether the findings are generalizable to other contexts.

Drawing on this second tradition, this book examines legislative perceptions of constituents and their impact on legislative behavior in the context of health policy and natural resources policy. This issue-specific approach best mirrors the reality of legislative perception and representation and dates back to at least Miller and Stokes's (1963) seminal article on constituency representation (see also Clausen 1973; Converse and Pierce 1986; Fenno 1986; Kingdon 1989). When a congressional enterprise considers the district's interests, it does so with respect to a given issue, or as Hall (1996, 59) notes, "the issue sets the context for how a member thinks about her constituency." Indeed, it is nonsensical for a

---

[2] Although the dominant (first) dimension is the liberal-conservative dimension (in modern times), NOMINATE also captures a second dimension that historically captures race-related issues. However, McCarty, Poole, and Rosenthal (2006) argue that this second dimension is no longer important after 1980 due to realignment in the South.

legislative enterprise to consider the interests of the district absent an issue by which those interests can be defined. Specifying the issue area in which to examine legislative perceptions of the district also facilitates the collection of much more precise data about perceptions, as well as measures of constituents' interests and legislators' actions.

The selection of health policy and natural resources policy as the empirical focus of this book stems from the importance of health care, energy, and environmental issues, and the fact that these issues include a wide range of policies that illustrate the variation in the types of bills addressed by the House. As a result, one should be able to generalize from these two rich, important issue areas. After the divided and contested presidential election in 2000, the 107th Congress (2001–2002) began with a newly elected Republican president in the White House and Republican majorities in both the House and the Senate. With the power of unified government to pursue their goals, the congressional Republican leadership pledged their support for President George W. Bush's agenda, including health care policy and natural resources policy. These issue areas had been mentioned frequently in the 2000 presidential campaign, as well as in a number of congressional races. Additionally, it was widely expected that health care and energy issues would play a role in congressional races across the country in the 2002 midterm elections (Gerber 2002).

An important similarity between these two policy areas is that the federal government traditionally has played a role in both health policy and resources policy, but the nature of this role was the subject of considerable political debate entering the 107th Congress. The federal government has long provided subsidized health care or medical assistance for low-income and fixed-income citizens, but with the rapidly rising costs of health insurance and the questionable financial solvency of Medicare, the nature of these programs was in the process of being reconsidered. In the case of natural resources policy, the federal government also has a history of involvement in programs such as the national parks system and support of energy production industries. With the shift from the Clinton administration to the Bush administration, however, the approach to land use was expected to change. The role of the federal government in these two issue areas is important because it illustrates that these policy domains are not temporary blips on the political agenda, but rather they are examples of issues that are part of the ongoing political dialogue, as are issues like agriculture, defense, transportation, and education. In this way, the findings drawn from health and natural resources issues should be applicable to the broader collection of issues that occupy much of the political agenda.

Another similarity between these two issue areas is the nature of the relevant constituency interests. Both health policy and natural resources policy affect large subconstituencies of relatively unorganized people (e.g., patients and consumers, respectively), as well as sizable industry interests (e.g., health insurance companies and energy industries, respectively). Consequently, legislative activity in these two policy areas is likely to be relevant to subconstituencies of different sizes and with different resources in districts across the country. The diversity of subconstituencies in the district relevant to health policy and natural resources policy mirrors the range of subconstituencies more generally, thereby increasing the generalizability of the findings presented here to other issue areas. In this way, the task of representing a district on health or natural resources policy approximates the general challenge of constituency representation faced by legislative enterprises in the U.S. House of Representatives across all issues.

Natural resources policy, however, differs from health policy in ways that make it an interesting issue area in which to examine legislative perceptions. One difference is that resources policy contains an element of regional politics that is largely absent in other issue areas. Specifically, there is a "Western perspective" on natural resources issues that reflects the greater proportion of public (including federal) lands in Western states and differences in attitudes about private property rights and land use. Legislators and their staff often refer to this political geography when talking about natural resources policy as evidenced by a Western Member of Congress's reference to the "common bond to almost all of us [Western congressmen]."[3] Indeed, the regional differences in natural resources politics highlight the importance of understanding how legislative offices see their district, since perceived constituency interests are likely to vary considerably across districts.

Health policy and natural resources policy, then, possess similarities and differences that make them important venues in which to examine legislative perceptions of the district. Furthermore, within each issue area this book focuses on two specific policy proposals. These bills were selected from among the bills on health issues and natural resources issues that reached the House floor during the 107th Congress (2001–2002). Each of the two health policy bills and the two natural resources policy

[3] Personal interview.

bills address substantively different issues that are of concern to different subconstituencies. Within each issue area, one bill addresses a broader policy that received considerable deliberation in the House, and one bill addresses a more narrow policy that was considered under an expedited process in the House. Although the substantive and procedural particulars of the four bills are different, a similar process is at work when legislators and their staff look back to the district from their vantage point on Capitol Hill and consider the policy interests of their constituents.

The selection of these four bills within the areas of health politics and natural resources politics not only illuminates important details about constituency representation in prominent issue areas but also provides a solid basis from which to draw broader conclusions about legislative perceptions of their constituents. Just as more and less salient bills are examined here, bills of varying political salience come before Congress every session. Similarly, the variation in the legislative path taken by the bills examined here reflects the various paths that legislation can take through the House. As a result, the insights into the role of legislative perception of constituents gained from the in-depth examination of these health and natural resources bills are applicable to a larger set of policies. The next section offers a more detailed discussion of each of these four bills, including the issues at stake in each bill and the subconstituencies to whom the policy was relevant.

HEALTH POLICY IN THE 107TH CONGRESS

In the case of health policy during the 107th Congress (2001–2002), concerns centered on issues such as the rising cost of health care, the dominance of health maintenance organizations (HMOs), and the reform of Medicare. Consistent with these concerns, the two policy proposals in which legislative perceptions and constituency representation are examined are the Patients' Bill of Rights and the Medicare Regulatory and Contracting Reform Act. Both of these bills were referred to the House Energy and Commerce Committee, but they differ in other important respects. Most notably, the bills vary in their salience, scope, and partisanship, as well as their paths through the chamber. These differences are important because the dyadic theory of subconstituency representation outlined in the previous chapters should apply regardless of the particulars of the bill. Additionally, legislation in general varies along these dimensions, thereby increasing our confidence that the findings are applicable to other policy contexts.

The Patients' Bill of Rights

At the heart of the debate over the Patients' Bill of Rights are the rights of patients insured by HMOs and the degree of liability faced by insurers and employers. The Patients' Bill of Rights, in some form, has been part of the health policy debate in the U.S. House of Representatives since 1994, and the bill debated during the 107th Congress reflected these previous negotiations. For instance, the consensus on the patient protection provisions was the result of agreements reached in previous years.[4] However, other key issues remained unresolved, including the contentious question of liability and damage caps. In fact, the main obstacle to the passage of the Patients' Bill of Rights in 2001 was disagreement over the amount of legal recourse patients should have if their insurer denied them care (Goldstein 2001).

The main piece of Patients' Bill of Rights legislation in the House in the 107th Congress was H.R. 2563, "The Bipartisan Patient Protection Act," which was cosponsored by Republican Greg Ganske of Iowa, Republican Charlie Norwood of Georgia, and Democrat John Dingell of Michigan. This bill was introduced to the House on July 19, 2001, and was referred to the Committee on Energy and Commerce, as well as to the Committees on Education and the Workforce, and Ways and Means.[5]

One of the most striking features of the debate over the Patients' Bill of Rights in the House is that it was highly partisan despite the fact that the champions of H.R. 2563 were a bipartisan group of legislators. This small, yet influential coalition worked together for several years to secure a Patients' Bill of Rights that included both strong patient protections and strong avenues of legal recourse for patients.[6] Although the congressional Republican leadership and President Bush supported patient protections, they strongly opposed liability provisions that they believed would promote frivolous lawsuits and allow for high damage awards. Consequently, the White House opposed H.R. 2563.[7]

---

[4] These provisions (often referred to as the Title I provisions) included direct access to OB/GYN physicians and pediatricians as primary care providers, patient choice of physicians, access to specialists, and access to clinical trials.

[5] H.R. 2563 replaced a previous version of the bill (H.R. 526), which was sponsored by Representative Ganske and introduced in February 2001.

[6] The central figures in the bipartisan coalition were Representatives Ganske (R-IA), Norwood (R-GA), and Dingell (D-MI), as well as Senators John McCain (R-AZ), Ted Kennedy (D-MA), and John Edwards (D-NC).

[7] In trying to understand why Representatives Norwood and Ganske were so active in their support for the Patients' Bill of Rights despite the opposition from the president,

In late July 2001, the three cosponsors of H.R. 2563 were working to pass their bill, which closely resembled the Senate's version of the Patients' Bill of Rights (S. 1052) that had passed at the end of June.[8] If the Norwood-Dingell-Ganske bill passed the House, the two chambers would call a conference committee to reconcile the final versions of S. 1052 and H.R. 2563. With few differences between the House and Senate versions, the Patients' Bill of Rights was expected to reach the desk of the president in the fall of 2001 (Goldstein 2001). However, this important bipartisan coalition of legislators soon crumbled under the weight of one member's defection.

At the beginning of August 2001, President Bush invited Representative Norwood to a closed-door meeting at the White House. During this meeting, Norwood struck a deal with the president, which reduced the limit on damage awards against HMOs from the $5 million cap in H.R. 2563 to the $1.5 million limit favored by the president and the Republican leadership. This compromise between Representative Norwood and President Bush shocked Capitol Hill, especially the bipartisan supporters of H.R. 2563. On August 2, 2001, the House considered H.R. 2563 on the floor. The Norwood Amendment, which reflected the deal brokered the previous day was offered and passed the House along party lines, 218–213. The amended version of H.R. 2563 passed the House later that night by a vote of 226–203.[9]

As passed, H.R. 2563 was no longer bipartisan, nor was it compatible with the version of the Patients' Bill of Rights that passed the Senate. The two chambers needed to resolve differences in the liability provisions in conference committee before the bill could be sent to the president. The events of September 11, 2001, however, precluded a conference committee and focused political attention away from HMO reform. Interestingly, the Patients' Bill of Rights did not disappear from the political agenda (see Gerber 2002). Rather, it was put on hold and reemerged in January 2002 when President Bush included the Patients' Bill of Rights in his State of the Union Address. Despite this potential injection of political momentum, little progress was made on resolving the differences between the House and Senate versions, and the Patients' Bill of Rights died with the close of the 107th Congress.

the Republican leadership, and many traditional Republican allies, it is interesting to note that both men are former health care professionals.

[8] S. 1052 passed the Senate on June 29, 2001, by a vote of 59–36.

[9] All legislative details are available through the U.S. Library of Congress and their *Thomas* Web site.

As a result of the congressional and executive activity on the Patients'
Bill of Rights during the 107th Congress, many subconstituencies were
active in voicing their support or opposition to the legislation. Interests
as varied as the business community, health professionals, insurers,
consumer advocates, seniors groups, unions, and trial attorneys took
a major interest in the discussion over the Patients' Bill of Rights and
actively participated in the political and public debate. The importance
of the issue to so many subconstituencies is notable because it indicates
that many constituents in each district would be affected by the Patients'
Bill of Rights. The question is whether legislators and their staff saw all
of these subconstituents.

Medicare Regulatory Reform

In sharp contrast to the highly visible debate surrounding the passage
of the Patients' Bill of Rights, the discussion of Medicare regulatory
reform during the 107th Congress was noncontroversial. The regulatory
process for Medicare was considered by patients, providers, administrators, and politicians alike to be burdensome, inefficient, and confusing.
After commissioning a major review of the programs administered by
the Centers for Medicare and Medicaid Services (the federal agency that
administers Medicare), the House Energy and Commerce Committee's
Subcommittees on Health and on Oversight and Investigations docu-
mented many of the complaints that health care providers and Medicare
beneficiaries voiced.[10] In response to these findings, Representatives
Shelley Berkeley (D-NV) and Patrick Toomey (R-PA) introduced legislation to address many of the regulatory problems. The Medicare
Regulatory, Appeals, Contracting, and Education Reform (RACER)
Act of 2001 (H.R. 3046) was introduced on October 4, 2001, and was
referred to the Committee on Energy and Commerce, as well as the
Committee on Ways and Means. After consideration and markup ses-
sions at both the subcommittee and committee levels, the Energy and
Commerce Committee reported the Medicare RACER Act to the House
in December of 2001. Once on the House floor, the Toomey–Berkeley bill
was incorporated into the Medicare regulatory proposal sponsored by
Representative Nancy Johnson (R-CT) entitled the Medicare Regulatory
Contracting Reform Act of 2001 (H.R. 3391). In its new form, H.R. 3391

---

[10] See the House Report 107–313 on the Medicare Regulatory, Appeals, Contracting,
and Education Reform Act of 2001.

passed the House under suspension of the rules on December 4, 2001. The use of this procedural shortcut illustrates the widespread appeal of the legislation, or as one staff member noted, "Usually suspensions are bills that are not controversial; they have not drawn a lot of opposition – they're pass-through kind of bills."[11]

The Medicare regulatory reform bill (H.R. 3391) that passed the House focused on protecting against fraud, educating providers, expediting claims, and reducing paperwork. These changes were not controversial, and they received bipartisan support. Furthermore, its sponsors stipulated that the final Medicare regulatory reform bill be budget neutral (i.e., require no additional funding or budget adjustments), thereby eliminating a potential source of opposition to the bill. As a low salience bill focused on regulatory changes to the administration of Medicare, H.R. 3391 received considerably less attention from the media, but remained important to numerous subconstituencies.

The Patients' Bill of Rights and the Medicare Regulatory and Contracting Reform Act were both referred to the Committee on Energy and Commerce in the 107th Congress, and both bills passed the House. The similarities, however, largely end there. Whereas the Patients' Bill of Rights was political, divisive, and visible, Medicare regulatory reform was technical, bipartisan, and inconspicuous. The passage of the Patients' Bill of Rights involved political drama and ended in a tight, party-line vote. In contrast, the passage of Medicare regulatory reform was non-controversial and was achieved under suspension of the rules. In short, these two issues provide important variation within the arena of health politics and allow for a richer examination of how legislative offices see the constituents in their districts on specific health policies.

NATURAL RESOURCES POLICY IN THE 107TH CONGRESS

The Bush administration and the Republican-controlled Congress were widely expected to address natural resources issues in the 107th Congress, including domestic energy production, clean air legislation, access to federal lands, and regulations implemented under the Clinton administration. Reflecting this agenda, the focus here is on two bills

---

[11] Personal interview. Suspension of the rules permits for only 40 minutes of debate, allows no amendments, and requires a two-thirds majority vote for passage. See Davidson and Oleszek (2000) for a more detailed discussion of suspension of the rules.

passed by the House of Representatives during the 107th Congress: the national energy bill entitled the Securing America's Future Energy (SAFE) Act of 2001 and the North American Wetlands Conservation Reauthorization Act. These bills were both under the jurisdiction of the House Resources Committee, but as with the two health policies, the energy bill and wetlands conservation bill vary considerably in their scope, salience, and divisiveness.

Securing America's Future Energy Act

A prominent item on the political agenda in 2001 was the creation of a national energy policy aimed at reducing dependence on foreign energy sources and increasing domestic production. Toward this goal, Republican Billy Tauzin of Louisiana sponsored H.R. 4, the Securing America's Future Energy Act of 2001, intended to "enhance energy conservation, research and development and to provide for security and diversity in the energy supply for the American people, and for other purposes."[12] However, creating a national energy policy was a difficult task because there was no existing policy on which to build new legislation and there were numerous components to include in a comprehensive policy. National energy policy encompassed many issues: extracting resources both on-shore and off-shore (including oil, natural gas, and coal); regulating the electricity industry; providing for alternative energy sources such as nuclear, water, wind, solar, and biodiesel; and funding research and development, conservation incentives, and industry and consumer tax incentives. In fact, the broad scope of the bill resulted in the bill being referred to the House Resources Committee as well as seven other House committees.[13]

Although numerous committee hearings were held and much debate occurred at the committee level, the main amendments to H.R. 4 were proposed on the House floor. Of these, three amendments received the most attention, and they reflect the salience of two key issues: drilling in the Arctic National Wildlife Refuge (ANWR) and increasing the Corporate Average Fuel Efficiency (CAFE) standard for automobiles and light trucks. The opening of ANWR to drilling for oil and gas

---

[12] Text of "H.R. 4: The Securing America's Future Energy Act of 2001," United States House of Representatives, July 27, 2001.

[13] The House Committees on Energy and Commerce, Science, Ways and Means, Education and the Workforce, Transportation and Infrastructure, Budget, and Financial Services.

was considered a political lightning rod, and two of the most contentious amendments addressed this provision. Democrat Edward Markey of Massachusetts, widely considered to be the staunchest opponent of ANWR drilling in the House, proposed striking from the bill the provision permitting drilling in ANWR. The Markey Amendment failed by a 206–223 vote. On the other side of the aisle, Republican John Sununu of New Hampshire proposed the "2,000 Acre Amendment," which limited the footprint of all drilling activities in ANWR's 1.5 million acres to 2,000 acres. Proponents of opening ANWR to drilling supported the 2,000 Acre Amendment and noted the political importance of having Representative Sununu offer the measure given his reputation as "moderate on these issues."[14] The Sununu Amendment passed the House by a vote of 228–201. The third prominent amendment was offered by Republican Sherwood Boehlert of New York and called for an increase in the CAFE standard plus further incentives for alternative fuel vehicles. Passage of this amendment failed by a vote of 160–269.[15]

On August 2, 2001 the amended version of the Securing America's Future Energy Act passed in the House of Representatives by a vote of 240–189, giving the Republican House leadership and President Bush a political victory. The SAFE Act was received in the Senate later that day; however, the events of September 11, 2001 would delay the Senate's consideration of a national energy bill until the spring. Ultimately, the Senate passed its own energy bill (S. 517) by a vote of 88–11 on April 25, 2002, but the House and Senate versions were worlds apart. Importantly, the Senate bill included no provision for drilling in ANWR, but instead increased support of renewable energies, especially ethanol fuel.[16] The Senate instructed conferees in May 2002, and the House followed suit in June 2002. However, the conferees were unable to reconcile the differences between the two versions before Congress recessed in October 2002.

The debate in the House surrounding the energy bill illustrates the importance of both party and region to the congressional debate over resources policy. The vote on H.R. 4 fell largely along party lines; 82% of Democrats voted against the legislation and 93% of Republicans voted

---

[14] Personal interview with House Resources Committee staff.
[15] Additional proposed amendments addressed issues ranging from changes to the royalties received by oil and gas companies, to promoting new technologies in mining and renewable energies, to controlling price volatility for consumers and businesses.
[16] This latter provision reflects, in part, the power of key senators from farm states and the greater representation of rural interests in the Senate than the House.

for the bill. Additionally, representatives from Western states generally were more likely to support multiple uses of federally owned land, including resource extraction, whereas representatives from the Northeast were more likely to be concerned with energy costs and environmental protection. The chairman and vice-chairman of the Western Caucus, Representatives George Radanovich (R-CA) and Christopher Cannon (R-UT), publicly attributed the regional divide to Eastern Members' lack of familiarity with the western landscape and their willingness to believe environmental propaganda (Kantin 2001). A common refrain among proponents of H.R. 4 included accusations that their opponents had never even been to Alaska (the location of ANWR).[17] On the other side of the debate, opponents of ANWR accused their colleagues of being in the pocket of big oil, as seen in these colorful comments by Representative Edward Markey (D-MA):

The Statue of Liberty National Monument, for example, could become the Statue of Fossil Fuels Production National Monument, with an actual flame burning on top of the torch. What an inspiring symbol that would be of the Bush Administration's public lands policy. Of course, we would have to change the inscription to read, give me your drill bits, your rigs, your huddled oil companies yearning to drill free, to dump their wretched refuse on our pristine shores. Send your well-heeled executives to me.[18]

It is important to note that increased regional party dominance reduced some of the regional variation within parties. As one insider noted, "the oil and gas industry used to be more bipartisan but now region overlaps with party so it's more partisan."[19] In contrast, the coal industry was considered bipartisan but regional. Additionally, some issues such as energy independence transcended partisan and regional divisions. Proponents of increased drilling, mining, and renewable energies all used the same argument that increasing domestic energy production would decrease American reliance on foreign oil sources (Kantin 2001). This shared goal of reducing dependence on Middle Eastern oil became even more prominent after September 2001. Overall, the passage of a comprehensive bill was widely supported by Members of Congress, but the details of how to achieve this goal were hotly debated.

---

[17] Personal interview with House Resources Committee staff. This same argument can also be found in media accounts of the debate and in the debate in the *Congressional Record*.

[18] Transcript of hearing held by the Energy Subcommittee of the House Committee on Energy and Commerce, March 15, 2001.

[19] Personal interview with House Resources Committee staff member.

Wetlands Conservation

In contrast to the energy bill, wetlands conservation was not at the top of the resources policy agenda. However, widespread support for the North American Wetlands Conservation Act (NAWCA) made it one of the few bills addressing natural resources issues to pass the House in the wake of the events of September 11, 2001. The North American Wetlands Conservation Act of 1989 established a federal program providing matching grants to private and public organizations for the purchase of wetlands for conservation in the United States, Mexico, and Canada.[20] With the original authorization for NAWCA set to expire at the end of fiscal year 2003, Republican James Hansen of Utah, chairman of the House Resources Committee, sponsored H.R. 3908 to reauthorize the program in March 2002. The bill was referred to the House Resources Committee, which held hearings on H.R. 3908 the following month. The primary changes to the bill were made during the subcommittee markup session by Republican Wayne Gilchrest of Maryland, who offered an amendment authorizing additional funding and requiring a greater percentage of programs to be located within the United States.[21] These changes were accepted by the Subcommittee on Fisheries Conservation, Wildlife, and Oceans, and shortly thereafter, the full Resources Committee held hearings on NAWCA and reported H.R. 3908 to the floor. The legislation received widespread support, and on May 7, 2002, the House of Representatives passed H.R. 3908 under suspension of the rules. The Senate then passed the legislation in November 2002 and sent it to the White House. On December 2, 2002, President Bush signed the legislation, and what began as H.R. 3908 became Public Law 107–308.

The North American Wetlands Conservation program enjoyed bipartisan support and was widely seen as a model conservation program around which a viable political coalition had been built. One important feature of NAWCA was that it used financial incentives rather than regulatory tools to increase wetlands conservation. Federal funding was used to match private or public organizations' contributions, and the money was then used to buy land and put it into conservation. Therefore, the market was allowed to determine the price of the land and individual land owners, including farmers, retained the right to decide whether or not to

---

[20] These grants are administered by the U.S. Fish and Wildlife Service.
[21] According to H.R. 3908, a minimum of 50% of NAWCA funding must be for conservation within the United States.

sell their land to conservation organizations. Consequently, NAWCA was lauded by many politicians who were generally skeptical of conservation efforts for showing greater sensitivity to property rights than other types of conservation programs. The nature of the federal–local partnership created by the matching grants also reduced traditional opposition to federal involvement in conservation stemming from concerns over federal involvement in local land management issues. An additional benefit of the matching grant design is that it generated nonfederal funds and therefore was a budget-friendly approach to conservation.[22] A final characteristic of NAWCA crucial to its political support was that its goal – the conservation of wetlands – appealed to a wide range of constituents including birdwatchers, environmentalists, anglers, and sportsmen. As an illustration of this unlikely coalition, the two organizations that provided the most matching money under NAWCA at the time were the Nature Conservancy and Ducks Unlimited.[23] Even more surprising is the fact that both the Sierra Club and the National Rifle Association supported the North American Wetlands Conservation Act.

Given this diverse coalition, it is no surprise that the reauthorization of NAWCA was not a controversial issue and did not spark heated debate in the House as did other environment and energy issues. In fact, when explaining the broad appeal of NAWCA, a staffer for the House Resources Committee remarked that H.R. 3908 was considered "an easy green vote" for members.[24] As a result, legislators who generally were not supportive of environmental legislation were supportive of H.R. 3908, including the House Sportsmen's Caucus.

The diversity of support for NAWCA, however, did not mean that support for the program was uniform. By providing incentives for conservation, NAWCA limited development in certain areas. Consequently, proponents of commercial and residential development often found their interests at odds with wetlands conservation. Similarly, local and state governments interested in expanding roads and highway systems ran afoul of NAWCA if proposed routes included wetlands. The potential impact of NAWCA on development also meant that NAWCA affected rural and suburban communities in different ways. Since NAWCA provided financial incentives to put wetlands into conservation easements,

---

[22] Committee staff noted that even though the legislation requires a 1:1 matching ratio, the current ratio is closer to 4:1 for nonfederal to federal funding.

[23] Personal interview with House Resources Committee majority staff member.

[24] Personal interview with House Resources Committee minority staff member.

some farmers considered NAWCA an alternate economic use of the land. In this way, NAWCA had the effect of providing "subtle but direct assistance to rural communities."[25] As with the national energy policy, there was also a regional element to support for wetlands conservation programs. For instance, not only did Western states maintain a different tradition of property rights, but they also contained far fewer wetlands than coastal states.

Taken together, then, these four policies provide a deliberate and varied set of contexts in which to examine how legislative enterprises perceive the constituents in their district. The cognitive theory of legislative perceptions developed in Chapter 3 applies to legislators and their staff across policy environments, and the analyses that follow provide empirical evidence of this theoretical assertion. With the health policy and natural resources policy contexts established, attention now turns to identifying the subconstituencies relevant to the four policies that legislative offices reasonably could be expected to see when they look at their district.

IDENTIFYING SUBCONSTITUENCIES

Since the analysis of legislative perception is rooted in the dyadic theory of subconstituency representation, defining the subconstituencies relevant to each of the four policies is essential. Once the relevant subconstituencies for each issue are identified, the presence of each of these subconstituencies in each legislator's district can be measured empirically using district-specific data from the U.S. Census, government agencies, and other sources.[26] Moreover, by focusing only on subconstituencies relevant to the policy at hand, the legislative enterprise–subconstituency pairings used to examine constituency representation are not inflated by the inclusion of nonsensical or improbable representative relationships. The identification of subconstituencies relevant to each of the four policies was done prior to the collection of data on legislative perceptions of their constituents, and utilized multiple information sources, including media reports, committee staff, and other policy experts.[27] The

---

[25] Personal interview with House Resources Committee minority staff member.

[26] More details about how each subconstituency in each district is measured are provided in Chapter 5 as well as in Appendix C.

[27] The background interviews and media research used to identify policy-relevant subconstituencies were conducted during the 2001–2002 congressional session and preceded the collection of data on legislative perceptions on the specified policy.

constituents relevant to each policy were carefully identified through contemporaneous media reports of the issue in Washington, D.C.–based outlets such as *The Hill* and *Roll Call*, as well as more general outlets like *The Washington Post*. In addition, personal interviews were conducted with policy experts on both the majority and minority party committee staff.[28] These interviews were particularly helpful for identifying subconstituencies relevant to the issue who may not be well known or obvious to the general public. From these sources, a list of subconstituencies that policy experts widely acknowledged to have interests in the specified health or resources policy was generated.

As a result of this process, the identified subconstituencies are not necessarily organized interest groups; rather they are defined by their common policy interests. The list of subconstituents relevant to each of the four bills exhibit variation in their degree of political organization, which reflects the diversity of constituents affected by health policy and natural resources policy. Congressional scholars interested in the influence of constituency considerations on legislative behavior note the difficulty in separating interest groups from less formal constituency interests (e.g., Evans 2002; Kingdon 1989). In particular, Evans (2002) notes that the common use of similar tactics including letter-writing campaigns, phone calls, and mobilization efforts "further complicate the distinction between constituent interests and organized groups" (p. 274). The difficulty of separating organizations and constituents is echoed by congressional staff members on Capitol Hill, one of whom commented that sometimes organizations "are not very active in our district, but people are members and so those folks will write to us."[29] Given the goal of understanding legislative perceptions of the district, including both unorganized and organized constituents most accurately captures the practice of congressional representation. In sum, legislative staff members realistically can be expected to be aware of the importance of the specified policies to any of the relevant constituents in their district.

In the case of the Patients' Bill of Rights, numerous subconstituencies expressed their support or opposition to the proposed legislation. The Patients' Bill of Rights was widely identified as being important to seven subconstituencies in each district: businesses, physicians,

---

[28] Interviews were conducted with several professional committee staff members "on background" to benefit from their insight and expertise in the specific policy areas. Note that committee staff are distinct from legislators' personal staff.

[29] Personal interview.

patients, organized labor, senior citizens, insurers, and attorneys. The business community was primarily concerned with the costs to employers, especially the possibility that employers would be held liable for coverage decisions. Physicians' interests focused on preserving the primacy of the doctor–patient relationship and the right of physicians, not insurance companies, to make decisions about medical care. Attorneys, particularly trial attorneys, were attentive to the provisions allowing patients to sue HMOs for damages, including noneconomic and punitive damages. The Patients' Bill of Rights was also relevant to insurers since it addressed issues including appeals of coverage decisions, liability, and limits on damage awards. Lastly, patients, senior citizens, and organized labor had common interests in protecting the quality of patient care, the ability to appeal insurers' decisions to deny coverage, and the right to sue HMOs.

Six subconstituencies were widely acknowledged to be relevant to policy that changed the regulation and contract procedures under Medicare. Hospitals and hospices were attentive to the legislation because they stood to benefit from attempts to streamline Medicare regulations. Physicians were primarily interested in legislative efforts to reduce Medicare fraud, including reforms of the appeals process and other safeguards for providers. Medicare patients were cautious about changes to the Medicare system but supportive of efforts to expedite claims and improve patient care. Not surprisingly, insurers also were attentive to Medicare regulatory reform, particularly provisions for streamlining the claims procedures and reducing fraud, which results in financial losses for insurers. Senior citizens constituted a broader subconstituency of citizens who had a more indirect interest in Medicare regulatory reform. Lastly, although primarily interested in changes to Medicare prescription drug coverage, the pharmaceutical industry also was attentive to any changes to Medicare regulatory and contracting procedures.

Like the two health care policies, natural resources issues were important to a diverse set of subconstituencies in each district. Nowhere is this more apparent than in the case of national energy policy, where the comprehensive nature of the bill would potentially affect many subconstituencies. Energy producers were interested in provisions that provided financial incentives to increase production whether in the form of reducing royalties (oil and gas exploration), providing incentives for technological improvements (coal mining), providing subsidies (ethanol, biodiesel), or funding research and development. Furthermore, each type of energy producer worried that the bill would advance the interests of competing energy producers. Businesses (including manufacturers and agribusiness) were concerned with the possibility of rising energy costs and their effect on production costs. Similarly, consumers were interested in reducing the cost and price volatility of energy for residential consumption. Utility companies found themselves concerned about the costs of energy production, their ability to recover such costs, and the risk of reduced energy supply.

Environmentalists were also relevant to the national energy bill and focused on the impact of energy development on the environment, especially on protected lands such as national parks, wilderness areas, and ANWR. Native American communities, particularly those tribes with land rich in natural resources, were also attentive to issues regarding energy development on protected lands.[30] Their concerns largely focused on Native Americans' right to decide whether (and how) to extract resources from their land, an issue that pitted potential economic benefits against potential environmental costs. Organized labor also was interested in the Securing America's Future Energy Act because of the potential impact on union jobs. The Teamsters supported drilling in ANWR and the Republican-sponsored energy bill due to the inclusion of a project labor agreement in which oil and gas companies pledged to hire unionized labor. As a result, drilling in ANWR was expected to result in thousands of jobs for union members. In describing the Teamsters' unusual support for a Republican-backed bill, one Republican staff member colorfully noted, "someone reached out and told the unions that 'the environmentalists are eating your lunch' and that there are a ton of jobs out there. Basically, someone said that if 'you help us get it done, you'll get the jobs.'"[31] Similarly, the United Auto Workers joined the automobile manufacturers in opposing increases in the fuel efficiency standards (CAFE standards) for cars and light trucks out of concern that increased standards would increase the cost of automobile production and lead to auto industry job losses. Finally, veterans were interested in the energy bill as a means to reduce American dependence on foreign energy sources and build energy independence. In fact, proponents of the national energy bill included veterans' support in their press materials

---

[30] Particular attention focused on Native American communities with land in the coastal plains of the Arctic National Wildlife Refuge. This land was set aside in 1980, and even though studies for oil and gas exploration have been conducted, no drilling can occur until Congress opens up the tract.

[31] Personal interview.

as illustrated by this tag line: "American veterans fought to protect our independence. Now it's your turn: open ANWR."[32]

Lastly, wetlands conservation legislation was relevant to six widely identified subconstituencies in each district. As discussed previously, developers and state and local governments were concerned that conservation programs would limit the growth of commercial, residential, and transportation projects. Consequently, these subconstituencies had an interest in the terms under which the North American Wetlands Conservation Act was extended. Environmentalists and conservation advocates were interested in NAWCA because it facilitated efforts to place sensitive lands into conservation. Sportsmen, including anglers and hunters, were also attentive to this wetlands conservation legislation because it protected areas that support fish and wildlife. Another subconstituency identified as relevant to the issue of wetlands conservation was residents who would benefit from increased green space and natural drainage in their communities. The final subconstituency interested in wetlands conservation legislation was farmers, for whom NAWCA provided the option of selling their land into conservation and the security of an alternate, economically viable use for their land.

MEASURING PERCEPTIONS

Having identified the relevant district subconstituencies for each of the four issues, the next step is to measure who is in "the mind's eye" of the legislative office when these issues are considered on Capitol Hill. The task of measuring legislative perception of constituents is far from straightforward because perceptions are not readily observable, and hence, they are inherently difficult to measure. However, the cognitive psychology literature provides a way to address the challenge of measuring perception. Since perceptions – or how legislators and their staff see the district – are based on the information most accessible to the perceiver, knowing about the accessibility of information about the different constituents in the district provides a measure of legislative perceptions (e.g., Houston and Fazio 1989; Schwarz 1998). Put differently, if one can ascertain what information is more (or less) accessible to a legislative staff member when he looks at his district, then one knows how he perceives the district. The accessibility of information about the

---

[32] Arctic Power, a grassroots, nonprofit citizens' organization in support of oil exploration and production in ANWR (see www.anwr.org).

different relevant subconstituencies in the district, therefore, captures legislative perceptions of constituents. Put differently, perceptions of the district draw on the information about subconstituencies that is most accessible, and this accessibility can be measured.

The psychology literature commonly employs an individual's spontaneous recall of information in response to open-ended questions to measure the accessibility of the information to an individual (e.g., Schwarz 1998; Wyer and Srull 1989). When an open-ended question is posed, an individual's answer draws on the information that he recalls most easily. Political scientists have adopted this measure of information accessibility and use recall in response to open-ended questions to determine the accessibility of political information to citizens (e.g., Chong 1993; DeSart 1995; Lau 1989; Lodge, Stroh, and Wahlke 1990; McGraw, Hasecke, and Conger 2003).[33] As Hagen (1995, 52) notes in his study of citizens' consideration of racial issues, "the readiness with which a political issue comes to mind when talking about politics naturally is best assessed with survey questions that are 'open-ended,' asking respondents to speak for themselves." Translated into the congressional context, this approach means that a legislative staff member's recall of information about subconstituencies in response to open-ended questions about the relevance of a policy to the district measures the accessibility of information about the subconstituents in the district.

In order to examine legislative recall and the accessibility of information about constituents, however, it is necessary to talk with the legislators and staff members who are responsible for representing constituents in Washington. To this goal, eighty-one offices are selected using purposive sampling designed to create a sample representative of the 435 Members of the U.S. House of Representatives, as well as the relevant committees, on key dimensions such as party, seniority, and region (see Appendix A). These dimensions are important because they reflect the structure of the chamber and the distribution of power within it, which may help to explain variation in legislative perceptions of their districts. The sample is split between offices in which the interviews focused on health policy (forty offices) and those that concentrated on energy and environment

---

[33] Latency data, or the amount of time that elapses before a respondent answers, is another measure of accessibility used in both the psychology literature (e.g., Fazio 1990; Hastie 1986; E. Smith 1984) and the political psychology literature (e.g., Bassili 1995; Lavine et al. 1996; Zaller 1992). However, this measure is poorly suited for interviews with elites where interviews are not computer assisted and greater emphasis is placed on maintaining a collegial rapport.

policy (forty-one offices).[34] Within each policy sample, half of the legislators serve on the committee with primary jurisdiction for health or natural resources policy, the House Committee on Energy and Commerce and the House Committee on Resources, respectively. The total sample (eighty-one offices) and each policy sample have a near equal number of Republican and Democratic offices, which reflects the close partisan balance of the 107th Congress. Additionally, the sample reflects the distribution of freshmen, junior, and senior legislators in the 107th Congress, as well as the regional distribution of legislators (see Appendix A for more details).

As noted previously, the choice to interview legislative staff members reflects the fact that staff members play an important role in congressional offices as both policy experts and constituent liaisons (e.g., Salisbury and Shepsle 1981). Legislators are stretched thin across a range of legislative and political obligations, and staff members assume a wide range of duties essential to the success of the legislator. In recognition of the importance of the legislative enterprise, some scholars have turned to interviews with legislative staff to examine legislative behavior (e.g., Evans 1991a; Evans 2004; Hall 1996; Kingdon 1989; Koger 2003; Schiller 1995). Given the focus here on the practice of constituency representation on Capitol Hill, interviews with staff members are an invaluable source of information about the way a legislative enterprise sees the constituency and how this perception of the district shapes the legislative actions taken on its behalf.

In-depth interviews were conducted with the professional staff member responsible for either health care policy or resources policy, as appropriate, in each office in the sample. The initial contact and interview request were made by phone and all interviews were conducted in person on Capitol Hill (see Appendix B for more details). Using this protocol, the response rate to requests for personal interviews was 80% as defined by the number of offices in which the correct staff member was contacted and granted an interview. Since the division of labor within congressional offices varies, the exact position held by the staff member responsible for health policy or resources policy varied across the offices interviewed. Of the eighty-one staff members interviewed, 64% of respondents were legislative assistants or senior legislative assistants,

---

[34] Forty-one offices were selected in the natural resources policy because the staff member in one office was not involved with the national energy bill and therefore this office is only included in the analysis of wetlands conservation.

22% were legislative directors, and 14% were other senior staff members. Although interviews with professional staff members are the primary source of data, interviews were also conducted with a half dozen Members of Congress (see Appendix B). These interviews provide additional insight into legislative perceptions of constituents and confirm the findings based on the staff interviews.

The interviews consist of pretested, primarily open-ended questions in which the staff member was asked how the office sees constituents' interests on each of the selected issues.[35] Given the substantial evidence on the effects of question ordering (e.g., Converse and Presser 1986; Weisberg, Krosnick, and Bowen 1989), the order in which the two health care policies (or two natural resources policies) were addressed in the interview alternates. This precaution reduces any potential order effects that might occur if one issue was consistently discussed before the other. Additionally, the interviews were conducted "on location" on Capitol Hill in order to more accurately capture legislative enterprises' view of their districts and the practice of congressional representation. All interviews were confidential and off the record. Given both written and verbal assurance that their names and the names of their bosses would not be used, no respondent refused to answer a question. In fact, with the guarantee of confidentiality, over 75% of staff members agreed to have the interview recorded, and all respondents were remarkably candid and forthcoming.

Consistent with the psychology literature's use of information accessibility to operationalize perceptions, staff members' responses to an open-ended question are used to measure the accessibility of information about subconstituencies, and hence legislative perceptions of constituents. Scholars who employ open-ended questions when interviewing legislative elites have found the use of such questions to be invaluable in shedding light on legislative preferences and judgments (see Evans 1991a, 1991b; Hall 1996; Sinclair 1989). After specifying the first of the two health (or natural resources) issues, the legislative staff member was asked, "to whom in the district is this issue [relevant health or natural resources issue] important?" The staff member's response, therefore, reflects the information about constituents in their district that is most accessible and is part of their mental picture of their constituency.

A policy's importance to the district is an integral feature of daily life on Capitol Hill, where staff members quickly call to mind information

---

[35] See Appendix B for a more detailed discussion of the interview protocol.

about constituents' interests on an issue and assess the importance of a policy to the district.[36] In meetings and conversations, staff members regularly are asked by legislators, other legislative staff members, and policy makers to succinctly assess a policy's relevance to constituents in the district. By focusing on legislative staff members in their Washington, D.C., offices, therefore, the interview replicates this routine feature of constituency representation on Capitol Hill with minimal artificiality.

The question asked of staff members deliberately invokes an inclusive notion of district constituents and does not ask about organized interests, or "interest groups." There is no limit to the number of subconstituencies that a staff member could include in his response. The result is a measure of whether or not each legislative office saw each relevant subconstituency when considering the importance of a policy to the district. This measure is unique to each legislative enterprise–subconstituency pairing and is consistent with the dyadic model of subconstituency representation. In the case of the Patients' Bill of Rights, there are 280 observations in which to evaluate legislative perceptions because there are 40 legislative offices in the sample, each with 7 relevant subconstituencies that could be perceived. Similarly, there are 240 observations (40 legislative offices multiplied by 6 subconstituencies) in the case of Medicare regulatory reform, 400 observations in the case of national energy policy (40 legislative offices multiplied by 10 subconstituencies), and 246 observations in the case of wetlands conservation (41 legislative offices multiplied by 6 subconstituencies).[37]

Although a concern common to data gathered in interviews or surveys is that respondents may behave strategically and give the response they think the interviewer wants to hear, the likelihood of such behavior in these interviews is quite small. The interviews were carefully crafted to minimize the possibility of strategic behavior. For one, the interviews were not for attribution and were solely for academic purposes, two conditions that are unlikely to foster strategic responses (see Herbst 1998). Indeed, legislators and their staff do not find academics to be an especially daunting audience. Additionally, the questions focus on a specific policy, which minimizes the risk of rationalization or strategic

---

[36] This is not to suggest that deliberative decision making does not occur in congressional offices but rather that the question of a policy's relevance to constituents is posed every day in every office.

[37] In the natural resources cases, one legislative office was interviewed regarding only wetlands conservation policy because the staff member was not involved on national energy policy.

behavior by the respondent (see Kingdon 1989). Despite these precautions, there remains the possibility that staff members acted strategically. If so, what would be the impact of such behavior? A staff member's strategic response to the question of to whom in the district is an issue important would be to recall as many constituents as possible in order to demonstrate the legislative enterprise's familiarity and responsiveness to the district. However, as the remainder of the chapter details, the data clearly show that legislative enterprises recall only a small subset of relevant subconstituencies in the district. Thus, if staff members answer questions strategically, then their truncated view of the district actually *overstates* legislative perceptions of constituents.

Legislative staff members' responses to open-ended questions about the importance of policies to constituents are used in two important ways. First, responses to this question are used to create a dichotomous measure of whether or not a given legislative office recalls a given subconstituency. This office-specific, subconstituency-specific measure of legislative perception serves as the dependent variable in the analysis of legislative perception in Chapter 5 as well as the primary independent variable in the analysis of dyadic representation in Chapter 6. Second, the collection of subconstituencies recalled with respect to a given issue in each office captures a legislative enterprise's aggregate perception of the district, or the sum of perceived relevant subconstituencies in the district. This measure of legislative perception of the totality of the district is the primary independent variable in the analyses of legislative behavior in Chapter 7. In sum, the examination of legislative perceptions of constituents and their impact on legislative behavior must encompass an understanding of both which subconstituencies legislators and their staff see in the district as well as how perceptions of specific subconstituencies come together to create a perception of the district as a whole. Amid the many interested subconstituencies on each bill, then, who do legislators and their staff see in the district?

WHO LEGISLATIVE ENTERPRISES SEE IN THE DISTRICT

Two striking patterns of legislative perceptions of constituents in the district are evident from the data: (1) Legislative perceptions of the district are limited; (2) some subconstituents are more likely to be seen than others. First, legislative staff members do not recall the full range of relevant subconstituencies in their district, but instead recall a small subset of relevant constituents. Across all four policies, 75% of legislative offices

TABLE 4.1. *Number of Subconstituencies Seen by Legislative Office*

	Patients' Bill of Rights (max = 7)	Medicare Regulatory Reform (max = 6)	National Energy Policy (max = 10)	Wetlands Conservation (max = 6)
No subconstituencies	0	2	0	3
One subconstituency	16	19	10	15
Two subconstituencies	14	12	15	15
Three subconstituencies	10	6	12	7
Four subconstituencies	0	1	3	1
Five subconstituencies	0	0	0	0
Six subconstituencies	0	0	0	0
Seven subconstituencies	0	n/a	0	n/a
Eight subconstituencies	n/a	n/a	0	n/a
Nine subconstituencies	n/a	n/a	0	n/a
Ten subconstituencies	n/a	n/a	0	n/a

saw two or fewer subconstituencies in their district. This limited view of the district is particularly striking when considering that there were six or more subconstituencies relevant to each policy (see Table 4.1).

In the case of Medicare regulatory reform, the Patients' Bill of Rights, and wetlands conservation, legislative staff members saw an average of fewer than two of the relevant subconstituencies, or less than one-third of the relevant subconstituencies in the district. In addition, legislative staff saw an average of only 2.2 out of 10, or about one-fifth, of the relevant subconstituencies when asked about district interests in the national energy bill. These patterns are especially striking because only those subconstituencies who were widely identified as relevant to the policy at hand are included. In other words, these assessments of legislative perceptions are not based on all constituents in the district, but rather are limited to only those subconstituencies who are widely considered by policy experts and political journalists to be relevant to the issue in question.

One possible explanation for this limited perception of the district is that not every subconstituency is present in every district and thus legislative offices should not be expected to see a subconstituency that is not there. In other words, when a legislative office does not see a subconstituency, is it because that subconstituency does not exist in their district? Although this is a sensible hypothesis, the construction of the legislative office–subconstituency dyads are specifically designed to minimize this potential problem since each of the relevant subconstituencies is present in each district.[38] Subconstituencies who were not seen by legislative offices did indeed have a presence in their districts, and this is true across all four issues. In fact, not only do subconstituencies exist in the districts where legislative staff members did not see them, but half of the identified subconstituencies were larger on average in districts where they were *not* recalled by legislative enterprises as compared to offices in which they were recalled. For instance, legislative offices that did not perceive the importance of Medicare regulatory reform to physicians had an average of 4,600 physicians in their district as compared to an average of 3,700 physicians in districts where staff members saw the issue as important to physicians. In the case of the national energy bill, legislative offices who did not recall the interests of low-income consumers in the legislation had an average of 80,200 low-income consumers in their districts, which is substantially larger than the 58,300 low-income consumers in the average district of offices that saw consumers when asked about their district.[39]

In addition, more often than not, legislative offices did not recall the largest subconstituency in their district relevant to the policy in question. Sixty percent of offices did not recall the largest subconstituency in their district relevant to the Patients' Bill of Rights, and this figure only grows when looking at the other three issues: wetlands conservation (76%), energy policy (77%), and Medicare regulatory reform (85%). This means that despite a strong presence in the district relative to other subconstituencies, the largest subconstituency is far from guaranteed to be seen by a legislator and his staff members. Additionally, legislators on the committee with jurisdiction for the policy do not have a more comprehensive view of their district, nor do majority party legislators. In short, legislators' limited view of their districts is widespread and indicates that information shortcuts are being used.

Given that legislative enterprises do not see all of the relevant constituents in their district, the focus shifts to which subconstituencies are seen.

---

[38] Based on the empirical data (see Appendix C for measurement details), this is true across the four issues with very few exceptions. In the case of Medicare regulatory reform, there are 15 out of 240 observations in which there is not an objective subconstituency presence in the district. Similarly, in the case of national energy policy, there are 31 of 400 observations in which there is not an objective subconstituency presence in the district.

[39] See Appendix C for details on the measurement of these subconstituencies.

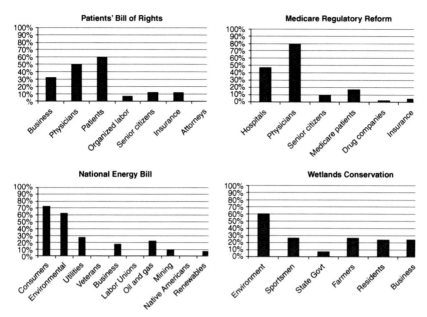

FIGURE 4.1. Legislative Recall of Subconstituencies (Percentage of Offices).

If legislative staff members see a random sample of the policy-relevant subconstituencies in their district, this would indicate that legislative perceptions are limited, but are nonetheless representative of the collection of constituency interests. However, the data reveal that legislative enterprises are systematically more likely to see some subconstituencies than other relevant subconstituencies in their district. Figure 4.1 illustrates the percentage of legislative offices that saw each of the relevant subconstituencies.

Not all legislative enterprises see the same subconstituencies, but across the sample, certain subconstituencies are more likely to be seen than others. For instance, in the case of wetlands conservation, the environmental subconstituency is recalled by 61% of legislative offices, whereas farmers are recalled by only 27% of offices interviewed, and state and local governments are recalled by a mere 7% of offices. When asked about district interests in the national energy bill, 73% of legislative offices recalled the interests of consumers, but only 18% of offices recalled the business subconstituency in their district. Physicians were recalled by 80% of legislative offices when asked about Medicare regulatory and contracting reform, which reflects one staffer's sentiment that "this bill is all about the doctors."[40] Or consider the case of the Patients' Bill of Rights, where 60% of legislative offices recalled patients as a subconstituency in their district to whom the issue was important – a rather low percentage considering that "patients" is in the very title of the legislation. In short, when legislative enterprises consider the interests of their district, some subconstituencies assume a more prominent place in the office's perception of district interests on that issue.

The data presented here illustrate the shortcomings of legislative perceptions of the constituents in their district across health and resources policies. One can comfortably conclude that legislative staff members do not engage in exhaustive information searches, which would have resulted in far more subconstituencies being recalled as relevant to the specified policies (Miler 2009). However, what remains unclear is why legislative enterprises see some constituents and not others. The next chapter takes up this question.

CONCLUSION

Legislators and their staff on Capitol Hill see the constituents in their district in a particular policy environment. Therefore, it is essential that any study of legislative perception be attentive to the policy context in which legislative enterprises represent their constituents in order to more closely reflect the reality of the political world. Additionally, an issue-specific approach makes it possible to identify the relevant subconstituencies that legislative enterprises can reasonably be expected to see when considering the interests of their districts, which benefits the tractability and precision of our analyses of legislative perceptions.

The presence of multiple, relevant subconstituencies in a district is central to the notion of legislative enterprise–subconstituency dyads advanced in this book and reflects the practice of constituency representation. When asked about the Patients' Bill of Rights, one Republican staffer replied that it was important to "subgroups" before going on to discuss the importance of the issue to specific subconstituencies in his district. Further illustrations of the attention to subconstituencies can be found in the responses from Members of Congress when asked about the relevance of health policy or resources policy to their districts. These members responded by talking about some subconstituencies in their district, and not talking about other relevant subconstituencies. For

40 Personal interview.

instance, one Member of Congress described his district by saying "we have big hospitals [names omitted] and we have small clinics.... Also, there are other folks in the district like [a medical device manufacturer] and [a pharmaceutical company]."[41] Another legislator discussed his view of his district on natural resources issues, noting that "you know who certain groups are in your district. You know who the environmentalists are, who the conservative businesses are."[42] Consequently, in order to understand constituency representation through the eyes of the legislative enterprise, the district must be broken down into its relevant subgroups.

Another requirement for understanding legislative perceptions of the district is to determine whether or not a legislative office sees a given subconstituency. Drawing on measurement techniques from the cognitive psychology literature and original personal interviews with professional legislative staff members, legislative perceptions of constituents in the district are captured by measuring the accessibility of information about relevant subconstituencies. The data reveal that legislative perceptions of their districts are far from exhaustive. In fact, legislative offices see less than one-third of relevant subconstituencies in their districts when they consider the importance of health, energy, and environmental policies to their districts. Even though the data presented here rely only on descriptive statistics, they strongly suggest that legislative perceptions of constituents in the district are incomplete. Moreover, they reveal an underlying pattern of variation in legislative perceptions that is not readily attributed to the composition of the district or other obvious explanations. The next chapter addresses the question of what explains the variations in legislative perceptions identified here.

[41] Personal interview.
[42] Personal interview.

5

Explaining Legislative Perceptions

The preceding chapters reveal that legislative enterprises are responsible for representing districts made up of many subconstituencies that vary according to the policy at hand. Yet we know remarkably little about where a legislator's sense of his constituency comes from. Dexter (1957, 2, italics added) calls attention to the origins of perceptions of the constituency and writes, "The fact is the congressman represents his image of the district or of his constituents (or fails to represent his, or our, image of them). *How does he get this image? Where does it come from?*"

This chapter is motivated by Dexter's observation that scholars know little about the origins of legislators' images of their district. Consequently, the factors that determine which constituents a legislative enterprise sees, and the reasons why one congressional enterprise sees a subconstituency but other legislators do not, remain unknown. Consider the case of the national energy bill, where for every three legislative offices who perceived the interests of environmentalists in energy policy, two offices did not see the environmental subconstituency in their district as relevant to the bill. Similarly, in the case of the Patients' Bill of Rights, only a slim majority of legislative offices perceived patients' interests despite the fact that every congressional district includes patients enrolled in managed care programs. In fact, across the four policies examined, not a single subconstituency was perceived by all legislative enterprises.

A further illustration of the differences in how legislative offices perceive their districts on the same issue can be found in a comparison of legislative staff members' perceptions of their districts on the issue of wetlands conservation. The legislative office of one Mid-Atlantic Democratic House member described NAWCA as being "very much an environmental issue" with environmentalists as the primary subconstituency, while the office of a Midwestern Democrat described the same wetlands conservation bill as about "wildlife and waterfowl" with hunters and sportsmen as the constituencies to whom the issue is important.[1] Offering yet another view of the importance of wetlands conservation to their district, the staff of a Southern Republican House member described the issue as about the tension between development and conservation and saw developers, businesses, and local government as the subconstituencies to whom the issue is important.[2] Since the same six relevant subconstituencies are present in each member's district, what varies in this example is not whether a subconstituency is in the district, but which subconstituencies legislative enterprises see. These examples show the variation in legislative perceptions, and beg the question of how legislative perceptions of their constituents are formed.

According to the information-based theory of legislative perceptions, differences in perceptions reflect differences in the accessibility of information about subconstituencies to legislative enterprises. Therefore, in order to understand why congressional offices perceive some relevant constituents and not others, it is necessary to focus on the factors that affect the accessibility of information among legislative enterprises. The cognitive psychology literature is again a valuable foundation for the development of hypotheses about the accessibility of information about constituents. These primary information-based hypotheses are presented alongside alternate arguments common to the congressional literature that focus on the strategic considerations of electorally minded legislators.

INFORMATION ACCESSIBILITY

"Readily accessible, easily processible, crucially relevant" (Carmines and Kuklinski 1990, 248) describes the type of information that is most likely to be used by legislative offices when considering the interests of the district. Given the flood of information that can overwhelm a legislative enterprise, legislators and their staff have adapted to their environment by relying on information that is easily accessible. As discussed in Chapter 3, the psychology literature concludes that accessible information is more likely to shape perceptions, including legislative

[1] Personal interview.
[2] Personal interview.

perceptions of constituents' interests on public policy issues. Accessible
information, however, does not necessarily produce the best judgments
because information that is accessible is not necessarily representative of
all relevant information. Recall that several factors make information
more accessible, four of which are of interest here: frequency, familiarity,
salience, and predisposition. The information-based theory of legislative perception provides a framework for adapting these four factors to
the congressional context and examining their impact on constituency
representation.

Frequency of Information

One factor that affects the accessibility of information about a
subconstituency is the frequency with which a congressional enterprise
encounters that information. Information that is encountered more frequently will be more easily accessible from memory, thereby increasing
the probability it will be recalled (e.g., Carlston and Smith 1996; Conover
and Feldman 1986). Congressional scholars recognize that frequent contact between constituents and congressional offices is an important part
of the representative relationship precisely because it provides legislative offices with information about constituents' preferences (e.g., Clapp
1963; Dexter 1956; Evans 2002; Hansen 2001; Kingdon 1989).

Of particular interest here is constituency-initiated contact with a legislative office through letters, email, phone calls, and visits on Capitol
Hill. Although journalists and scholars often rely on surveys to gauge
public opinion, legislative offices need a measure of constituency opinion that can keep pace with the ever-changing issues being considered in
Congress. Given these needs, the costs of relying on surveys are prohibi-
tive. Consequently, legislative enterprises typically use meetings, letters,
and phone calls to keep track of constituency opinion and rely on district
survey data only infrequently (see Jacobs et al. 1998).

In fact, responding to constituent inquiries and meeting with constituents is a large part of what legislators and their staff do on a daily
basis. When talking about policy issues such as health care, legislators
and their staff often refer to direct communication with their constituents. A comment from Representative Michael Bilirakis (R-FL) regarding Medicare reform reflects the pervasive importance of contact from
constituents:

I have heard often and forcefully from constituents that honest, law-abiding
providers have a difficult time understanding the rules, let alone following

them. I know other members have heard similar views from providers in their districts.[3]

Constituents, such as these health care providers, who frequently contact their legislator's office are not only voicing their opinion on a given issue but also making themselves more mentally accessible to the staff member. Frequent contact from a subconstituency has the effect of increasing the likelihood that the enterprise will perceive that subconstituency when considering the interests of the district. In interviews, a number of House staff members referred to the proverbial "squeaky wheel" in describing the subconstituencies from whom they hear most frequently. While these staffers did not use the language of cognitive psychology, they are describing the fact that frequent contact increases the accessibility of information about the interests of certain subconstituencies in the district.

There are two primary ways in which a subconstituency can make their interests known to a legislative office: mail contact and personal contact. These two measures correspond to the way in which legislative staff distinguish between types of constituency contact. Mail contact includes all written contact (letters, postcards, email, and fax correspondence) and personal contact includes in-person visits as well as phone contact. The most comprehensive source of information about this full range of constituency contact is the legislative office.[4] Legislative enterprises in the contemporary House routinely keep track of incoming mail, email, faxes, phone calls, and personal visits.[5] Some offices use computer software to track incoming constituent contact, and other offices rely on old-fashioned sorting; however, attentiveness to constituency contact is common to all offices.

Data on the amount of mail and personal contact from subconstituencies was collected during interviews with legislative offices. Using two forms administered at the end of the personal interviews (see Appendix B), legislative staff members indicated the amount of contact they received from each relevant subconstituency on a specified issue in the preceding twelve months. The first form provides a list of subconstituencies and asks how much mail the office received from each subconstituency – no

---

[3] House Report 107–23, 90.
[4] An alternate approach is to use individuals' reports of contact with their elected officials as the source of these data (see Bartels 2005, 2008). However, this approach requires district-level survey data and excludes contact by any groups or organizations.
[5] Personal interviews with staff members. See also Whiteman (1995).

mail, a little mail, some mail, or a lot of mail. Similarly, a second form is administered to collect data on how frequently a legislative office spoke with each of the listed relevant subconstituencies in the preceding twelve months. The amount of personal contact from a subconstituency in each legislative office is measured using a count variable (see Appendixes B and C for further measurement details).

It is both important and beneficial to collect data on subconstituency contact with legislative offices during the interviews because of the absence of public records of incoming mail or telephone calls to congressional offices. Information about personal contact between constituents and legislative offices, in fact, remains notoriously difficult to obtain. Records filed by lobbyists in compliance with the Lobbying Disclosure Act of 1995 are often quite vague regarding the legislation on which they lobbied and incomplete regarding the offices they lobbied. Moreover, these requirements apply only to registered lobbyists, which means that the records do not contain information about contact from nonlobbyists and constituents. In contrast, legislative staff members are well equipped to answer questions about the volume of mail and personal contacts from relevant subconstituencies.

One concern with gathering data directly from congressional offices is that the interviews are also the source of information about legislative perceptions. A number of steps were taken in the design and implementation of the interview to minimize concerns about measurement validity. The variables were obtained using very different instruments and were taken at different points in the interview. The dependent variable measure of legislative perception comes from an open-ended question that is posed at the beginning of the interview, whereas the contact variables come from close-ended survey instruments administered at the end of the interview (see Appendix B). Furthermore, when measuring the contact variables, staff members were provided with a list of relevant subconstituencies so they did not have to recall subconstituencies. Additionally, in the time between these two questions, the interviews focus on the specified policy issue and all relevant subconstituencies, not just those recalled in response to the first question. The structure of the interview, therefore, reduces the possibility of the earlier recall question influencing responses to later questions. In short, the time elapsed, the intervening questions, and the different cognitive tasks required of the respondent increase confidence that the recall measure and contact measures capture distinct information.

Familiarity of Information

A second factor that affects the accessibility of information is an individual's familiarity with the information. According to the cognitive psychology literature, information that is more familiar to an individual is more easily accessible and therefore more likely to be recalled (e.g., Jones 1998; Wyer and Srull 1989). Since individuals rely on only a subset of all available information, it is logical that a primary cognitive short-cut is to rely on the information that is most familiar, and thus least cognitively taxing to recall. A legislative enterprise may be more or less familiar with information about constituents for three reasons: past professional experience, committee-based expertise, and seniority.

The first source of familiarity is rooted in the previous careers of legislators and their staff since these experiences increase a congressional enterprise's familiarity with a subconstituency. Media accounts of congressional politics call attention to the revolving door of employment on Capitol Hill, especially the ease with which individuals move between the halls of Congress and the corridor of K Street, resulting in arguably unseemly ties.[6] Scholars also have examined career experience to explain gender differences in legislative recruitment (Friedman 1993; Fulton et al. 1996; Gertzog 1995) and policy specialization (Burrell 1994; Foerstel and Foerstel 1996; Thomas 1994). In general, past professional experience has been found to affect the types of campaigns that legislators run (e.g., Fenno 1978, 1996) and their committee activity (Hall 1996). It is only logical, then, to expect that previous career experience also may influence a legislative enterprise's view of the district.

Since the congressional enterprise is the primary actor here, the previous professional experiences of both legislators and staff members responsible for health and resource policy in each office are examined. Legislative offices in which the legislator or staff member shares previous professional experience with a specified subconstituency are more familiar with that subconstituency's concerns and policy interests. This familiarity, in turn, renders information about the subconstituency more easily accessible to the enterprise, and increases the likelihood that the office will perceive the policy as important to the subconstituency. For instance, a legislator who was a medical professional before being

---

[6] For a sample of recent coverage of the Washington revolving door, see Akers and Kane (2007), Birnbaum (2007), Gettleman (2005), Kirkpatrick (2006), Kornblut (2006), McIntire (2006), and Stolberg (2006).

elected to the House is likely to be intimately familiar with the concerns and interests of physicians and is likely to see their interest in health policy. The familiarity generated by past experience is illustrated by the comments of one staff member to a Republican legislator when asked about the health care interests in the district:

My boss, before he came to Congress had his own marketing and consulting business and primarily what he was doing was hospital consulting. And so he knows all of these people, he knows all the physicians.... He knows the industry very well.[7]

Similarly, when talking about the importance of national energy policy to the district, a staff member in another House office said:

[He's] a former small business guy and so he understands how difficult it is in the regulatory environment of California to run a business.... You know, a lot of his friends are small businessmen.[8]

A second measure of familiarity with information about a subconstituency focuses on the role of congressional committees as a source of issue-specific expertise. Krehbiel (1990, 1993) argues that the House committee system provides a division of labor among members and promotes specialization and expertise. Committee members bear the costs of gathering issue-specific information on behalf of the chamber, but they also reap the benefits of this expertise through the chamber's deference to committees (Krehbiel 1991). There is considerable evidence that legislators specialize according to their committee assignments and gain expertise in areas within the committee's jurisdiction (e.g., Adler and Lapinski 1997; Cox and McCubbins 1993; Hall 1996).[9] The general continuity of committee jurisdiction (and committee membership) also means that committee members address the same issues over time. Consequently, committee members and their staff are particularly well informed about the issues that come before the committee and the subconstituencies relevant to those issues.

Consistent with the literature on House committees, issue-specific constituency information is hypothesized to be more accessible to members of the committee with jurisdiction in a policy area as compared

---

[7] Personal interview.

[8] Personal interview.

[9] One should note the unresolved debate over the extent to which this expertise is a function of self-selection in committee assignments or primarily a function of the information advantages created by specialization (e.g., Hall and Grofman 1990; Kollman 1997, 1998; Krehbiel 1990; Shepsle 1978).

to nonmembers. In turn, members who serve on a committee with primary responsibility for health care issues or natural resources issues should be more likely to recall relevant subconstituencies. Legislators are expected to be more familiar with health policy if they are members of the House Committee on Energy and Commerce, which has primary jurisdiction for health issues. Similarly, legislators who serve on the House Committee on Resources, which is the primary committee of jurisdiction for policy involving natural resources, are expected to be more likely to perceive relevant subconstituencies. Given the potentially important effects of committee membership, the sample of legislative enterprises in this study is equally divided between offices of legislators who serve on committees with jurisdiction for health policy or resources policy and those who do not.[10]

Lastly, familiarity with information can be due to a longer tenure of service representing a district. More senior legislators, by definition, have been reelected repeatedly by the plurality of their district, thereby indicating some degree of successful representation of their constituents. Moreover, it is likely that a legislator and his staff have developed a familiarity with the issues affecting the district, as well as the subconstituencies within the district, over the years. This increased familiarity should make information about the importance of health policy and natural resources policy to constituents more readily accessible in the offices of more senior House members. For instance, a legislative office in which the legislator has represented a district for twenty years is expected to be more familiar with both the issues and the district's interests on those issues than the office of a first-term legislator. Accordingly, these enterprises also should be more likely to perceive the interests of relevant subconstituencies in their districts, all else equal. A measure of legislative seniority, which is the number of years of service in the U.S. House of Representatives, including their service during the 107th Congress, is included in the analyses of legislative perceptions.

Salience of Information

A third factor that increases the accessibility of information about a subconstituency in the district is the salience of the information to the legislative office. Information may be salient because it is particularly vivid or compelling, and therefore it is more likely to be recalled by a

---

[10] See Appendix A for further details.

congressional enterprise when asked about the interests of the district. The challenge, however, is to define the salience of information about a subconstituency. What does it mean for information to be salient to a congressional enterprise? Here, the salience of information about subconstituencies is conceptualized in terms of financial contributions to the legislator. The average House member spent close to $1 million on his reelection bid in 2000, and the cost of congressional campaigns continues to escalate.[11] Since legislators must raise an enormous amount of money every two years, financial contributions are both vivid and compelling to the office. Information about subconstituencies who contribute more money to a legislator is more likely to be recalled than information about other subconstituencies relevant to the issue who do not make a financial contribution because the salience of the contribution makes information about the contributing subconstituency more accessible.

While the popular press and political pundits generally argue that money buys Congress (e.g., Lewis 1998; Stern 1988), political scientists have reached far less conclusive results. Studies have largely concluded that money does not "buy votes" (e.g., Grenzke 1989; Wawro 2001; Wright 1990), although there is also evidence that money does influence access to legislators (e.g., Austen-Smith 1995; Langbein 1986; Wright 1996) and legislative participation (e.g., Hall and Wayman 1990; Witko 2006).[12] Of interest here is whether financial contributions affect legislative offices' perceptions of the district. Put differently, does money buy "mental access"? At an intuitive level, money seems to matter in congressional politics, but tracing its influence has proven to be far more difficult. If money affects "mental access" and shapes how legislators see the constituents in their district, then this would provide evidence of the subtle but pernicious influence of money in congressional politics. Financial contributions might allow constituents to become salient in the minds of legislators and their staff, which then could affect the actions taken by Members of Congress. The impact of financial contributions on legislative perceptions is examined using the total amount of financial contributions received by each legislator from each given subconstituency during the 2000 election cycle.[13]

---

[11] According to Federal Election Commission (FEC) records reported by the Center for Responsive Politics, the average amount of money spent by Members of the House in the 1999–2000 cycle was $948,608.

[12] But see Fleisher (1993) and Strattman (2002).

[13] These totals include contributions from individuals and organized groups associated with the specified subconstituency both inside and outside the district. The inclusion of

Predisposition to Information

A fourth and final factor believed to influence the accessibility of information about subconstituencies is a legislative enterprise's predisposition toward the information. Recall that the cognitive psychology literature largely asserts that an individual's predisposition to agree with information makes that information more easily accessible (e.g., Eagly and Chaiken 1998; Festinger 1957). However, some scholars contend that disagreement with information actually renders the information more accessible (e.g., Hastie and Kumar 1979; Higgins and Bargh 1987). In the congressional context, then, how do predispositions toward information about subconstituencies affect legislative perceptions?

The psychological notion of predisposition is defined here as a partisan predisposition between a legislator's party and a specified relevant subconstituency. A legislator's party affiliation indicates shared preferences with certain subconstituencies, and therefore, the legislative enterprise is considered predisposed toward information about those subconstituencies (see Bailey and Brady 1998). Information about subconstituents with whom a legislative enterprise has party-based ties, therefore, is expected to be more accessible to legislative enterprises, and consequently more likely to be recalled when legislative staff consider the policy interests of their districts. Thus, although parties play many roles in congressional politics, the role relevant to legislative perceptions of constituents is rooted in parties' traditional ties with certain subconstituencies.

A survey of political science accounts and journalistic accounts of partisan politics are used to determine traditional ties between subconstituencies and the Republican and Democratic Parties. For instance, in the case of natural resources issues, the environmentalist subconstituency is coded as having traditional ties with the Democratic Party, whereas the business and development subconstituency is considered to be traditionally linked with the Republican Party.[14] A simple dichotomous variable is then used to indicate the presence of a traditional partisan tie between each legislative office–subconstituency pair.

---

all sources of contributions is important since some constituents support and contribute to groups that have a state or national office through which political donations are made. Consequently, if financial contributions were limited to only the district, these important sources of financial support to legislators would be excluded (see Hall 1996; Jackson 1988). See Appendix C for more details on measurement.

[14] For a full account of the classification of subconstituencies across the four issues, see Appendix C.

ALTERNATE ARGUMENTS

Information accessibility is not the only theoretical approach to understanding legislative perceptions. Indeed, an alternate approach might be
to treat the question of what explains legislative perceptions as a variant
of the more frequently examined question of what determines legislative voting behavior. This approach produces hypotheses that are based
on models of strategic legislators and posits the constituents legislative
enterprises see when they look at their districts are the result of deliberate
decisions rather than cognitive processes. However, this alternate logic
fails to recognize that legislative perception of constituents is deeply different from legislative behavior.

Legislative perceptions are the picture of the district that the legislative
enterprise has in mind when working to represent constituents on Capitol
Hill. This is a fundamental distinction when examining perceptions of
the district as compared to the conventional focus on calculated decision making, especially regarding voting behavior. The strategic decision
to take legislative action involves opportunity costs (e.g., Hall 1996;
Kingdon 1989), and as a result, legislators and their staff make deliberate decisions about their activities and their votes. This is *not* the same
process by which perceptions of constituents' interests are formed. There
is no decision by legislators to perceive or not to perceive a constituency.
Rather, underlying cognitive processes and the way in which legislators
and their staff use information when evaluating the relevance of policy to
the district determine legislative perceptions of the constituents.

Nevertheless, given the prominence of strategic behavior in the congressional literature, this alternate logic is considered alongside the
information-based hypotheses. According to this alternate approach,
it is assumed that a legislator's primary goal is reelection and that the
office's view of the district systematically will reflect this goal. In this
regard, legislators are believed to be vote-maximizers concerned with the
promise of electoral support (or punishment) from larger subconstituencies. Consequently, if legislative perception is based on strategic decisions,
then congressional enterprises should see larger subconstituencies instead
of smaller subconstituencies in the district because they have the greatest
potential impact on a legislator's reelection goal. Underlying this hypothesis is the assumption that individuals in the district are equal. In other
words, a legislative office should be more likely to perceive the shared
interests of 10,000 district residents (i.e., potential voters) as opposed to
a subconstituency of 2,000 constituents without regard for who these
individuals are. This assumption is put to the test when examining

congressional representation in practice. For instance, on the issue of Medicare regulatory reform, are legislative enterprises more likely to perceive the concerns of the more numerous senior citizens in their district or the concerns of physicians who constitute a smaller group?

For each issue examined, a measure of relevant subconstituency size in the district, as a proxy for electoral calculations, is constructed from detailed data on the number of district residents who are identified as part of each subconstituency relevant to the issue at hand (see Appendix C). Census data are used to identify relevant subconstituencies in each district, including data from the U.S. Census, the U.S. Small Business Administration, the Economic Census, the Bureau of Labor Statistics, and the U.S. Country Business Patterns. For instance, the total number of individuals employed by "insurance carriers and related activities" in each district is used to measure the size of the insurance subconstituency in each district. When there is no relevant Census data on the subconstituency in question, alternate measures are used. For instance, a relevant subconstituency to wetlands conservation are sportsmen; however, this is not a subconstituency identified by government statistics. Instead, the size of the sportsmen subconstituency is measured by the number of Ducks Unlimited members in each district based on membership records from the organization. Appendix C provides full details on the measurement of these variables.

A second hypothesis based on this alternate logic of electoral calculation is that a congressional enterprise's view of the district is affected by the electoral "safety" of the legislator. A legislator's past electoral performance is believed to influence the enterprise's calculations about the district and the legislator's reelection prospects. This logic suggests that legislators who were elected with a smaller percentage of the vote will be more likely to see a wide range of constituents in the district because of the legislator's precarious electoral position (e.g., Fiorina 1974; Hall 1996; Kingdon 1968). Indeed, a rational reaction to electoral uncertainty is for a congressional enterprise to expand his relationships with constituents in the district. Therefore, those offices in which legislators won by a smaller percentage of the vote in the 2000 general election are hypothesized to be more likely to recall any given subconstituency.[15]

---

[15] One possibility is that there might be an interactive effect between electoral security and subconstituency size, as well as with subconstituency contributions. However, the interaction terms are correlated with the parent terms at .97 and .98, respectively. Because of this degree of multicollinearity, all three variables are included without an interaction term.

Although these final hypotheses are consistent with the existing literature on legislative voting behavior, this alternate approach fails to recognize that perception is a unique cognitive process that is distinct from the cost-benefit calculations undertaken by legislators in other aspects of their jobs. As a result, the alternate logic is considered alongside the information-based hypotheses, but it is not expected to explain which constituents legislative enterprises see when they look at their district.

AN EMPIRICAL MODEL OF LEGISLATIVE PERCEPTIONS

To test these hypotheses regarding which subconstituencies a legislative enterprise sees in the district, it is essential to have a measure of legislative perception. Drawing on the psychology literature, perceptions here are measured by the spontaneous recall of information in response to open-ended questions about the policy interests of the district administered in personal interviews with legislative staff members. For example, when asked to whom in the district Medicare regulatory reform is important, one Member of Congress promptly replied, "That was hospital administrators and doctors."[16] Similarly, when asked about the importance of the national energy bill to their district, the staff of one Midwestern Republican recalled, "Farmers and coal miners are the top two that it would be important to."[17] These examples illustrate how legislators and their staff recall certain subconstituencies much more readily than other subconstituencies that are equally relevant to the issue in question. As discussed in the preceding chapter, the ease with which legislative staff recall information about a subconstituency reflects the accessibility of information about that subconstituency. Legislative perceptions of the district are dominated by subconstituencies about whom information is most accessible. Based on the dyadic theory of subconstituency representation, the dependent variable of legislative perceptions is a dichotomous variable indicating whether a given legislative enterprise recalled a specified, policy-relevant subconstituency.

The dyadic, or paired, structure of the data also means that there are multiple observations (each subconstituency–legislative office pair) within a single legislative office. This characteristic of the data violates the assumption of independent observations that underlies many

---

[16] Personal interview.
[17] Personal interview.

estimators such as ordinary least squares (OLS) and logit. In other words, it is likely that the relationship between a legislative enterprise and the insurance subconstituency in the district is not fully independent of the legislative enterprise's relationship with the physician subconstituency in the district because characteristics of the legislative enterprise are common to these two relationships. Similarly, it is likely that there are subconstituency-specific traits that exist across the insurance subconstituency's relationships with all legislative offices that make these relationships not fully independent of each other.

The use of a multilevel model captures this structure of the data and incorporates both within-group (i.e., subconstituencies within a legislative office) and between-group relationships in a single model. The particular multilevel model employed here is a random effects model, which is distinguished from typical estimators by the inclusion of explanatory variables at both levels of the model (legislative office and subconstituency), error terms for each of the two levels, and random intercepts for each observation (see Rabe-Hesketh and Skrondal 2005; Snijders and Bosker 1999). In short, the estimation technique employed takes into account the possibility of legislative office-specific patterns, as well as subconstituency-specific patterns. Since the dependent variable of whether a legislative enterprise sees a given subconstituency in their district is dichotomous, a logit function is specified when estimating the model.

This random effects model can by illustrated by the following formula:

$$Y_{ij} = \gamma_{oo} + \gamma_{1o}\chi_{1ij} + \cdots + \gamma_{po}\chi_{pij} + \gamma_{o1}z_{1j} + \cdots + \gamma_{oq}z_{qj} + U_{oj} + R_{ij}$$

In the equation, j denotes the legislative office, or group, (j = 1, 2, ..., N), and i denotes the subconstituencies within the office (i = 1, 2, ..., n_j). In addition, the explanatory variables at the subconstituency level are denoted $X_1, ..., X_p$, and the explanatory variables at the legislative office level are denoted $Z_1, ..., Z_q$.[18]

---

[18] See Snijders and Bosker 1999. The model is also estimated using alternate estimators, and the results are substantively and statistically robust. Since previous studies have addressed the nonindependence of observations in dyadic data by employing robust standard errors (Evans 1996) or clustered standard errors (Carpenter, Esterling, and Lazer 2004; Hojnacki and Kimball 1998, 1999), the model is also estimated using a logit model with standard errors clustered by legislative office, and the results are robust. Additionally, the model is robust when using a negative binomial estimator. The results of the multilevel model are presented because the theoretical foundation is most appropriate given the nature of the data.

Given the hypotheses described previously, this equation can be rewritten as

$$Y_{ij} = \beta_1 M_{ij} + \beta_2 C_{ij} + \beta_3 F_{ij} + \beta_4 E_{ij} + \beta_5 T_j + \beta_6 P_{ij} + \beta_7 S_{ij} + \beta_8 V_j$$

In this equation, Y_{ij} is the likelihood that congressional enterprise j perceives subconstituency i when asked about the importance of an issue to the district. M is a categorical measure of the amount of mail sent by constituency i to legislative office j, while C is a count of the number of personal and phone contacts initiated by subconstituency i with enterprise j. F is the amount of financial contributions (in thousands of dollars) from subconstituency i to office j in the 1999–2000 electoral cycle preceding the 107th Congress. E is an indicator variable of shared previous career experience between the legislator and staff members in congressional enterprise j and subconstituency i. T is a dichotomous variable of whether legislative office j serves on the committee of jurisdiction for the policy area. P indicates whether there are traditional partisan ties between the party of legislative office j and subconstituency i. S is the number of individuals identified as belonging to subconstituency i in the district represented by legislative enterprise j. Finally, V represents the percentage of the general election vote won by legislator j in the 2000 general election. These relationships are estimated for each of the four policies separately.

DETERMINANTS OF LEGISLATIVE PERCEPTIONS

The estimated results of the four multilevel models of legislative perceptions of constituents are presented in Table 5.1 (the Patients' Bill of Rights and Medicare regulatory reform) and Table 5.2 (the Securing America's Future Energy Act and the North American Wetlands Conservation Act reauthorization). The set of parameter estimates in each table indicates the impact of the independent variables on the likelihood that a staff member recalls a given subconstituency when asked about the specified issue.

A quick survey of these tables reveals consistent results across all four policy issues, which are summarized briefly here and then discussed in more detail. The most striking finding is the strong support for the information-based theory of legislative perception. Legislative staff are more likely to recall constituents about whom information is more accessible. In particular, there is compelling evidence that legislative staff members

TABLE 5.1. *Legislative Recall of Subconstituencies on Health Care Policy: Logit Results for the Hierarchical Linear Model*

	Likelihood of Subconstituency Recall	
	Patients' Bill of Rights	Medicare Regulatory Reform
Information Accessibility		
Subconstituency Contact		
Mail Contact	0.314	0.508**
	(0.230)	(0.196)
Personal Contact	0.068**	0.043
	(0.025)	(0.047)
Contributions (in $1,000s)	0.003**	0.004*
	(0.001)	(0.002)
Shared Professional Experience	0.160	−0.958
	(0.453)	(0.600)
Membership on Committee of	−0.395	−0.427
Jurisdiction	(0.315)	(0.380)
Legislative Seniority	0.001	0.003
	(0.030)	(0.024)
Partisan Ties	−0.489	−0.317
	(0.334)	(0.368)
Alternate Argument		
Subconstituency Size (in 1,000s)	−0.001	−0.019**
	(0.002)	(0.007)
Electoral Safety (2000 Election)	0.005	−0.009
	(0.012)	(0.014)
Constant	−2.629	−0.499
	(1.127)	(1.099)
N	273	240
Wald Chi-Squared (9)	38.49	23.80
p > Chi-Squared	0.000	0.005
Panel-Level Variance (σ_u)	0.001	0.117
	(0.364)	(1.304)

Robust standard errors in parentheses: * p < .05, ** p < .01 (two-tailed test).

are more likely to recall subconstituencies who contact the legislative office more frequently about an issue. Similarly robust is the finding that legislative enterprises are more likely to recall subconstituencies who contribute more money to the legislator. At first blush, the impact of these two variables – constituency contact and financial contributions – may seem intuitive, but they indicate that legislative perceptions are affected

TABLE 5.2. *Legislative Recall of Subconstituencies on Natural Resources Policy: Logit Results for the Hierarchical Linear Model*

	Likelihood of Subconstituency Recall	
	National Energy Bill	Wetlands Conservation
Information Accessibility		
Subconstituency Contact		
Mail Contact	0.834**	0.305
	(0.188)	(0.213)
Personal Contact	0.092**	0.155**
	(0.028)	(0.055)
Contributions (in $1,000s)	0.003**	0.005*
	(0.001)	(0.002)
Shared Professional Experience	−0.442	−0.603
	(0.598)	(0.460)
Membership on Committee of Jurisdiction	−0.022	−0.241
	(0.277)	(0.315)
Legislative Seniority	−0.020	−0.020
	(0.019)	(0.022)
Partisan Ties	0.308	0.482
	(0.282)	(0.338)
Alternate Argument		
Subconstituency Size (in 1,000s)	0.013**	−0.001
	(0.005)	(0.001)
Electoral Safety (2000 Election)	0.017	0.007
	(0.011)	(0.013)
Constant	−4.937	−2.053
	(0.926)	(1.059)
N	390	240
Wald Chi-Squared (9)		
p > Chi-Squared	61.10	26.98
Panel-Level Variance (σ_u)	0.000	0.001
	(0.002)	(0.001)
	(0.023)	(0.208)

Robust standard errors in parentheses: * $p < .05$, ** $p < .01$ (two-tailed test).

by constituency activity in ways previously unexamined. Additionally, the data reveal that legislative perceptions are not based on rational, electoral calculations. Across three of four policies, larger subconstituencies are not more likely to be seen by legislative enterprises than smaller subconstituencies, and there is no evidence that electoral vulnerability shapes legislative perceptions of constituents in the district.

Support for a Theory of Information of Accessibility

The data provide strong evidence that more frequent contact from a subconstituency increases the likelihood that the subconstituency will be perceived by a legislative office (see Tables 5.1 and 5.2). Frequent contact increases the accessibility of information about a subconstituency, thereby making it more likely that a legislative enterprise will recall the subconstituency when considering the importance of a policy to the district. Indeed, the relationship between constituency-initiated contact and legislative recall is positive and statistically significant at conventional levels across all four policies examined.[19] This makes it the single most consistent predictor of perceptions across the analyses.

Whether this influence is primarily the result of written or personal contact varies by policy. In the case of the Patients' Bill of Rights, there is evidence that legislative enterprises are more likely to see subconstituencies in their district that personally contact the office more frequently (see Table 5.1). Figure 5.1 illustrates the increase in the likelihood of legislative recall as the amount of phone and personal contact from a subconstituency increases, holding all else equal.

For example, as compared to a subconstituency that initiates no contact, a subconstituency that calls a legislative office twice a month for the (usually) ten months that the House is in session is three times more likely to be seen by a staff member when asked to consider the importance of Patients' Bill of Rights legislation to the district. Even a modest amount of personal contact from a subconstituency increases the likelihood of being seen by a legislative office. A legislative office is almost twice as likely to see a subconstituency that calls or visits a legislative office a total of ten times in a year (or about once a month) about the Patients' Bill of Rights as compared to a subconstituency that does not contact the office (see Figure 5.1).

Similarly, in the case of wetlands conservation, legislative offices are significantly more likely to perceive the interests of subconstituencies

---

[19] For purposes of robustness, a logged measure of personal contact is substituted in the model. The change in the functional form of the variable does not change the magnitude or significance of other variables, and the logged measure of personal contact remains positive and statistically significant.

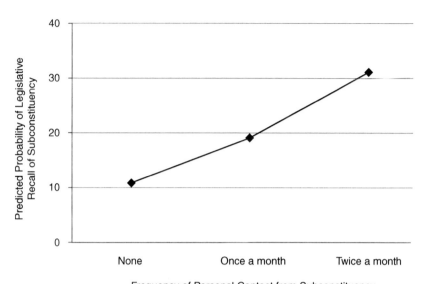

FIGURE 5.1. The Effects of Contact on the Probability of Subconstituency Recall: The Patients' Bill of Rights.

who frequently contacted them via phone or personal visits. A congressional enterprise who is contacted by a subconstituency ten times (once a month) is almost three times more likely to see that subconstituency in the district as compared to a subconstituency who does not contact the office (see Table 5.3). It is little surprise, then, that of the six subconstituencies identified as relevant to wetlands conservation, the two that were most active in personally contacting House offices – environmentalists and sportsmen – were also the two subconstituencies most often seen by legislative enterprises.[20] These two subconstituencies repeatedly contacted legislative offices to make their voice heard on the issue of wetlands conservation policy. As one staff member described his experience, "They [Ducks Unlimited] were my pen pal, or phone pal, for a while about it. We had a number of conversations."[21]

In addition to phone calls and personal visits, subconstituents also can make their interests in a policy known by contacting their legislator by mail, email, and fax. Scholars and practitioners both acknowledge the importance of mail from constituents to the relationship between

[20] The environmental subconstituency was seen by 61% of legislative offices and the sportsmen subconstituency was seen by 27% of legislative offices. See also Chapter 4.
[21] Personal interview.

TABLE 5.3. *The Effects of Personal Contact on the Probability of Subconstituency Recall*

Amount of Personal Contact	Patients' Bill of Rights	Wetlands Conservation	National Energy
No Contact	10.9	16.4	9.2
Once a Month Contact	19.1	47.9	20.3
Percentage Increase	175%	292%	221%

representatives and the represented: Hansen (2001, 193) notes that "[mail] is the most important communications link with the constituency," while a House staff member declared that constituent mail is "a good eye into the soul of the constituency."[22] In the case of Medicare regulatory reform, legislative offices are more likely to recall those subconstituencies who frequently contacted the office via mail. An office that received "a lot" of mail from a subconstituency is almost three times more likely to recall that subconstituency as compared to a subconstituency who did not contact the office (see Figure 5.2).

Across Republican and Democratic offices of committee members and non–committee members alike, legislative staff members are significantly more likely to perceive Medicare regulatory reform as important to subconstituencies who were active in contacting the office. For instance, physicians were active in contacting House members regarding Medicare regulatory reform – they contacted 78% of offices in this sample – and were also the most frequently recalled subconstituency on the issue. In fact, 87% of offices who received at least a little mail from physicians on this issue recalled physicians when asked about the interests of the district.

Contact from constituents is particularly influential in shaping legislative staff members' perceptions of the importance of the national energy bill to their district because both personal contact and mail contact affect their view of their constituency. The importance of both forms of contact reflects the prominence and scope of the energy legislation. In fact, 70% of legislative offices in the sample were personally contacted by at least one subconstituency in their district concerning the national energy bill, and 87% of offices were contacted via mail, email, or fax by at least one subconstituency in their district. Furthermore, more than 30% of legislative enterprise–subconstituency pairs were characterized

[22] Personal interview.

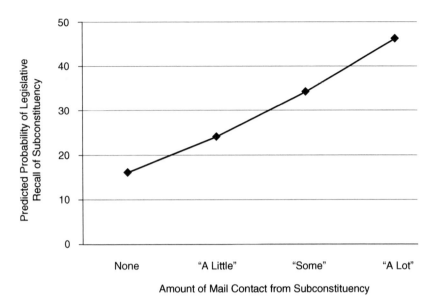

FIGURE 5.2. The Effects of Contact on the Probability of Subconstituency Recall: Medicare Regulatory and Contracting Reform.

by "a lot" of mail contact from the specified subconstituency, and 20% of legislative office–subconstituency pairs were marked by ten or more personal contacts from the given subconstituency regarding the energy bill. Even the bill's designation as H.R. 4 signals its prominence because the first ten bills (i.e., H.R. 1 through H.R. 10) are reserved for key pieces of legislation in each congress (see Oleszek 2004).

More important, however, is the impact of this frequent contact on the perceptions of legislators and their staff. Personal contact with a legislative office about once a month during the congressional session (or a total of ten times) doubles the predicted probability that a legislator and his staff will perceive the subconstituency when considering the relevance of the national energy bill to the district. Similarly, if phone and personal contact is held constant, a congressional enterprise that receives "a lot" of mail from a subconstituency is more than twice as likely to see that subconstituency as relevant to the national energy bill debate as compared to a subconstituency who sent only "some" mail to the office.[23]

---

[23] Holding other features at their mean or median values, the predicted probability that a legislative enterprise perceives a subconstituency who sends "a lot" of mail on the energy bill is 23% as compared to 10% when a subconstituency sends "some" mail.

The fact that contact influences legislative perception of constituents has two important implications. First, a subconstituency must be active if it is to increase the likelihood of being seen by a legislative office. Relevant subconstituencies are unlikely to be seen if they do not contact the legislative office either by mail or in person. The notion that constituents themselves can impact legislative perception is important because it locates control of the congressional representation relationship partially in the hands of constituents. This leads to a second implication, which is that contacting a legislative office is a meaningful form of political action that is available to all citizens and has relatively low barriers to participation. Although resource-rich constituents are more likely to participate in politics by contacting their legislator (e.g., Verba, Schlozman, and Brady 1995), the fact that relatively low-cost means of communication like mail affect who legislative enterprises see when they consider their district suggests that resource-poor constituents may still be able to take steps to increase their mental access.

The data presented in Tables 5.1 and 5.2 offer further robust support for an information-based theory of legislative perception since salient information also is strongly related to legislative perceptions of constituents in the district. The coefficient estimates for the salience of contributions are positive and significant at conventional levels of statistical significance across all issues.[24] Information about subconstituencies who contribute more money to legislators' campaigns is more easily accessible to legislative staff members when considering the importance of a policy to the district. Consequently, legislative enterprises are more likely to see subconstituents in their district who make generous campaign contributions.

In fact, subconstituencies that give a lot of money to a legislator are considerably more likely to be seen than those subconstituencies that make smaller contributions (see Figure 5.3). In the cases of Medicare regulatory reform and wetlands conservation, a subconstituency that gives $300,000 to a legislator has an approximately 50% chance of being seen by that legislative office, which is nearly 30 percentage points greater than for a subconstituency that did not contribute to the legislator's campaign. In a higher-profile case like the Patients' Bill of Rights, a subconstituency that contributes a sizable amount of money ($500,000)

---

[24] For purposes of robustness, contributions are also measured as a percentage of total receipts from a given subconstituency to a legislator's campaign, which takes into account the fact that some legislators receive more total contributions. The results of the model estimation are robust across measurement.

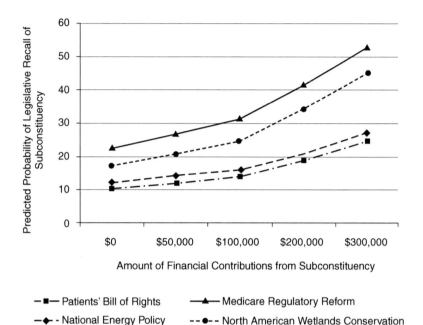

FIGURE 5.3. The Effects of Financial Contributions on the Probability of Subconstituency Recall.

is nearly three times more likely to be seen than a group that made only a small donation ($10,000).[25]

Given the high costs of congressional campaigns, it is not surprising that large contributions are salient to congressional enterprises and therefore influence which constituents they see in their district. Modest financial contributions have a positive impact on legislative perceptions, but it is clear that subconstituencies who contribute hundreds of thousands of dollars greatly increase the likelihood that they are seen by the legislative enterprise. The high costs of congressional campaigns weigh on legislative enterprises, and money is an undisputed aspect of the relationship between a congressional office and the district. The comments of one Member of Congress illustrate the salience of campaign contributions:

I'm talking about money here. It takes money to win elections. They don't know who you are if you're not on TV.... So you're hustling, raising money, going to fundraisers because that's what it takes to run a campaign.[26]

[25] Holding all else equal, the predicted probability that a subconstituency who contributes a total of $500,000 to a legislator will be seen is 41% as compared to 13% for a subconstituency who gives $10,000.

[26] Personal interview.

However, unlike contacting a legislative office, making financial contributions to a legislator is a form of political activity more common among resource-rich constituents (Verba et al. 1993). For this reason, the influence of money on legislative perceptions of constituents in the district raises normative questions about the equality of political representation in the House. Resource-rich subconstituencies are advantaged due to the increased mental access they enjoy, while legislative enterprises are less likely to see equally relevant subconstituencies in their district who have less ability to contribute financially to their campaign.

Figure 5.3 also illustrates an interesting pattern where financial contributions from subconstituencies have a stronger impact on legislative perceptions of the district when the policy itself is less prominent (i.e., Medicare regulatory reform and wetlands conservation). This finding is consistent with the popular belief that the influence of money in politics is greater in the dark corners of Capitol Hill. Indeed, the belief that openness and public scrutiny reduce the influence of money in politics is central to congressional reforms from the "sunshine laws" of the 1970s to more recent efforts to curb congressional earmarks and increase government transparency.

Overall, the finding that money affects legislative perceptions of constituents in the district is consistent with the conventional wisdom that money is important in congressional politics (e.g., Jackson 1988; Lewis 1998). Moreover, the information-based theory of legislative perception advanced here identifies a new mechanism by which money matters. Financial contributions increase the accessibility of information about the contributing subconstituency to the legislative enterprise when considering the importance of a policy to the district. As a result, the congressional office's view of the district favors those subconstituencies who contribute more money to the legislator's campaign. By providing new evidence of how money influences legislative perceptions of the district, this book also addresses the puzzle of why there is not more consistent evidence regarding the effects of money on legislative behavior (e.g., Grenzke 1989; Hall and Wayman 1990; Strattman 2002; Wawro 2001; Welch 1982; Wright 1985). In short, money matters in a more subtle way than previously examined – it shapes legislators' image of who they represent.

It is also worth noting that some mechanisms of information accessibility are less important. For instance, the data provide no evidence that legislative enterprises' familiarity or predisposition toward information about constituents shapes whom they see in their districts. The null finding concerning the familiarity of information is not predicted by the cognitive psychology literature, but the fact that a legislative enterprise's predisposition toward information about subconstituencies does not have a clear impact on perceptions of the district is not surprising given the conflicting evidence from the psychology literature. It is easy to imagine that a Democratic legislator would be aware of the importance of the Patients' Bill of Rights to businesses in his district even if the office were not predisposed to agree with the business community's position. In fact, more than 45% of legislative offices who perceived business constituents in their district were Democratic offices. Similarly, 32% of legislative enterprises who recalled the environmental subconstituency when considering the importance of a national energy bill to their district were Republicans. As one staff member said, "I deal with the pharmaceutical industry all the time. They can't stand this office."[27] This indicates both an awareness of the issues important to the pharmaceutical industry as well as a lack of shared preferences. Thus, the accessibility of information about a policy-relevant subconstituency does not appear to be affected by whether a legislative enterprise is predisposed in favor of, or against, that subconstituency.

Assessing the Alternative Arguments

Although Tables 5.1 and 5.2 offer clear support for an information-based theory of legislative perceptions, the data offer relatively weak support for the vote-maximizing argument common to studies of legislative decision making. Across all four bills, the data offer little evidence to support the first alternate argument that reelection-minded legislative enterprises should be more likely to see larger subconstituencies in their district based on the desire to gain votes. In three of the four cases, the data reveal that legislative staff are not more likely to see larger subconstituencies in their district as compared to smaller subconstituencies. In the cases of the Patients' Bill of Rights and wetlands conservation, the size of a subconstituency has no discernible impact on legislative perception of constituents (see Tables 5.1 and 5.2). Legislative staff are no more likely to see large subconstituencies in the district than they are to see small subconstituencies.

The case of Medicare regulatory reform provides further evidence that vote-maximizing attention to large subconstituencies does not

---

[27] Personal interview.

determine which subconstituencies a legislative enterprise sees as relevant to the issue at hand. In this case, the data indicate a negative relationship between subconstituency size and the likelihood of being seen by a legislative office, which is the opposite of the expected vote-maximizing relationship (see Table 5.1). When considering the collection of subconstituencies in the district, legislative staff members are half as likely to see a subconstituency of 60,000 people as compared to a subconstituency of 10,000.[28] The substantive impact of this finding is notable; legislative staff are more likely to see smaller subconstituencies such as doctors and hospital administrators than Medicare patients when considering the importance of the issue to their district.[29]

Only in the case of the national energy bill is there any evidence of a positive relationship between the size of a subconstituency and the likelihood that a legislative enterprise will perceive that subconstituency when considering the district. On this piece of legislation, legislative staff are more likely to recall larger subconstituencies like businesses than smaller subconstituencies like renewable energy. The likelihood that a legislative enterprise sees a subconstituency of 10,000 is about 11%, all else equal, and this increases to 19% for a subconstituency of 60,000.[30]

Additionally, the data presented in Tables 5.1 and 5.2 do not provide support for the argument that electoral vulnerability influences legislative perceptions of constituents in the district.[31] In three of the four cases, the relationship between electoral vulnerability and legislative perception is indeterminate, and in the fourth case there is a weak, positive relationship between a legislator's electoral support in the 2000 general election and the likelihood that the legislative enterprise sees a subconstituency in the district. Thus, even this weak relationship does not support the

---

[28] The predicted probability that a subconstituency of 10,000 is recalled is 22.4% as compared to 10.5% for a subconstituency of 60,000. All other variables are held at their median values.

[29] One might wonder whether the size of the patient subconstituency is driving this relationship. In order to address this concern, the data are analyzed excluding all dyads between legislative offices and Medicare patients and find that subconstituency size still has a negative and statistically significant impact on the likelihood of recall.

[30] Predicted probabilities are calculated holding all other variables at the median values.

[31] The alternate argument that legislators are more likely to perceive larger subconstituencies conditional on the electoral security of the legislator is also considered. A model that includes an interaction term between subconstituency size and electoral vulnerability, as well as the two parent terms, is estimated. The interaction term does not achieve standard levels of statistical significance, and there is generally no change in the other relationships.

strategic argument that electorally vulnerable legislators are more likely to see subconstituencies in the district.

Taken together, the findings across these four policies are consistent with a cognitive psychology–based theory of legislative perceptions. Again, the details of the Medicare reform case are illustrative. Physicians represent a relatively small number of votes, yet they actively influence the way legislative offices see their districts on the issue through their financial contributions and direct contact. In contrast, the Medicare patient population is as an example of a subconstituency made up of many voters who are not seen by many offices. In fact, 80% of legislative offices saw physicians, whereas only 18% of offices saw Medicare patients. Those offices in which physicians were seen by staff members had nearly 1,000 fewer physicians in the district but received an average of $25,000 more in financial contributions than offices who did not see physicians.[32]

The evidence provided in this chapter demonstrates that active and resource-rich constituents dominate legislative perceptions of the district from the vantage point of Capitol Hill. Additionally, the voice of a subconstituency on Capitol Hill is distinct from the size of a subconstituency. This comment by a legislative staff member provides an example of the frequent discrepancy between the two: "the number of the environmentals – they may not be as large as some of those other people, but they try to make as much noise as they can to make sure they're not forgotten about."[33] Consistent with Olson's (1965) argument that larger subconstituencies may suffer from problems of collective action, one key implication of this chapter, then, is that we cannot assume that larger constituency groups will have their interests reflected in Congress.

CONCLUSION

The empirical analyses of legislative perceptions of constituents across four distinct legislative proposals provide support for the information-based theory of legislative perception articulated in this book. The findings reveal that the district perceived by legislators and their staff is systematically skewed in favor of those subconstituencies active in

[32] The average legislative office that recalled doctors when asked about Medicare regulatory reform has 3,700 physicians in the district and received $60,000 in campaign contributions. The average legislative office that did not recall doctors had 4,600 physicians in the district and received $35,000 in campaign contributions.

[33] Personal interview.

contacting and contributing to the legislative office. Information about these subconstituencies is more accessible to legislative staff members when they consider the importance of a policy to their districts as compared to information about other policy-relevant subconstituencies. One implication of these findings is that constituents can play an active role in shaping how a legislative enterprise views the district from Capitol Hill. However, not all subconstituencies are equally likely to contact or make contributions to the legislative office. Consequently, the findings are simultaneously promising and disheartening for congressional representation. Constituents have the ability to affect legislative perceptions, but resource-rich and active constituents are systematically more likely to avail themselves of this opportunity, which can result in legislative misperceptions of the constituents in the district.

Overall, the findings presented here demonstrate that perceptions are rarely accurate reflections of the objective reality of district composition. Legislators and their staff see a district that does not look like the collection of constituents who reside in the district. It is precisely this discrepancy that is essential to understanding congressional representation through the eyes of the legislative enterprise. In addition to the normative concerns raised here, the limited nature of legislative perceptions of constituents also has implications for legislative behavior. If legislative enterprises do not see the importance of issues to constituents – if these constituents are not on their proverbial "radar screens" – then they are unlikely to provide accurate political representation, and this casts doubt on the health of representative democracy. Predicting legislators' actions and votes, therefore, requires knowing not only the strategic incentives they face, but also the image of the district held by the congressional enterprise (see Jones 2001). The next chapter, then, addresses the question of how legislative perceptions of the constituents in their districts affect legislative behaviors.

6

The Effects of Legislative Perception on Participation

The widespread consensus in the literature on congressional representation is that "constituents matter" when explaining legislators' voting and nonvoting behavior. This familiar phrase provides a useful summary of the relationship between constituents and legislators, but it also leaves much to the imagination. In particular, when concluding that constituents matter, *which* constituents matter and *how* do they matter? The preceding chapter reveals that legislators and their staff see an incomplete and unrepresentative subset of their constituents when they look back at their district from Capitol Hill, which suggests that all constituents may not be represented equally. The central question addressed in this chapter, then, is whether biases in perception become biases in representation. More specifically, do legislative perceptions of the constituents in their district affect the actions legislators take on behalf of their district during the policy-making process?

In order to examine the effect of perceptions on representation, it is necessary to consider the practical actions legislators take to represent their constituents on Capitol Hill. An important form of representation is legislators' participation in the committee and floor debate in the House. Participation in these venues is an integral part of the development of public policy in Congress and is consequential for both representation and lawmaking. Furthermore, participation in the congressional debate provides legislators with the opportunity to represent multiple district interests. This flexibility to represent many constituents is critical to analyzing which constituents are represented and how legislative perceptions affect constituency representation. For these reasons, participation is a uniquely appropriate way to examine legislators' representation of the multiple subconstituencies in their district.

There are two ways by which legislative perceptions are expected to affect legislators' participation. First, legislative perceptions should affect whether or not a subconstituency is represented by a legislator. Legislators are expected to be more likely to act on behalf of those constituents that they see in their district. Second, legislative perceptions should also affect how much a legislator represents a subconstituency during the House debate. Subconstituencies that have a more prominent place in a legislator's mental image of the district should also figure more prominently in legislator's participation in the policy debate. Based on legislators' participation on two important pieces of legislation during the 107th Congress, the Patients' Bill of Rights and the Securing America's Future Energy Act, this chapter finds strong support that legislative perceptions of the district influence legislators' participation. Furthermore, the independent effects of perception on participation remain statistically and substantively significant even when standard factors known to affect participation are taken into account.

REPRESENTING SUBCONSTITUENCIES THROUGH PARTICIPATION

In addressing the question of whether constituency considerations affect legislative behavior, much of the literature conceives of representation as the "match" between a single district preference and a legislator's vote. Votes are one important component of representation and lawmaking, but legislative behavior in practice is not solely about casting votes. Writing a generation ago, Eulau and Abramowitz (1978, 263) note in their assessment of the literature on legislative behavior that "Roll-call behavior usually serves as the dependent variable, even though it is agreed to be a poor indicator of political life in Congress." As a result, efforts have been made in the literature to better reflect the range of ways legislators represent their constituents.

Congressional scholarship on legislators' nonvoting behavior includes a number of different concepts of legislative activity. Across all of these, the most striking and consistent finding is that participation is not universal; some legislators are active in the stages before the roll-call vote, but many are not. One approach to studying legislative activity is through the characterization of members as either "workhorses" or "showhorses," which reveals variation in legislators' participation in the day-to-day business of Congress (e.g., Matthews 1959; Payne 1980). Continuing in this tradition, Wawro (2000) identifies legislative entrepreneurs who are willing to bear costs in the policy-making process rather than free-ride on their colleagues' efforts. A second approach is to examine legislators' actions to represent their constituents through constituency service and casework (e.g., Cain, Ferejohn, and Fiorina 1987; Fiorina 1989; Mayhew 1974). Still a third approach focuses on legislators' speeches and partici- pation in the congressional dialogue (e.g., Burgin 1991; Hill and Hurley 2002; Maltzman and Siegelman 1996; Morris 2001). These scholars echo John Stuart Mill's argument that what legislators say is not "merely" talk, but rather has consequences for policy making and representation.[1] A fourth approach highlights the importance of legislators' involvement in congressional committees as central to the division of labor within the House and Senate (e.g., Esterling 2007; Evans 1991b; Fenno 1973; Gamble 2007; Hall 1996; Hall and Evans 1990; Krehbiel 1991).

Among more recent work, Hall's (1996) study of members' participa- tion in the subcommittee, committee, and floor stages of policy making in the U.S. House is one of the most extensive and influential. Hall identi- fies both formal and informal modes of participation and offers insights into the myriad ways in which legislators can be active in the lawmaking process (see also Evans 1991b; Hall 1987). Despite the comprehensive measurement of participation, Hall finds that participation is selective and the amount of activity varies greatly even among those legislators who choose to participate. Hall argues that this selective participation reveals individual legislators' choices about how to allocate their time, energy, and resources. Legislators decide whether to be active on a given issue, as well as how active to be, and these decisions reflect legislators' ability and willingness to bear the costs associated with participation. As a result, participation in Congress is dominated by a subset of legislators with greater capacity and interest in the issue.

This shift in focus away from voting is particularly relevant when examining congressional representation of multiple subconstituencies within a district as opposed to a single district interest. Invoking Pitkin's (1967, 126) notion of representation as acting "in behalf of" constitu- ents, meaning acting in the interest of constituents, legislators are able to represent numerous district preferences on a given issue by their partici- pation in the policy debate. Indeed, Mill (1861, 61) argues that a central

[1] John Stuart Mill (1861). See Chapter 5.

function of legislative bodies is to provide a venue for the representation of contested interests: "When it is necessary or important to secure hearing and consideration to many conflicting opinions, a deliberative body is indispensable." More recently, Hall (1996, 26) asserts that one of the advantages of studying legislative participation is "that the expression of a wide range of alternative points of view is central to the practice of democratic consent." In short, because participation involves more than an up-or-down vote, legislators can act on behalf of multiple subconstituencies in the district by giving voice to their interests and concerns.

Measuring Participation

Drawing upon these literatures, participation is defined here as "legislators'" activity during committee and subcommittee markup sessions, committee and subcommittee hearings, and the floor debate. These policy-making activities comprise what Hall (1996) refers to as "formal participation" and they are the venues in which the House considers legislative proposals. Markup sessions provide members of the committee or subcommittee the opportunity to make a case for a bill (or specific provisions of the bill), to debate the proposed legislation, to offer (and debate) amendments, to vote on the proposed legislative language, and to actively revise the policy proposal (see also Evans 1991a, 1991b; Hall and Evans 1990). In fact, Hall (1996, 37) calls attention to the importance of markup hearings: "By raising or redefining issues or by taking and defending specific positions, participants in the markup debate can give expression to the views and interests of citizens in their district." Hearings are also held at both the committee and subcommittee stages. These are more structured venues in which members express their opinions, make arguments for (or against) specific provisions, ask questions of witnesses, and debate the legislation and related policy issues. Lastly, the floor debate provides a final opportunity for legislators to debate the proposed bill and any floor amendments before the House votes on the legislation. Again, during the floor debate legislators have the opportunity to make statements on behalf of their constituents, and all members can choose to participate in the floor stage regardless of committee membership and participation (or lack thereof) in the earlier stages of the policy-making process.[2]

---

[2] It is important to note that committee members have inherent institutional advantage because they have access to all three venues for participation, whereas members who

Two pieces of legislation – the Patients' Bill of Rights and the Securing America's Future Energy Act – received multiple committee hearings and were debated on the House floor during the 107th Congress, thereby providing numerous opportunities for legislators to participate. Since the other two bills discussed (Medicare regulatory reform and wetlands conservation) were less contentious, there were not as many opportunities for legislators to formally participate in hearings or debate on these bills, and they are not included in the analysis of legislators' participation.[3] The examination of legislators' participation on the two relevant bills is based on the official transcripts of all hearings, markups, and debates concerning the Patients' Bill of Rights and the Securing America's Future Energy Act during the 107th Congress. Relevant legislative activity includes all instances when legislators pose questions or make statements in these three venues on the issue of interest.[4] Transcripts of committee (and subcommittee) hearings and markups come from House committees, and the Congressional Record provides transcripts of the floor debate on each issue.[5] All of these documents are examined consistently and coded for statements that invoke the interests of the subconstituencies relevant to the policy examined. In the case of the Patients' Bill of Rights, transcripts are coded for legislators' references to the seven relevant sub-constituencies (business, doctors, patients, labor, seniors, insurance, and attorneys) on whose behalf legislators are expected to participate. Similarly, all transcripts pertaining to the Securing America's Future Energy Act are coded for legislators' references to the ten subconstituencies relevant to national energy policy (consumers, environmentalists, Native Americans, veterans, businesses, labor, oil and gas, mining, utilities, and renewables). Using an issue-specific coding scheme to establish

---

do not serve on the committee have unrestricted access to participating in the floor debate, but not the committee or subcommittee stages. This is discussed again later in the chapter and it is taken into account in the statistical analyses.

[3] Recall that both the Medicare regulatory reform bill and wetlands conservation bill passed the House under suspension of the rules, a procedure designed to facilitate passage of noncontroversial bills by limiting debate (see Oleszek 2004).

[4] Although scholars sometimes refer to all statements by legislators in congressional hearings as questions (see Esterling 2007), the terms "statements," "arguments," and "questions" are used here interchangeably to refer to any comment made by a legislator in markup, hearings, and floor debate.

[5] Nearly all of these documents are available online through the official House committee Web site, the Library of Congress, or the U.S. Government Printing Office (GPO). Markups held by the House Ways and Means Committee and House Energy and Commerce Committee are not available online, but they are available through committee offices on Capitol Hill.

the words and phrases indicative of each subconstituency, each sentence spoken by each legislator is evaluated with respect to whether the legislator invokes a specified subconstituency and their interests (see Appendix D for more details).[6]

Legislative participation on behalf of constituents can be conceptualized two ways: whether a legislator participates and how much the legislator participates. The first measure of legislative participation is an indicator variable of whether or not a given legislator invokes a given subconstituency during the policy debate. The second measure of legislative participation is a count of the number of times that a legislator invokes a specified subconstituency relevant to the national energy bill or the Patients' Bill of Rights. In order to faithfully capture Pitkin's notion of representation as acting in the interest of constituents, negative comments made by legislators are omitted from these measures of participation on behalf of subconstituents in the district. Negative comments are infrequent; nonetheless, it is a worthwhile distinction to draw since a legislator speaking against a subconstituency can hardly be considered to be representing the interests of that subconstituency.[7]

THE EFFECTS OF LEGISLATIVE PERCEPTION
ON PARTICIPATION

Earlier scholars theorized about the importance of legislative perceptions of constituents for legislative voting behavior (e.g., Fiorina 1974), but with the notable exception of Miller and Stokes (1963), the empirical congressional literature has largely neglected the link between perception and behavior. The shortage of empirical work stems from both the difficulty of the empirical task and the lack of discussion about the mechanisms by which perceptions shape legislative activity. With a theory of legislative perception developed and tested in the preceding chapters, however, the effect of these perceptions on legislative behavior can be examined.

The central argument is that when a legislative office perceives a subconstituency in the district, it increases the likelihood that the legislator

---

[6] All transcripts were coded independently by multiple coders, and any discrepancies in coding were resolved by the author (see Appendix D).

[7] When looking at legislators' participation in the policy debate on these two bills, legislators made exclusively negative comments less than 2% of the time. On occasion, legislators made a negative comment about a subconstituency as part of a broader series of positive comments; this occurred in only 8% of observations.

acts for that subconstituency in Congress. When participating in the congressional policy-making process, legislators have both normative and strategic reasons to represent their constituents, but the district they represent is the district as they see it. For instance, one Midwestern legislative enterprise saw "the coal mine, all the coal companies" when asked to whom in their district the national energy bill is important.[8] In this case, the mining subconstituency is central to the legislative enterprise's perception of the district. Moreover, this legislator participated in the House debate on energy policy and voiced the concerns of the coal mining subconstituency in his district on the House floor, including comments that "The state and [local university] in particular have been at the forefront of using clean coal technology funds to find clean ways of burning coal."[9] Legislators participate on behalf of perceived subconstituencies because doing so is consistent with the picture of the district in their heads.

Perception and Participation: Initial Patterns

Legislative enterprises are more likely to perceive certain subconstituencies in their district as compared to other relevant subconstituencies, but are legislators also more likely to act for these perceived constituents? The first step in answering this question is to look at the patterns of participation by legislators on the Securing America's Future Energy Act and the Patients' Bill of Rights. One striking pattern of legislators' participation on these two important pieces of legislation is that not all legislators participate in the debate, which is consistent with previous work on selective participation (e.g., Esterling 2007; Evans 1991a, 1991b; Hall 1996). During the debate over the national energy bill, legislators participate on behalf of a relevant subconstituency only 30% of the time, and this figure falls to 21% when looking at participation in the Patients' Bill of Rights case. Put differently, legislators do not take advantage of 70 to 80% of the opportunities to voice the interests and concerns of their constituents during the policy-making process in the House.

There are two principal explanations for the low levels of participation on behalf of constituents. First, some legislators do not participate on behalf of any subconstituency in their district. As Figure 6.1 reveals, 40% of the legislators studied do not participate at all in the debate

---

[8] Personal interview.
[9] Statement in the *Congressional Record.*

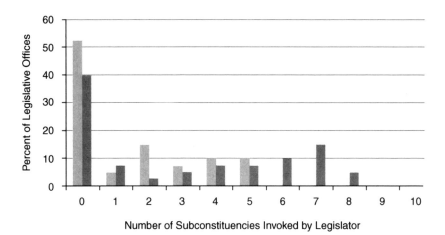

FIGURE 6.1. Participation on Behalf of Relevant Subconstituencies.

over the national energy bill, and 52% do not participate regarding the Patients' Bill of Rights. The first pair of columns in Figure 6.1 illustrates the prevalence of legislators' decisions not to act on behalf of their constituents on these two major issues.

Second, legislators who do participate are active on behalf of only a small fraction of the relevant subconstituencies (see Figure 6.1). The Patients' Bill of Rights provides an opportunity for legislators to speak on behalf of the seven relevant subconstituencies present in every district, but only 20% of legislators participate on behalf of at least half of their district subconstituencies who are relevant to the issue.[10] In the case of the national energy bill, there are ten relevant subconstituencies in each district, but only one-fifth of legislators act for a wide range of constituents.[11] Across both issues, no legislator participates on behalf of all the policy-relevant subconstituencies who reside in his district.

Additionally, legislators are not active on behalf of the same subconstituencies. Almost all subconstituencies are invoked by at least a few

[10] Only eight of forty legislators participated on behalf of four or more subconstituencies during the debate over the Patients' Bill of Rights.

[11] Twenty percent of legislators participated on behalf of a wide range of constituents, as defined by seven or more of the ten subconstituencies relevant to the national energy bill.

TABLE 6.1. *Legislators' Participation on Behalf of Subconstituencies*

The Patients' Bill of Rights

Subconstituency	Percentage of Legislators Who Participated on Behalf of Subconstituency
Doctors	32.5%
Business	27.5%
Patients	47.5%
Labor Unions	0%
Senior Citizens	2.5%
Insurance	27.5%
Attorneys	10.0%

The National Energy Bill

Subconstituency	Percentage of Legislators Who Participated on Behalf of Subconstituency
Consumers	42.5%
Environmentalists	45.0%
Utilities	32.5%
Veterans	0%
Businesses	30.0%
Labor Unions	2.5%
Oil and Gas	45.0%
Mining	35.0%
Native Americans	17.5%
Renewables	52.5%

Note: Legislators' participation includes participation in committee markup, committee hearings, and floor debate in the House.

legislators, but no single subconstituency dominates legislators' statements (see Table 6.1). In fact, in only one case did a majority of legislators speak on behalf of a subconstituency – the renewable energy subconstituency. Table 6.1 also illustrates the varying frequency with which subconstituencies are invoked. For instance, 45% of legislators speak on behalf of the oil and gas subconstituency during the debate over the Securing America's Future Energy Act, while one-third fewer legislators (or 30% of legislators) participate on behalf of businesses. In short, legislators participate on behalf of different subconstituencies, but the data reveal that some subconstituencies have their preferences represented on Capitol Hill far more often than other relevant subconstituencies.

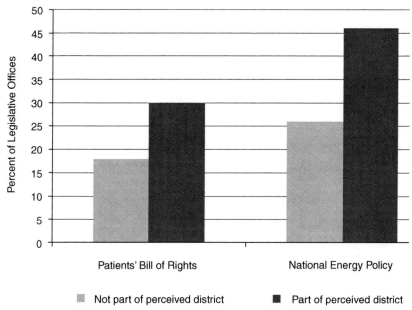

FIGURE 6.2. Legislative Perception and Participation on Behalf of Relevant Subconstituencies.

These data provide an overview of legislative participation and paint a picture of limited participation on behalf of relevant district subconstituencies, but they do not address the central question of whether perception affects participation. However, the raw data provides initial evidence of a strong relationship between perception and participation. In the national energy case, legislative enterprises are almost twice as likely to participate on behalf of subconstituencies that they see in their districts as compared to those that they do not see (see Figure 6.2).[12] The overall rates of participation in the debate over the Patients' Bill of Rights are slightly lower, but again legislators are nearly two times more likely to participate on behalf of those subconstituencies that they perceive in the district.[13] These differences are statistically and substantively important; legislators are more likely to speak for the subconstituencies they see.[14]

[12] The likelihood that a legislator speaks on behalf of a subconstituency seen in the district is 46%, but the chance of participating for a subconstituency that was not initially perceived is 26%.

[13] The likelihood that the legislator will participate on behalf of a perceived subconstituency is 30%, but this drops to only 18% if the legislator does not see the subconstituency when looking at the district.

[14] Differences are statistically significant at p < .001.

The data provide important, early evidence that legislators are more likely to participate on behalf of constituents in their district they see, but this is only an initial test. Perceptions are not the only determinant of legislators' participation. A well-established literature on legislative participation establishes a number of institutional, partisan, and conventional constituency considerations that influence legislative activity. Legislative perceptions need to be considered alongside these other factors, which present a more difficult test of the independent effect of perceptions on legislators' actions. If perceptions still affect participation in this more rigorous test, then congressional scholars need to take perceptions seriously in our theories of constituency representation.

ALTERNATE EXPLANATIONS OF LEGISLATORS' DECISIONS TO PARTICIPATE

Constituency considerations, namely the size of the relevant constituency and the intensity of the constituency's interest in the issue at hand, are two factors that are expected to affect legislative participation. These conventional, strategic constituency considerations are important because legislators' decisions are assumed to be motivated by their desire to represent their constituents and gain electoral benefits (e.g., Fenno 1973; Fiorina 1974; Mayhew 1974). Since the focus here is on participation on behalf of specific constituents within the district (as opposed to participation on behalf of "the district"), the task of measuring conventional constituency considerations is somewhat more complex than usual. Instead of a single, summary indicator of the district interest in each bill, there is one indicator for each subconstituency relevant to each bill.[15]

The first aspect of constituency influence is the size of the subconstituency, as measured by the number of individuals associated with each subconstituency in each district. This variable is a subconstituency-specific adaptation of the conventional objective measure of district interests (see Krehbiel 1993).[16] Legislators are hypothesized to be more likely to participate on behalf of larger subconstituencies in the district due to the possible electoral gains of speaking on their behalf.

---

[15] See also Hall's (1996) discussion of the Universal Telephone Preservation Act and its effect on three distinct interests in the district (Chapter 7). Kau and Rubin (1982) and Kalt and Zupan (1984) also provide earlier treatments of multiple district interests.

[16] One important exception to the general reliance on this type of objective measure is Hall's (1996) use of whether a legislative office considers an issue to be of negligible,

Measuring constituency interest in an issue by the size of the subconstituency, however, may miss variation in the intensity of constituents' interests. A legislator is expected to be more likely to speak on behalf of constituents who have a stronger interest in an issue because it is more likely that those constituents will reward (or punish) him based on his actions. Two measures of the intensity of subconstituency interest are employed: financial contributions and subconstituency-initiated contact. First, legislators who receive financial contributions from a subconstituency are expected to be more likely to participate on behalf of that subconstituency (Hall 1996; Hall and Wayman 1990). The measure of contributions is the total dollar amount of contributions made from a subconstituency to a given legislator during the 2000 election cycle as reported by the Federal Election Commission.[17] Second, legislators are hypothesized to be more likely to speak on behalf of subconstituencies who contact the office more frequently.[18] Consistent with the previous chapters, subconstituency-initiated contact is separated into mail contact and personal contact. Mail contact is measured as a categorical variable denoting whether the legislative office received no mail, a little mail, some mail, or a lot of mail from the subconstituency on the issue, while the personal contact variable is a count of the number of times the legislative office was contacted by the subconstituency in the past year regarding the issue.[19]

Given the underlying assumption that electoral motivations shape legislators' decisions to participate, a measure of legislators' electoral security based on the percentage of the vote they received in the prior general election (in 2000) is included in the model. Legislators with greater

minor, moderate, or major interest to the district. Hall's results show that the magnitude of district interest has a positive influence on legislators' participation, and the use of a subjective measure of district interest expands the literature's definition of "constituency considerations."

[17] For more details on the measurement of subconstituency contributions to legislative offices, see Appendix C.

[18] Note that legislators may be attentive to active subconstituencies because they believe this reflects the best policy choices for the district or because they make electoral calculations about the benefits of their actions (see Wawro 2000). Since it is not possible to distinguish between these motivations here, this research is agnostic between them. Moreover, for the purposes of understanding the impact of legislative perceptions on participation, the distinction between these motives is not consequential, and they both suggest a positive relationship between subconstituency-initiated contact and participation.

[19] For more information about the source of these data and measurement details, see Appendix C.

electoral support in their district are expected to be more likely to spend their limited time and resources participating in the policy debate as compared to vulnerable legislators who may choose to spend their time on constituency service or other district-focused activities.[20]

Institutional position is also expected to shape legislators' decisions to participate on behalf of a subconstituency because it affects the costs of participation (e.g., Evans 1991a; Hall 1996; Sinclair 1989). The primary component of a legislator's institutional position is his committee membership, specifically whether or not a legislator is a member of the committee with jurisdiction over the issue at hand. Committee membership, therefore, is expected to increase the likelihood that a legislator participates on behalf of a subconstituency because committee members have more opportunities to do so. A dichotomous variable is used to indicate whether a legislator is a member of the House Energy and Commerce Committee (for participation on the Patients' Bill of Rights) or the House Resources Committee (for participation on the Securing America's Future Energy Act).[21]

A second aspect of a legislator's institutional position is whether the legislator holds a committee leadership position. Previous studies find evidence that legislators in leadership positions are more likely to participate in the policy-making process in both the House (e.g., Hall 1987, 1996) and the Senate (e.g., Evans 1991a; Sinclair 1989). Legislators who are leaders on the relevant committee enjoy increased resources, expertise, and authority, all of which reduce the costs of participation and thus may increase the likelihood of participation on behalf of constituents in the district. An indicator variable denotes whether a legislator is a chair or ranking minority member of the relevant committee or any of its subcommittees.

A legislator's partisanship is another factor expected to influence legislators' propensity to participate on behalf of their constituents. Majority party members in the House enjoy a number of institutional advantages that can leave minority party members excluded from policy making

---

[20] A legislator's electoral security may also affect decisions about participation because it affects the influence of other factors on participation. For instance, subconstituency interest in health policy (or resources policy) may have a greater impact on vulnerable legislators' decisions about participating on behalf of constituents in the policy debate as compared to "safe" legislators' decisions. In the analyses to follow, the impact of electoral security on participation is considered, as are the possible interactive effects.

[21] Complex bills such as the two examined here are often referred to multiple committees, so the primary committee of jurisdiction for each bill is chosen, which facilitates the sampling of an equal number of committee members and non-committee members.

(Binder 1997; Cox and McCubbins 2005). As a result, Hall (1996) argues that minority party legislators may see participation in hearings, markup, and debate as important opportunities to express their views and to influence the development of proposed legislation. Minority party legislators, therefore, are expected to be more likely to participate as compared to legislators in the majority party. The analyses focus on the 107th Congress during which the Republicans were the majority party, so an indicator variable denotes Democratic legislators.

ESTIMATION OF LEGISLATORS' DECISIONS TO PARTICIPATE

Drawing on the preceding hypotheses about the importance of legislative perception for participation, as well as other potential predictors, a model of the probability of legislative participation on behalf of subconstituents on a given policy is estimated using multiple regression. The dependent variable is an indicator variable of whether a legislator participates at all on behalf of a given subconstituency during the policy debate. Since the data consist of legislator–subconstituency dyads, the observations are not fully independent, which violates the assumptions underlying standard logit and probit estimators. As discussed in the previous chapter, this feature of the data can be addressed by using standard errors clustered on the legislative office (see Carpenter et al., 2004; Hojnacki and Kimball 1998, 1999) or a multilevel model (see Miler 2007; Rabe-Hesketh and Skrondal 2005; Snijders and Bosker 1999).

One issue to note is that some factors hypothesized to affect participation also shape legislative perceptions (see the discussion in Chapter 5). Theoretically, this is not a problem. Indeed, it is logical that the factors that affect the accessibility of information about subconstituencies also may affect the likelihood that a legislator will decide to participate on their behalf. Methodologically, however, the fact that features of the subconstituency may influence both perceptions and participation is less desirable because it introduces the possibility that perception might be endogenous to the model of legislative participation. Statistical analyses conducted to determine whether endogeneity is a feature of the data that needs to be accounted for in the model demonstrate that legislative perception is not endogenous in the model of legislative participation on national energy policy, but the data indicate potential endogeneity in the case of the Patients' Bill of Rights.[22] Consequently, legislative

---

[22] Before estimating the models, statistical analyses are conducted to determine whether endogeneity is a feature of the data that needs to be accounted for in the structure of

participation on the national energy bill is estimated as a single equation using a probit model with standard errors clustered by legislative office. Legislative participation on behalf of subconstituents regarding the Patients' Bill of Rights, however, is estimated while taking into account the endogeneity of legislative perceptions.[23]

The results of the pair of models of legislators' decisions to participate on behalf of subconstituencies are presented in Table 6.2. The primary finding of interest is that when legislators perceive a subconstituency in their district, they are significantly more likely to participate on its behalf. This finding is especially striking because conventional constituency considerations (e.g., subconstituency size and activity) are also included in the model. In other words, perceptions of constituents influence participation above and beyond the standard ways that constituency considerations are believed to shape legislative behavior.

Not only do the effects of legislative perception hold up to the inclusion of well-established explanations of legislative behavior, but their effects are highly substantively meaningful. In the debate over the Patients' Bill of Rights, whether or not a legislative enterprise perceives a subconstituency significantly increases the probability that a legislator will speak on behalf of that subconstituency. For a legislator who serves on the committee, but is not a committee leader, the predicted probability of participating on behalf of a subconstituency that he does not see in the district is 21%.[24] If a legislator perceived a subconstituency in his district when considering the Patients' Bill of Rights, then the likelihood that the legislator acts on its behalf in the House debate increases to 75% (see

the model. Specifically, tests are conducted to determine whether the error terms in the participation equation and the perception equation are correlated, which would indicate the potential presence of endogeneity. The null hypothesis is that the correlation parameter between the residuals in the two equations (ρ) is equal to zero (H_0: $\rho = 0$). In the case of the national energy bill, the null hypothesis cannot be rejected at the $p < .10$ level; therefore, one can conclude that legislative perception is not endogenous in the model of legislative participation. In the case of the Patients' Bill of Rights, however, the null hypothesis that the correlation parameter is equal to zero (H_0: $\rho = 0$) is rejected at the $p < .05$ level, indicating that endogeneity is present in the data.

[23] Three instruments identify the endogenous perception variable (legislative seniority, traditional partisan ties, and relevant career experiences), and the two models are estimated simultaneously using bivariate probit regression with clustered standard errors. Note that Table 6.2 reports only the results of the participation model (the estimates of the endogenous perception equation are omitted for ease of presentation and are presented in Appendix E).

[24] In these calculations, the features of the subconstituency (size, financial contributions, mail contact, and personal contact) and legislator's electoral safety are held at their mean or median values (for continuous and discrete variables, respectively).

TABLE 6.2. *Probability of Legislative Participation on Behalf of Subconstituencies*

	Patients' Bill of Rights	National Energy Bill
Legislative Perception of Subconstituency	1.481***	0.433*
	(0.390)	(0.223)
Subconstituency Size (in 1,000s)	−0.001	−0.004
	(0.001)	(0.002)
Financial Contributions (in $1,000s)	0.001	−0.001
	(0.001)	(0.001)
Contact from Subconstituency		
Mail Contact	0.053	0.272***
	(0.151)	(0.110)
Personal Contact	0.020	0.037
	(0.021)	(0.025)
Electoral Safety (2000 Election)	0.027***	0.003
	(0.008)	(0.010)
Membership on Committee of Jurisdiction	0.869***	0.791***
	(0.277)	(0.317)
Committee Leadership	−0.154	0.496***
	(0.381)	(0.151)
Minority Party	−0.140	0.009
	(0.248)	(0.268)
Constant	−3.86	−1.98
	(0.862)	(0.824)
N	273	390
Wald Chi-Squared (17)	479.26	–
Wald Chi-Squared (9)	–	95.16
p < Chi-Squared	.001	.001

Two-tailed hypotheses test: * $p < .10$, ** $p < .05$, *** $p < .01$.

Note: Reported estimates are coefficients for a probit model with robust standard errors clustered by legislative office in parentheses. For the Patients' Bill of Rights, the reported coefficients are for a probit model of legislative participation estimated using seemingly unrelated bivariate probit regression with standard errors clustered by legislative office; results of the endogenous regressor equation are not shown.

Figure 6.3). Similarly, in the debate on national energy policy, the predicted probability that a legislator participates on behalf of a subconstituency that the legislative enterprise does not see in the district is 36%.[25]

---

[25] Calculations are performed for a legislator on the Resources Committee, holding all constituency characteristics (size, contributions, mail contact, personal contact) and electoral security at their mean or median values (for continuous and discrete variables, respectively).

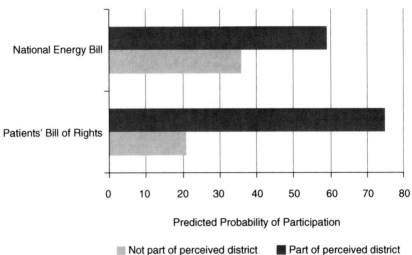

FIGURE 6.3. Predicted Probability of Participation on Behalf of Subconstituencies.

However, if a subconstituency is part of the perceived district, the probability that this same legislator participates on behalf of the subconstituency during the House debate increases to 59%.

These findings are important not only because they provide evidence that perceptions affect legislative participation but also because of the implications that this relationship has for constituency representation. If legislators are considerably less likely to voice the interests and concerns of constituents in their district that they do not see, then policy debate on Capitol Hill and legislative outcomes are less likely to reflect the interests of these constituents. In short, the influence of legislative perceptions of subconstituencies on legislators' participation is both statistically and substantively consequential. Whether a legislator perceives a subconstituency in the district is a major determinant of whether he acts on behalf of those constituents in Washington.

In addition to the important role played by legislative perceptions of constituents in determining legislators' participation, a limited number of other constituency considerations also affect legislative behavior. For instance, legislators who receive more mail from a subconstituency are more likely to act on behalf of that subconstituency during the debate over national energy policy. This finding provides further evidence of the importance of constituency-initiated contact for congressional representation, which has already been shown to affect legislative perceptions of the district. It is interesting to note that the positive effect of contact from constituents on the likelihood of participation on their behalf is not a function of the size of the subconstituency, as large subconstituencies may or may not be active in sending letters and email to their legislator.[26] In fact, this exchange between then Representative Sherrod Brown (D-OH) and Michael Mangano, the Acting Inspector General for the Department of Health and Human Services, during the hearings on Medicare regulatory reform held by the House Energy and Commerce Committee illustrates this dynamic:

Brown: "You know, I hear over and over the threat of doctors going to jail, and I hear it from my district ... if doctors make a mistake, they go to jail." Mangano: "... In the last 3 years, we criminally prosecuted an average of 18 physicians a year, out of 650,000 physicians." Brown: "Do all 18 of them – since I hear so much about it – do all 18 live in my district?"[27]

The results presented in Table 6.2 also confirm the importance of committee membership and electoral security for legislative participation, which are consistent with previous studies. First, legislators who serve on the committee with jurisdiction are more likely to be active in the congressional policy debate. In the case of the Patients' Bill of Rights, the likelihood that a committee member is active on behalf of a given subconstituency is 21% as compared to 5% for members not on the committee.[28] Legislators on the House Resources Committee are predicted to participate on behalf of a subconstituency 36% of the time as compared to 12% of the time predicted for their colleagues not on the committee. Additionally, holding a committee leadership position increases the probability that a legislator will be active in the debate over the national energy bill, an effect that is not evident in the debate over the Patients' Bill of Rights.

Second, legislators who were elected with a larger percentage of the vote in the last election were more likely to participate on behalf of constituents in the debate over the Patients' Bill of Rights. This finding is

---

[26] The inclusion of an interaction term for subconstituency size and mail contact is not significant at conventional levels and does not change any of the other relationships. In fact, the size of a subconstituency and the amount of mail contact with the legislative office regarding the energy bill are negatively correlated at –.16.

[27] U.S. House of Representatives, Committee on Energy and Commerce, Report 107–23, p. 170.

[28] Calculations are performed holding all variables at their median or mean values (for discrete and continuous variables, respectively). Since there are an equal number of Democrats and Republicans, the legislator is assumed to be a Democrat.

consistent with the argument that more secure legislators are able to
spend their time being active on Capitol Hill, while legislators who are
electorally vulnerable must devote their time to activities in the district
that more directly build electoral support.[29]

Overall, legislators' decisions to participate on behalf of a subconstituency are shaped to a large degree by their perceptions of their constituents.
Legislators are more likely to act for subconstituencies they see in their
district, and they are unlikely to participate on behalf of those constituents that they do not see. Since legislative perceptions are incomplete and
biased views of the collection of relevant constituents in a district, the fact
that they shape legislative decisions about behavior, even after controlling
for alternate explanations, has important consequences. In sum, the flaws
in legislative perception are reflected in legislative participation.

THE EFFECTS OF LEGISLATIVE PERCEPTION ON THE EXTENT OF LEGISLATIVE PARTICIPATION

The decision to participate on behalf of a subconstituency is an important
part of representing the interests of constituents in Congress; yet, when
a legislator invokes a subconstituency, there is considerable variation in
the extent to which he does so. Legislators sometimes speak on behalf
of a subconstituency a handful of times, while in other instances legislators participate on behalf of a subconstituency several dozen times. *How
much* a legislator participates in the policy-making process is meaningful
because a legislator who repeatedly speaks on behalf of a subconstituency more actively represents those constituents' interests.[30] Therefore, it
is important to understand the effects of perception on not only *whether*
legislators participate but also whether legislative perceptions play an
additional role by influencing the *extent* of legislators' actions on behalf
of constituents. This second question, when added to the first, presents a
more complete picture of congressional representation.

[29] As a robustness check in models not presented here, electoral security is included as
an interaction term with subconstituency size, subconstituency contact, and financial contributions. The results of these models are not substantively different from the
results presented in Table 6.2.

[30] In general, a greater number of mentions of a constituency demonstrates a greater
activity level on behalf of the constituency. However, there may be situations in which
this general relationship is less straightforward. To this point, the dependent variable
of legislative participation is analyzed as both a count variable and a dichotomous
variable. When legislators' participation is examined without regard to the amount
of participation, legislative perception of a subconstituency is a strong predictor of
whether a legislator participates on behalf of that subconstituency (see Table 6.2).

Perception and the Extent of Participation: Initial Patterns

To capture the extent of legislative participation on behalf of subconstituencies, a count of the number of times a legislator invokes a specified
subconstituency during the debate over either bill is employed. This variable is once again based on content analysis of official transcripts of committee and subcommittee hearings and markup, as well as the debate on
the House floor. In the case of the Patients' Bill of Rights, the extent of
participation ranges from speaking on behalf of a subconstituency once
to voicing the interests of a subconstituency forty times, with the average active legislator participating on behalf of a subconstituency almost
5½ times. The overall amount of legislative participation in the debate
over national energy policy is greater, since more committee hearings
were held on the issue, which provides more opportunities for legislators
to speak on behalf of their constituents. During the House debate over
the Securing America's Future Energy Act, legislators' activity varies
from participating on behalf of a subconstituency once to invoking the
concerns of a subconstituency more than one hundred times, with the
average active legislator acting on behalf of a subconstituency 13 times.

The descriptive statistics for this second question about the extent
of legislative participation continue to suggest that legislative perceptions of subconstituencies increase the amount of legislative participation (see Figure 6.4). When legislators do not perceive a subconstituency
in their district, they make an average of about half a comment on behalf
of that subconstituency during the debate over the Patients' Bill of Rights.
However, when legislators see a subconstituency in the district, they
make an average of 2½ comments on behalf of that subconstituency, ceteris paribus. Similarly, legislators who perceive a subconstituency in the
district relevant to the national energy bill participate on behalf of that
subconstituency three times more frequently than they do on behalf of
a subconstituency that is not part of their view of their districts, or an
increase from an average of 2½ comments to 7½ comments. These sizable
differences in the extent of legislators' participation on behalf of subconstituencies are statistically significant at conventional levels.[31] As before,
it is necessary to consider the relationship between perceptions and the
amount of legislative participation after controlling for the same set of
alternate explanations.

---

[31] The differences presented in Figure 6.4 are significant at p < .01. There are 280 observations in the case of the Patients' Bill of Rights and 400 observations in the case of the
national energy bill.

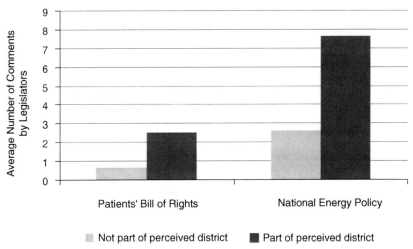

FIGURE 6.4. Legislative Perception and the Amount of Legislative Participation on Behalf of Relevant Subconstituencies.

ESTIMATION OF THE EXTENT OF LEGISLATORS' PARTICIPATION

The factors likely to shape the extent of legislators' participation on behalf of constituents mirror the factors initially hypothesized to influence the likelihood that legislators participate at all. In addition to legislative perceptions of subconstituencies, institutional, partisan, and conventional constituency factors are also hypothesized to affect the number of times a legislator participates in the congressional debate on behalf of a subconstituency, although it certainly is possible that the effects of these variables on the extent of participation will differ from their effect on whether legislators participate.

In order to assess the influence of legislative perceptions of the district, as well as the alternate considerations discussed earlier, multiple regression is used to estimate the extent of legislators' participation in the congressional debate. The extent of legislative participation on behalf of constituents is conceived of as a two-step process in which legislators first choose whether to participate on behalf of a subconstituency, and then choose how active to be on behalf of that subconstituency. Consequently, these relationships are estimated using a zero-inflated count model that takes into account what we know about legislators' initial decision to participate in order to estimate the amount of participation.[32] This type of model is well suited for count variables where the large number of zeros (which indicate no participation on behalf of a subconstituency) is inflated by a systematic process (see Hall and Miler 2008; Long 1997). The case of legislative participation on behalf of constituents is indeed such a case.[33] The first-stage model of the likelihood that a legislator will not participate on behalf of a subconstituency (i.e., a zero count) is informed by the results of the previous analysis of legislators' decisions to participate (see Table 6.2). The second stage of the model examines the extent of legislators' activity given their decision to participate and the influence of legislators' perceptions, as well as institutional, partisan, and constituency considerations on the extent of their participation. A separate model is estimated for the Patients' Bill of Rights and the Securing America's Future Energy Act, and each model uses standard errors clustered on the legislative office to take into account the fact that the observations are not fully independent.

The results of the zero-inflated count models of legislators' participation on behalf of subconstituencies are presented in Table 6.3.[34] In the case of the national energy debate, legislative perception of a subconstituency increases both the probability that a legislator participates on behalf of a subconstituency and increases the number of times he does so. The effects of whether a legislator perceives a subconstituency in the district are statistically significant at the $p < .10$ level in both models. Predicted probability estimates indicate that a legislator participates 3½ times on behalf of a subconstituency that he perceives in the district as compared to only 1½ times if the subconstituency is not part of the perceived district, all else equal.[35] Put differently, whether or not a legislative enterprise sees a subconstituency in the district more than doubles the expected amount of legislative activity on behalf of that subconstituency during the policy-making process.

[32] Zero-inflated count models estimate a first stage binary model of the probability that an event count will be zero (i.e., a legislator will not participate on behalf of a subconstituency) and a second stage count model of how many times a legislator speaks on behalf of a subconstituency.

[33] The Vuong test comparing the zero-inflated count model to the traditional count model confirms that the zero-inflated version is more appropriate for these data (see Table 6.5).

[34] Note that the coefficients on the parameter estimates in the binary stage are negative, whereas they are positive in Table 6.2 because the binary stage in a zero-inflated count model estimates the probability of *no* action.

[35] In these calculations, all other variables are held at their mean values (for continuous variables) or median values (for discrete variables).

TABLE 6.3. *Count of Legislative Participation on Behalf of Subconstituencies*

	Patients' Bill of Rights Participation Count	National Energy Bill Participation Count
Count Stage: Number of Actions		
Legislative Perception of	−0.327	0.448**
Subconstituency	(0.374)	(0.214)
Subconstituency Size (in 1,000s)	−0.002**	−0.013***
	(0.001)	(0.005)
Financial Contributions (in	0.002***	−0.001
$1,000s)	(0.001)	(0.026)
Contact from Subconstituency		
Mail Contact	−0.460**	−0.071
	(0.202)	(0.167)
Personal Contact	0.063***	0.116***
	(0.013)	(0.026)
Electoral Safety (2000 Election)	0.004	0.022**
	(0.011)	(0.010)
Membership on Committee of	1.016***	−0.789**
Jurisdiction	(0.391)	(0.416)
Committee Leadership	0.498*	0.312**
	(0.273)	(0.133)
Minority Party	−0.005	0.385
	(0.263)	(0.347)
Constant	0.184	0.264
	(1.271)	(0.821)
Binary Stage: Probability of No Action		
Legislative Perception of	−1.080***	−0.901*
Subconstituency	(0.369)	(0.553)
Membership on Committee	−1.187**	−1.970***
	(0.535)	(0.782)
Committee Leadership	–	−0.894***
		(0.334)
Electoral Safety	−0.038*	–
	(0.021)	
Mail Contact from Subconstituency	–	−0.740**
		(0.307)
Constant	4.840	3.211
	(1.663)	(0.698)
N	273	390
Wald Chi-Squared (9)	317.75	150.45
p < Chi-Squared	.001	.001
Vuong z-Statistic	2.96	4.55
p < z-Statistic	.002	.001

Two-tailed hypotheses tests: * p < .10, ** p < .05, *** p < .01.

Note: Reported estimates are coefficients for the count process of the zero-inflated count model with robust standard errors clustered by legislative office in parentheses.

In the case of the Patients' Bill of Rights, the effect of legislative perception on participation continues to predict whether a legislator will participate on behalf of a subconstituency, but there is no evidence that perception has an additional influence on the extent of participation. The negative and statistically significant coefficient on legislative perception of the subconstituency in the binary stage of the model indicates that a legislator who perceives a subconstituency in the district is unlikely to *not* act on behalf of that subconstituency (see the bottom half of Table 6.3). In other words, a legislator who sees a subconstituency is more likely to act on their behalf. However, the coefficient does not achieve conventional levels of statistical significance in the count stage of the model, which indicates that the data are inconclusive regarding the impact of perceptions on the amount of legislators' participation. In sum, on the Patients' Bill of Rights, legislators continue to be more likely to act on behalf of constituents they see, but whether they participate at high levels is not predicted.

In addition to the impact of legislative perception of district constituents, conventional constituency considerations also affect how actively legislators represent their constituents. Across both cases, legislators participate more frequently on behalf of subconstituencies who make their interests known through personal contact with the legislative office. The effects of constituency-initiated phone and personal contact are statistically and substantively meaningful. For instance, a legislator who was contacted ten times by a subconstituency is more than twice as active on behalf of those constituents as compared to subconstituencies that do not contact the legislator.[36] In contrast, there is no evidence that mail contact increases the amount of legislative activity on behalf of a subconstituency, although it continues to increase the likelihood that a legislator will participate for a subconstituency in the case of national energy policy (see Table 6.2 and the bottom half of Table 6.3). Additionally, legislators are not more active on behalf of subconstituencies comprised of a larger number of constituents in the district. In fact, there is evidence that the size of subconstituency is negatively related to the extent of legislative participation, which means that legislators participate more frequently on behalf of smaller subconstituencies in their district.

---

[36] Holding all other variables at their median values, the expected amount of legislative participation on behalf of a subconstituency increases from 0.7 to 1.3 acts in the case of the Patients' Bill of Rights, and increases from 2.2 to 6.9 acts in the case of the Securing America's Future Energy Act.

The results in Table 6.3 also provide mixed evidence concerning the influence of money on the extent of legislative participation on behalf of constituents. Only in the case of the Patients' Bill of Rights are legislators who receive more money from a subconstituency more active on that subconstituency's behalf, and even then, the substantive impact is quite modest.[37] As shown in Chapter 5, the primary influence of money in congressional representation is in shaping legislative perceptions of the constituency, not in directly buying legislators' behavior. These results add to the literature on the different ways that money can shape congressional politics (e.g., Esterling 2007; Grenzke 1989; Hall and Wayman 1990; Wawro 2001). Money may not buy legislative activity in a direct and unseemly way, but money shapes legislators' image of their constituency. By buying mental access, financial contributions shape the pre-conscious stage of representation and can have a corrupting influence on constituency representation even when legislators are not active accomplices.

The data also illustrate that committee membership and committee leadership significantly increase legislative participation in the policy-making debate. In the case of the Patients' Bill of Rights, committee members are more likely to participate, and they also are more active when they do participate. When looking at the Securing America's Future Energy Act, committee members are more likely to participate on behalf of constituents, but among active legislators, committee membership does not increase the amount of participation. Overall, however, the substantive impact of congressional committees is rather modest.[38] Additionally, across both policies, legislators who are committee leaders are significantly more active on behalf of subconstituencies in their district than legislators who are rank and file committee members.[39]

---

[37] A subconstituency that contributes $300,000 to a legislator can expect less than one additional comment on its behalf during the House debate as compared to a subconstituency that made only minor contributions ($10,000) to the legislator. Calculations are performed while holding all other variables at their mean and median values.

[38] The total effect of committee membership amounts to an expected increase of less than one comment in both cases.

[39] On the Patients' Bill of Rights, a committee member is expected to make one comment while a committee leader is expected to make two comments on behalf of constituents. In the case of the national energy bill, a committee member is expected to make 3½ comments as compared to 5½ for a committee leader. When calculating these predictions, all other variables are held at their median or mean values, except for party because there are an equal number of Democrats and Republicans. The legislator is assumed to be a Democrat.

Taken together, these findings illustrate that the extent of legislators' participation on behalf of subconstituents is affected by their perceptions of subconstituencies as well as a handful of institutional factors (i.e., committee position) and features of the subconstituency (i.e., personal contact). A legislator's perceptions determine both whether or not he acts on behalf of a subconstituency, and in some circumstances, how much the legislator acts for the subconstituency. Furthermore, across the analyses in this chapter, legislators' perceptions of their constituents have a strong and independent effect on participation even when alternative explanations are included.

CONCLUSION

This chapter began by asking whether legislative perceptions of constituents in the district affect legislative behavior on their behalf. The central argument is that the district a legislator sees is the district that a legislator acts for during the policy-making process. To evaluate this argument, legislators' initial decision to participate and their subsequent decision of how much to participate are examined. The findings are clear – legislators are more likely to participate, and to do so more frequently, on behalf of constituents that they see when they look back at their district from Capitol Hill.

Moreover, the real-world impact of perceptions on legislative behavior is significant. When participating in the debate over the Patients' Bill of Rights, legislators are over three times more likely to speak on behalf of constituents that they see in their district as compared to constituents they do not see. Similarly, in the case of the Securing America's Future Energy Act, legislators are nearly two times more likely to participate on behalf of subconstituencies they see in their district, and they are two times more active on behalf of these perceived subconstituencies. Overall, legislative perceptions are one of the three most substantively important factors in explaining constituency representation as captured by legislators' participation on behalf of constituents.

The fact that legislative perceptions are a significant predictor of legislators' participation is important because it contributes to a fuller understanding of what determines legislative activity on behalf of constituents. By defining congressional representation as a collection of relationships between a legislative enterprise and the relevant subconstituencies in the district, this chapter takes an important step toward unpacking the notion that "constituents matter" in order to understand *which* constituents matter for legislative behavior as well as *how* they matter. This research reveals that *perceived* constituents influence legislators' participation in the policy-making process, and that they do so both by affecting whether or not a legislator participates and how much he participates. As a result, legislative perceptions influence whether a subconstituency is represented and the extent to which it is represented on Capitol Hill. The findings are significant because they provide valuable evidence of the consequences of biased district perceptions. If there was evidence that the flaws of legislative perceptions do not translate into systematic biases in legislative behavior, then this would suggest that perhaps the concerns identified in the previous chapter are less troubling in practice than in theory. However, the analyses clearly demonstrate that flawed perceptions of the district do impact legislators' decisions about participation in the policy-making process. Some constituents are systematically not being seen by legislators and their staff and, as a result, not being represented on Capitol Hill.

In sum, legislative perception is an essential piece of the story of congressional behavior. As Fenno (1978, 244) writes, "To put the point most strongly, perhaps we can never understand his [a legislator's] Washington activity without also understanding his perception of his various constituencies." The findings across this chapter validate Fenno's concern. Perceptions shape the way that legislators behave above and beyond the conventional measures of constituency influence on behavior. This conclusion amplifies normative concerns about the partial and unrepresentative nature of legislative perceptions by revealing that biases in perception become biases in representation.

7

Reassembling the District as a Whole

In representing the various subconstituents in their districts, legislators often cannot avoid taking a larger view and thinking of "the district" as a collective. However, the district legislators see from Capitol Hill is not a perfect reflection of the objective reality of their district, but rather some filtered summary. This chapter identifies the legislator's perception of the district as a whole and examines its effects on his behavior. Given the evidence about the impact of perceptions of subconstituencies in Chapter 6, there is good reason to expect that the way legislators see the totality of their district also will affect their actions on Capitol Hill. The primary question explored in this chapter, then, is how these aggregate perceptions shape legislators' involvement at earlier and later stages of the lawmaking process.

Overall perceptions of the district are characterized by two important features: their *completeness* and their *balance*. Completeness of a district perception emphasizes the extent to which legislators perceive all subconstituency interests in the district relevant to the policy in question. The balance of district perception, on the other hand, shifts attention to the competing preferences among district interests. As this chapter shows, these two characteristics of perceptions are consequential. Legislators who perceive a more complete district are more active in introducing legislation than their colleagues with a narrower vision. Moreover, legislators who perceive a balanced district are not hesitant to sponsor legislation, despite the conventional wisdom that legislators representing competing constituents will be less active. Perhaps less surprisingly, but not less importantly, legislators who see a balanced district vote more moderately than do legislators who see constituents on only one side of the issue. These findings suggest that legislators are, in fact, quite attentive to the district as they see it. They do not shy away from the challenges of representing a complex constituency but instead are active in sponsoring legislation on the issues they believe to be important to their constituents. Additionally, the influence of legislators' perceptions of their district on their behavior is evident even when rational choice explanations of legislative behavior are taken into account. Legislators' perceptions of the district as a whole also have implications for the functioning of the House more broadly. Balanced district perceptions, regardless of the reality on the ground, correspond with individual legislators' moderate voting records. When considered in the aggregate, the moderating influence of balanced district perceptions thus may be a counterweight to the increased polarization and frequent stalemate that characterize the modern Congress.

PERCEPTIONS OF THE DISTRICT AS A WHOLE

In complicating the concept of "the district," this book has focused so far on the issue-specific subconstituencies a legislator sees in his district and how he represents these constituents in Congress. However, the dyadic theory of subconstituency representation does not preclude us from also wanting to understand legislators' perceptions of their districts as a whole. In fact, it is precisely because the conventional notion of "the district" has been broken apart into its subconstituency-based parts that it is now possible to rebuild a more informed notion of legislators' overall district perceptions. Perceptions of the district as a whole are defined with respect to a substantive policy area, but the policy context tends to be broader than an individual piece of legislation. Therefore, I examine how legislative perceptions are summarized by looking at the pairs of issues in health policy and natural resources policy.

Recall that the completeness of district perception emphasizes the extent to which legislators' perceptions of the district include all of the relevant subconstituencies in the district within an issue area. Since there are subconstituencies relevant to both proposals within health policy (or natural resources policy), these are counted only once for the purposes of measuring the completeness of district perceptions. Seven subconstituencies are identified as relevant to the Patients' Bill of Rights and six subconstituencies are identified as relevant to Medicare regulatory reform, which when put together results in eight distinct subconstituencies relevant to broader health policy. Similarly, ten subconstituencies are identified as relevant to national energy policy and six subconstituencies are identified as relevant to the wetlands conservation act, which results in eleven distinct subconstituencies relevant to natural resources policy.

The balance of district perception calls attention to whether legislative enterprises perceive subconstituencies with competing policy preferences within their district. The collection of relevant subconstituencies in a district shares an interest in a policy area, but they do not necessarily share preferences over that policy. As one staff member commented when reflecting on the district, "certainly, you know, opinion is not unanimous."[1] To paraphrase Fiorina (1974, 31), legislators perceive a "state of nature" in their district, which is based on the answers to the question: "Who cares, and on which side of the issue?" To these questions, I add: Do legislators perceive these competing sides within their district, and does it affect their behavior? In order to answer these questions, the competing sides of each issue must first be identified.[2] In the case of health policy, the key distinction is between a focus on the provision of health care benefits and a focus on the costs of health care.[3] The first of these competing sides is represented by patients, seniors, doctors, labor unions, and trial attorneys, whereas the side emphasizing costs is made up of employers, businesses, hospitals, and insurance providers. Likewise, subconstituency interests on natural resources issues can be divided into two sides based on their dominant approach to resource management. The first side focuses on restricted resource extraction and support for conservation and includes environmentalists, consumers, sportsmen, and renewable energy subconstituencies. The other side of the issue consists of subconstituencies supportive of resource extraction and multiple land use, including oil and gas, mining, utility companies, business, agriculture, veterans, and local government.[4]

[1] Personal interview.

[2] There are multiple ways in which districts can be divided (see Chapter 2), but the relevant dimension for explaining the influence of the constituency on legislators' policy activity is constituents' preferences on the issues at hand.

[3] See Baumgartner et al. (2004) for a discussion of the two sides of health policy issues and natural resources policy issues based on their extensive "Advocacy and Public Policymaking" project.

[4] Recall that the veterans subconstituency is coded as supportive of resource extraction given their interest in reducing dependence on foreign energy sources. The state and local government subconstituency is coded as being on the side of the issue that is more supportive of resource extraction. This characterization is accurate in the context of the policies examined here; however, the position of state and local governments on resource extraction might differ on certain policy questions or across localities. The

Legislative enterprises who see one or more subconstituencies on each side of the policy debate are considered to have a balanced view of their district. For instance, a legislative enterprise that sees both the environmental and mining subconstituencies is considered to have a balanced district perception, whereas an enterprise that sees the utility and mining subconstituencies is considered to have an unbalanced district perception. Legislators and their staff talk about their district in ways that clearly reveal whether or not they see constituents on both sides of an issue. In talking about natural resources issues, the office of one California Democrat highlighted that "there was a citizen side and there's a business side ... so we're trying to put one major fire out [national energy policy] that's dealing with two different interests,"[5] while the staff to a Southern Republican described the "tough line to walk"[6] between protecting national land in the district and supporting the local utilities. Every legislator's district includes subconstituencies on competing sides of health and natural resources policy, but the question is whether they see them and what effect this has on their behavior.

DISTRICT PERCEPTIONS AND BILL SPONSORSHIP

Bill sponsorship is an important way that legislators seek to achieve their electoral and policy goals. Sponsoring legislation is costly for legislators and their staff, and the decision to sponsor legislation in a policy area is a deliberate one (Hall 1996). As a result, bill sponsorship is "a strong indicator of which issues [the legislator] wants to be associated with" (Schiller 1995, 187) and an expression of legislators' priorities (Sulkin 2005). Bill sponsorship also reflects legislators' desire to advance the interests of their constituents and secure their own electoral success. As Kingdon (1977) argues, these two goals are inextricably linked in the empirical data and are at the heart of congressional representation. In her work on bill sponsorship in the U.S. Senate, Schiller (1995, 2000) argues that legislators are attentive to the issues that their constituents care about, and sponsoring legislation in these areas is an important way to demonstrate that attentiveness. Additionally, bill introduction allows legislators to both advertise and claim credit for their policy-relevant

results reported in this chapter are robust to specifications that omit the veterans and local government subconstituencies.

[5] Personal interview.

[6] Personal interview.

activities (Arnold 1990, 2004; Mayhew 1974; Sulkin 2005). Legislators' decision to sponsor legislation, therefore, is meaningful for both policy outcomes and constituency representation.

If bill sponsorship reflects legislators' perceptions of their district, then we would expect to see different patterns of sponsorship according to whether legislators have complete and balanced views of their constituency. Completeness and balance of district perceptions, however, can produce competing hypotheses. Legislators who have a more complete district perception are expected to sponsor more legislation, ceteris paribus. A legislator who sees a greater number of interests within his district will interpret this completeness as an indicator of the greater importance of the issue to the district. Given both electoral and good public policy motives (Fenno 1973; Mayhew 1974), legislators should prefer to spend their limited time and energy on policies that they believe reflects their district's interests. On the other hand, legislators who see a balanced district are expected to sponsor less legislation. As Fiorina (1974) argues, legislators representing districts with competing interests risk alienating part of their constituency with almost any action they take (see also Achen 1978; Hall 1996). Since legislators are risk-averse and reelection-minded (e.g., Mayhew 1974), when they see a balanced district, they should sponsor less legislation, all else equal, in order to reduce the likelihood of losing support among their constituents.

In order to assess the influence of legislators' overall district perceptions on bill sponsorship, the number of bills introduced by legislators regarding health policy and natural resources policy in the 107th and 108th Congresses (2001–2004) is examined.[7] The explanatory variables of primary interest are the completeness and balance of legislators' aggregate district perceptions. First, a complete district perception is measured by the number of relevant constituents a legislative office perceives in its district when asked about health policy or natural resources policy. For example, a legislator who considers his district's interests in resources policy and sees five of the eleven relevant subconstituencies is

---

[7] These data are taken from Sulkin (2009), and all bill introductions by a given legislator in a given congress are counted and coded according to substantive policy codes. Bill introductions are aggregated across the 2001–2004 period due to the fact that normal legislative activity during the 107th Congress (2001–2002) was affected by the events of September 11, 2001. As a result, terrorism issues dominated the congressional agenda, and numerous domestic issues were delayed until the 108th Congress. Looking at bill introductions across the two-congress period takes this important political event into account while also capturing the broader patterns of the congressional agenda.

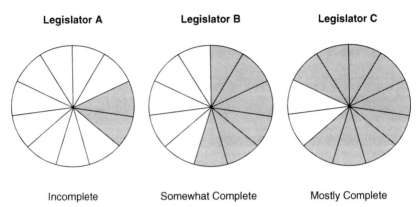

FIGURE 7.1. Completeness of District Perception: Resources Policy (Eleven Subconstituencies).

considered to have a more complete perception of his district as a whole than a legislator who sees only two of the eleven relevant subconstituencies when looking back at his district (see Figure 7.1).

Second, a balanced district perception is measured by an indicator variable denoting whether or not a legislative enterprise sees one or more subconstituencies on both sides of the policy debate. These two measures are related but conceptually distinct ways of measuring the perception of the district as a whole, and each is included separately in the analyses of legislators' bill sponsorship.

Perception of the overall district, however, is not the only factor that might affect bill sponsorship because the costs and potential benefits of introducing legislation differ systematically across legislators (Hall 1996). As a result, institutional, partisan, and electoral considerations are taken into account when examining the impact of district perceptions on bill introductions. First, legislators who serve on the committee with jurisdiction over the policy area are expected to be more active in introducing legislation. The costs of bill sponsorship are lower for committee members because they are more familiar with the policy and have more resources available to them than non–committee members (e.g., Hall 1996; Schiller 2000; Sinclair 1989). An indicator variable is used to capture committee membership on the primary committee with jurisdiction for health policy (House Energy and Commerce Committee) and natural resources policy (House Resources Committee) respectively. Additionally, committee leaders are expected to sponsor more legislation in the relevant issue area because their leadership position provides them with greater resources and expertise (e.g., Hall 1987, 1996; Sinclair 1989). Legislators who serve as chair or ranking minority member of the House Energy and Commerce Committee and its subcommittees (or the House Resources Committee and its subcommittees) are designated as holding relevant leadership positions.

Second, more senior legislators are expected to introduce more bills because they also enjoy lower costs of sponsorship relative to their more junior colleagues (see Schiller 1995, 2000). As a function of their experience in the U.S. House, senior legislators are more familiar with both the policy area and the lawmaking process, which makes sponsoring legislation less burdensome than for newer House members. Legislative seniority is measured by the number of years served in the U.S. House of Representatives prior to the beginning of the 107th Congress (2001–2002).

Third, that a legislator belongs to the majority party in the chamber – in this case, the Republican Party – is expected to increase the number of bills he sponsors. The majority party in the House enjoys numerous institutional advantages that reduce the costs of bill sponsorship as compared with minority party legislators. An alternate hypothesis is offered by Schiller (1995), who argues that Democrats are generally more supportive of government activity, whereas Republicans are less likely to believe in an active federal government. According to this competing argument, Democrats are expected to introduce more legislation as compared to their Republican colleagues, all else equal. In order to test these competing hypotheses about party, an indicator variable that takes a value of one when the legislator is a Democrat and a value of zero when the legislator is a Republican is included.

Fourth, legislators who were elected by a larger electoral margin are expected to sponsor more bills than their electorally vulnerable colleagues. Bill introduction is a costly behavior for all legislators, but it is especially costly for vulnerable legislators for whom the opportunity costs of sponsoring bills in Washington are the time and resources that could have been spent building greater electoral support. Legislators' electoral security is measured by the percentage of the vote they received in the 2000 general election.

Taken together, then, legislators' district perceptions, as well as considerations based on committee, seniority, party, and electoral security, are expected to affect sponsorship of legislation concerning health policy and natural resources policy. The dependent variable is a count of the number of health policy (or natural resources policy) bills sponsored by a legislator. In the multivariate analyses, then, each policy area is

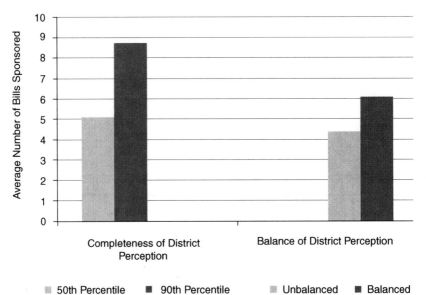

FIGURE 7.2. Complete and Balanced District Perceptions and Bill Sponsorship.

examined separately using a Poisson count model, which is appropriate for examining the impact of perceptions and other factors on the number of bills introduced by a legislator.

The Influence of Complete and Balanced District Perceptions on Bill Sponsorship

Before turning to the multivariate analysis, it is useful to consider some initial patterns. A brief look at the descriptive data offers preliminary support for the hypothesis that legislators with a more complete perception of their district as a whole are more active in introducing legislation. Legislators who perceive an average degree of completeness in their district sponsor 5.1 bills as compared to legislators who see a considerably more complete district (90th percentile) and sponsor 8.7 bills, or 70% more bills than their colleagues who see an average degree of completeness in their district (see Figure 7.2).

In order to more fully examine the effects of the completeness of legislators' district perceptions on bill sponsorship, multiple regression analysis is used to estimate the relationships. Table 7.1 presents the results of these analyses. The data provide some evidence that a more complete district perception increases legislators' activity in sponsoring legislation. Legislators who have a more complete perception

TABLE 7.1. *Complete District Perception and Bill Sponsorship*

	Count of Resource Policy Bills Sponsored	Count of Health Policy Bills Sponsored
Completeness of District Perception	0.225***	−0.001
	(0.084)	(0.133)
Electoral Safety (2000 Election)	−0.008	0.012
	(0.009)	(0.012)
Membership on Committee of Jurisdiction	1.337***	0.337**
	(0.302)	(0.375)
Committee Leader	0.673***	1.139***
	(0.182)	(0.415)
Seniority	0.017	0.001
	(0.017)	(0.010)
Minority Party	−0.228	0.082
	(0.295)	(0.241)
Constant	0.652	0.062
	(0.622)	(0.903)
N	41	40
Wald Chi-Squared (6)	93.79	43.23
p < Chi-Squared	.001	.001

Two-tailed hypotheses tests: * p < .10, ** p < .05, *** p < .01.
Note: Reported estimates are coefficients for a Poisson count model with robust standard errors in parentheses.

of their district on natural resources issues (see first column) sponsor significantly more bills addressing resources issues than do their colleagues with more limited district perceptions. The magnitude of this relationship is notable. For instance, based on the coefficients presented in Table 7.1, a Democratic legislator who serves on the House Resources Committee (but is not a committee leader) and has an incomplete district perception (defined as including approximately one-fifth of the relevant subconstituency interests) is predicted to introduce six bills on natural resources policy. In contrast, a similar legislator who has a more complete district perception (defined as including half of the relevant subconstituency interests) is predicted to sponsor almost 12 pieces of legislation (see Figure 7.3).[8] The increase in the number of

---

[8] Here, the legislator is assumed to be a Democratic committee member, and both seniority and electoral security are held at their mean values. The predicted probability for incomplete district perception assumes that the legislator's district perception includes two of eleven relevant subconstituencies, whereas the more complete district perception assumes a perception including five of eleven, or just over half, of the relevant subconstituencies in the district.

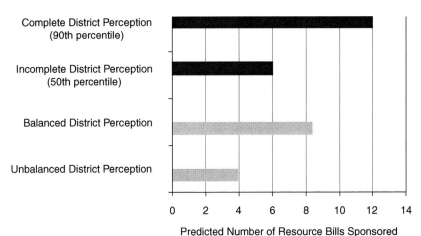

FIGURE 7.3. Predicted Amount of Bill Sponsorship on Natural Resources Policy.

bills introduced is quite large, especially given the modest increase in the completeness of district perception. In the case of health care, however, the data concerning the impact of complete district perceptions on bill sponsorship are inconclusive. Additionally, the results illustrate that committee membership and committee leadership are important predictors of bill sponsorship activity, which is consistent with expectations based on the literature.

The second feature of legislators' perceptions of the district as a whole is balance, or whether legislators see constituents on both sides of the policy debate. The standard story is that strategic legislators are risk-averse and thus are expected to sponsor fewer bills when they see a balanced district because some constituents in their district will oppose whatever action they take. A first glance at the data provides evidence to the contrary. Legislators who have a balanced district perception sponsor an average of 6.1 bills, but legislators who see homogenous preferences in the district propose only 4.4 bills, or roughly two-thirds as many bill introductions (see Figure 7.2).

Again, multiple regression analysis provides a more thorough examination of this relationship while taking into account other factors that might determine legislators' sponsorship activity (see Table 7.2). Contrary to expectations that legislators who see constituents on both sides of an issue will shy away from sponsoring legislation, there is consistent evidence that these legislators do not introduce fewer bills than their colleagues who perceive a more one-sided district. In fact, there is

TABLE 7.2. *Balanced District Perception and Bill Sponsorship*

	Count of Resource Policy Bills Sponsored	Count of Health Policy Bills Sponsored
Balanced District Perception	0.746**	−0.088
	(0.315)	(0.328)
Electoral Safety (2000 Election)	−0.007	0.012
	(0.009)	(0.011)
Membership on Committee of Jurisdiction	1.190***	0.343
	(0.276)	(0.373)
Committee Leader	0.707***	1.114***
	(0.206)	(0.380)
Seniority	−0.005	0.002
	(0.015)	(0.013)
Minority Party	−0.308	0.059
	(0.267)	(0.275)
Constant	1.032	0.182
	(0.527)	(0.765)
N	41	40
Wald Chi-Squared (6)	90.20	44.63
p < Chi-Squared	.001	.001

Two-tailed hypotheses tests: + p < .20, * p < .10, ** p < .05, *** p < .01.
Note: Reported estimates are coefficients for a Poisson count model with robust standard errors in parentheses.

even evidence in the case of natural resources that a balanced district perception increases the number of bills sponsored. As illustrated in the first column of Table 7.2, a legislator who sees constituents in the district on both sides of the resources debate actually introduces more legislation than a legislator who sees constituents on only one side, ceteris paribus. Based on the coefficients in Table 7.2, a balanced perception of the district more than doubles the number of bills a legislator introduces on natural resources. For instance, Figure 7.3 shows that a Democratic committee member who has a balanced district perception is predicted to offer almost eight bills as compared to just four bills sponsored by a similar legislator who sees constituents on only one side of the policy debate.[9] In sum, the data reject the conventional wisdom that legislators will avoid sponsoring bills when faced with perceived competing district preferences.

[9] The predicted values are 8.35 bills and 3.96 bills, respectively. The illustrative legislator is not a committee leader, and legislative seniority and electoral security are held at the mean values when calculating the predicted values.

DISTRICT PERCEPTIONS AND LEGISLATIVE VOTING

Given the extensive literature on congressional voting, there is little need to review the importance of voting as a valuable measure of legislative activity on Capitol Hill. What is less clear, however, is whether legislators' district perceptions shape the way they vote. Fiorina (1974) argues that "the representative's perceptions become the link between his constituents and his vote," but there has been little empirical research that examines this argument.[10] Here, legislators' perceptions of the overall district are expected to affect their votes by reducing patterns of extreme voting behavior. If legislators are responsive to their image of the overall district, then legislators who see a balanced district should have more moderate voting records than their colleagues who perceive a one-sided constituency. This relationship between balanced perceptions and legislative voting not only has implications for constituency representation but also suggests that an increase in the number of legislators who see a balanced district may foster compromise and mitigate some of the polarization in the House.

In this section, the focus is on the balance of perceptions of the district as a whole. A strong pattern of votes in support of one side of an issue carries the risk of angering constituents on the other side of the debate, and therefore legislators who see competing preferences in their district are expected to vote more moderately. As Stimson, MacKuen, and Erikson (1995) note, legislators' rational anticipation of the electoral implications of their behavior is one of "mechanisms of policy responsiveness." Furthermore, the potential for electoral punishment is sufficient incentive for a legislator to be responsive to his image of the district by moderating his voting behavior (see Arnold 1990; Hall 1996; Hansen 1991). As one Member of Congress said concerning the difficulty of voting on behalf of a diverse district, "You're representing a lot of people and you've only got one vote."[11] In contrast, legislators who perceive consensus in their district can more confidently vote in agreement with their image of the district, which allows them to take more extreme (or one-sided) positions.

[10] As discussed in the previous chapter, Miller and Stokes's (1963) study of constituency representation finds that legislative perceptions of the mean constituency opinion in the district influence legislators' votes on specific legislation, but their focus on the mean district opinion is significantly different from the conceptualization of complete and balanced district perceptions presented here.

[11] Personal interview.

Unlike the case of bill sponsorship, there is no clear theoretical expectation regarding the effect of completeness of district perceptions on the moderate (or extreme) nature of legislators' votes. The number of sub-constituencies a legislative enterprise perceives in its district could be used as a rough proxy for the diversity of constituency preferences if one assumes that legislators who see more constituents also see a more diverse set of constituents. However, the balance of legislators' district perceptions is a more accurate measure of competing district preference, which is why the balance of legislative perception is the primary focus of the remainder of the chapter.

Examining the pattern of votes cast by a legislator in a specified policy area rather than a single vote establishes the legislator's tendency to support (or oppose) the competing sides of the policy debate, and provides a useful overview of a legislator's voting record on that issue. Additionally, looking at legislators' voting patterns mirrors the practice of organizations that monitor the voting behavior of Members of Congress. Various media outlets (e.g., the *National Journal*) and many interest groups create indices of legislators' roll-call votes as a measure of each member's support for the organization's preferred policy positions. Organizations select votes within a specific policy area and generate a 0–100 score of legislators' record of support on legislation of interest to the group. Examples of these types of policy-specific voting records include the AFL-CIO on labor policy, the National Taxpayers Union on fiscal policy, and NARAL Pro-Choice America on abortion policy.[12] Furthermore, legislators are well aware of these voting scores, since they are used in the media and campaigns to summarize legislators' positions. In fact, when talking about legislators' activity on issues, legislative staff reference these voting scores as a point of reference for the legislator's history on the issue.[13]

Consistent with this tradition of policy-specific voting scores, the impact of legislative perceptions of the district is assessed in terms of legislators' voting patterns on health policy and on natural resources policy. Three key features of the measure of legislative voting patterns employed here are the use of multiple scores, the inclusion of scores from both sides of the policy debate, and the focus on the extremity of the

---

[12] One of the best known voting scores is created by the Americans for Democratic Action (ADA), which selects twenty votes to generate a measure of legislators' pattern of support for liberal policy positions. Although ADA scores are well known, they are unusual in that they are based on votes across a number of substantive policy areas.

[13] Personal interviews.

voting record. First, data from multiple sources is used to create an average of legislators' voting scores in support of one side of the health (or natural resources) policy debate. For instance, rather than rely only on one environmental organization's assessment of legislators' support for a restricted approach to resource management policy, legislator's support for this position is measured by scores from both the Sierra Club and the League of Conservation Voters.

Second, legislators' voting records are assessed by not only supporters of a particular policy position but also organizations on the opposing side of the issue. In order to create a single measure of voting behavior that includes both sides of the policy debate, a legislator's score from one side of the policy debate is averaged with the inverse of their record of support for the other side of the debate. The incorporation of the score from one side and the inverse of the vote score on the other side accounts for the fact that each side values different policy positions. This composite measure uses the same policy divisions between constituents' interests in health policy and natural resources policy that are used to define balanced districts earlier. Legislative votes cast in support of the provision of health care benefits are captured by vote scores compiled by Public Citizen, a consumer advocacy organization, and the U.S. Public Interest Research Group, both of which focus on patient care. Votes cast in support for the other side of the health policy debate (i.e., concern with the costs of health care) are based on vote scores from the U.S. Chamber of Commerce and the National Federation of Independent Business, which both focus on increased health care costs for employers and the business community. In the case of natural resources policy, votes in support of restricted resource extraction are taken from two leading environmental organizations – the Sierra Club and the League of Conservation Voters, as well as from Public Citizen, which advocates strong environmental protections. Votes cast in support of the benefits of resource extraction and development are based on scores created by the U.S. Chamber of Commerce, the National Federation of Independent Business, and the Associated Builders and Contractors.

Third, the extreme nature (or one-sidedness) of voting patterns is assessed based on the distance of each legislator's composite vote score (described earlier) from 50. This distance score captures both legislators' extreme support for a position (i.e., a score close to 100) and extreme lack of support for a position (i.e., a score close to 0). For instance, a legislator with a voting score of 90, indicating strong support for policies that focus on the provision of health care benefits, and a legislator with a voting score of 10, indicating very low levels of support for this side of the health care debate, are both coded as having rather extreme voting records on health policy that favor one side (i.e., a distance score of 40). In contrast, a legislator who has a moderately supportive (or a moderately opposed) position on health care may having a voting score of 60 (or 40, respectively), which is coded as a rather balanced voting record (i.e., a distance score of 10). For each policy area, then, the dependent variable is a 0–50 rating of the extreme nature of legislators' voting records on health and resources policy from 2001–2004.[14] The result is a richer measure of legislators' pattern of roll-call positions on health and natural resources votes.

As in the analysis of bill sponsorship, legislative perceptions of the district as a whole are the primary, but not the only, factor expected to influence the degree of moderation in legislators' voting records. Legislators' committee membership, electoral security, and party are also expected to affect their votes. First, in light of the debate in the congressional literature over whether committee members are preference outliers (e.g., Adler and Lipinski 1997; Hall and Grofman 1990; Krehbiel 1990; Shepsle and Weingast 1987), committee members are expected to have less moderate voting records, all else equal. An indicator variable captures whether legislators are members of the committee with jurisdiction for health (or natural resources) policy in the House. Second, legislators' electoral vulnerability is included to address the "marginality hypothesis" (Kuklinski 1977; Sullivan and Uslaner 1978) that legislators elected to their seat by a small margin of victory represent more competitive districts, and therefore will be more moderate on Capitol Hill. Legislators' electoral security is measured by the percentage of the vote they received in the 2000 election. Third, given the weight of the congressional literature that finds party to be an important determinant of voting behavior, legislators' partisan affiliation is included in the model as a dummy variable indicating the legislator belongs to the Democratic Party. The expected impact of party on the moderate nature of legislators' voting record, however, is not straightforward because the dependent variable is a nondirectional measure of distance (i.e., it treats extreme support for a position and extreme opposition to a position in the same way), and neither party has a monopoly on moderate (or extreme) policy positions.

[14] As with legislators' bill introductions, legislative voting records are averaged across the 107th and 108th Congresses to take into account the political disruption following the events of September 11, 2001.

The Influence of Balanced District Perceptions on Voting Behavior

An initial look at the raw data suggests that a balanced perception of the district as a whole does moderate legislators' voting behavior, at least in certain contexts. In the case of natural resources, legislators who see a balanced district are quite moderate in their support for the proconservation side of the argument, voting in support of this side of the policy debate just short of 40% of the time. On the other hand, legislators who only see proconservation constituents on this side of the policy debate are extremely supportive and vote for proconservation positions nearly 80% of the time. This example highlights the fact that whether legislators see constituents on both sides of a policy debate shapes the votes they cast on that issue.

In order to more fully examine whether balanced perceptions of the overall district have a moderating impact on legislators' voting records, the relationship is examined using an OLS estimator with corrections for robust standard errors. Recall that the dependent variable is a measure of the extreme nature of legislators' voting records such that a score of 0 represents a moderate voting record and a score of 50 represents the most extreme voting pattern on either side of the issue.

The results provide strong evidence that balanced perceptions of the district as a whole have a moderating effect on legislators' voting patterns on natural resources issues, as illustrated by the negatively signed coefficient estimates (see the first column of Table 7.3). This relationship is both statistically significant and substantively meaningful. The coefficient estimates show that a legislator with a balanced district perception has a voting history that is nearly seven points more moderate than a legislator who sees a homogenous district. The real-world impact of this reduction in support for extreme policies is illustrated by the case of a Democratic legislator who serves on the House Resources Committee. In this example, a seven-point reduction in this legislator's distance score, which is the result of his seeing constituents on both sides of the issue in his district, would equate to his proconservation rating going from a 76 to a more moderate 62.

In addition to legislative perceptions of the district as a whole, legislators' electoral safety and party status also have a consistent effect on the extremity of legislators' voting patterns. Legislators who were elected with a larger percentage of the vote consistently have more extreme voting records on health policy and natural resources policy. This finding is consistent with both the evidence that safe legislators represent

TABLE 7.3. *District Perceptions and Legislative Voting*

	Distance of Voting Score			
	Resources Policy		Health Policy	
Balanced District	−6.686**	−10.288***	3.988	4.104
Perception	(3.021)	(3.128)	(5.372)	(5.048)
Completeness	−	1.727**	−	−0.086
of District		(0.793)		(2.423)
Perception				
Electoral Safety	0.158**	0.161**	0.257*	0.256+
(2000 Election)	(0.078)	(0.077)	(0.150)	(0.155)
Membership on	3.041+	3.840+	−0.244	0.236
Committee of	(2.284)	(2.294)	(3.797)	(3.382)
Jurisdiction				
Minority Party	−12.933***	−12.342***	−13.955***	−13.927***
	(2.678)	(2.720)	(3.677)	(3.905)
Constant	36.354	32.423	18.810	19.009
	(6.651)	(7.574)	(13.790)	(15.809)
N	41	41	40	40
F-Statistic	7.46	8.94	5.18	4.07
P < F-Squared	.001	.001	.002	.005

Two-tailed hypotheses tests: * $p < .10$, ** $p < .05$, *** $p < .01$.

One-tailed hypotheses tests: + $p < .10$.

Note: Reported estimates are coefficients for OLS regression with robust standard errors in parentheses.

less competitive districts with more one-sided views and the argument that safe legislators may have more leeway to cast more extreme votes regardless of constituency opinion. There is also consistent evidence that Democratic legislators have significantly less extreme voting records on these two issues than their Republican colleagues.

With the relationship between balanced district perceptions and moderate voting records established, it is useful to briefly revisit the completeness of district perceptions. As discussed previously, when taken alone, it is not clear why a more complete district would result in legislators taking more (or less) extreme voting positions unless completeness is used as a poor substitute for balanced perceptions. Rather than assume this to be true, however, the completeness of district perceptions is added to the previous model of legislative voting, which is estimated a second time in order to determine the robustness of the moderating effects of balanced district perceptions on legislators' voting patterns. As shown in the second column of Table 7.3, when the completeness of aggregate district perceptions is included in the model, the moderating influence of a balanced district perception remains statistically significant and substantively strong in the case of natural resources policy. In fact, the moderating effects of a balanced district perception are even more pronounced. Legislators who see constituents on both sides of the natural resources policy debate have voting records that are more than ten points more moderate than their colleagues who see constituents on only one side of the policy debate. Completeness of district perceptions itself has no effect or a weak opposite effect on legislators' voting records. Additionally, the other relationships specified in the model of legislators' voting behavior on natural resources policy are robust to the inclusion of the measure of completeness of perceptions.

In contrast to the finding that legislative perceptions of the district as a whole have a significant influence on legislative voting patterns on natural resources policy, the data provide little insight into how district perceptions affect legislators' votes on health care policy. The results presented in Table 7.3 show that legislators who see a balanced district on health care policy are neither more nor less likely to take extreme positions, and these results do not change with the inclusion of the completeness measure. One reason that the balance of district perceptions does not significantly moderate legislators' votes on health care is that health care received considerable congressional attention in the 1990s, such that by the 107th Congress, the two sides of this policy debate were well known and had some history of compromise (see Chapter 4). As a result, the overall health care policy environment was less polarized than might be expected, and this curbed the extreme nature of legislative voting patterns even among legislators with an unbalanced (or homogenous) view of their district.

In contrast, the political environment surrounding natural resources policy in the 107th Congress was more polarized. Constituents in favor of greater conservation and limited resource extraction did not have a recent history of working together with constituents in favor of expanded resource extraction, and the result is a wider chasm between the policy preferences of the two sides. A quick glance at the data reveals that the average distance score across members on health policy is 32.7, which is significantly less extreme than the average distance score of 37.2 when looking at natural resources policy.[15] These findings suggest that the

---

[15] Distance scores are on a scale of 0 to 50 where 0 indicates a moderate voting record and 50 indicates an extreme voting record. The difference is statistically significant at $p < .10$.

relationship between legislative perceptions of the aggregate district and voting patterns likely varies across issue area, and further research on additional issues is needed to fully understand the relationship between legislative perceptions of their overall district and legislative voting.

Overall, the data from the two issue areas provide moderate support for the argument that legislators who perceive competing constituency interests have more moderate voting records that reflect the heterogeneity they see in their district. The moderating effects of a balanced district perception provide new support for Arnold's (1990) argument that legislators engage in rational anticipation. Reelection-minded legislators who see competing subconstituencies in their district are keen to minimize the chances of being characterized by opponents or the media as ignoring their constituents' interests. As a result, legislators vote in ways consistent with their image of the district as whole.

CONCLUSION

The central goal of this chapter has been to rebuild the notion of overall district perception and to examine whether the way legislators see their constituents in totality affects their behavior on Capitol Hill. The most striking evidence concerns the effects of balanced district perceptions on legislative behavior. Contrary to prior expectations that reelection-oriented legislators shy away from being active in policy areas where there is no district consensus, legislators who see competing constituents in the district are not less likely to introduce bills than legislators who see a one-sided district. In addition, the balance of legislators' district perceptions affects their votes on natural resources policy and results in more moderate voting records than those of legislators who see constituents on only one side of the issue.

The implications of these findings extend beyond predicting the behavior of individual legislators to address broader concerns of representation and polarization in the House. There is no evidence that legislators avoid the tough task of representing the complexity of their districts – *if* they see that complexity. This is good news for constituency representation. Legislators are responsive to the district they see, even if that district is complex and contains opposing subconstituencies.

Finally, the finding that more balanced district perceptions can result in less extreme voting patterns among House members also has broader implications for the chamber. More balanced district perceptions may actually reduce some of the party polarization that characterizes the modern House. An increase in the number of legislators with a balanced district perception would result in an aggregate reduction of extreme voting patterns. Therefore, a positive implication of balanced district perceptions is that they may promote legislators' ability to work across the party aisle to pass legislation in exactly the types of prominent policy areas examined here.

8

Perception, Reform, and Representation in Congress

Legislative perceptions of the district are an essential part of constituency representation in Congress. Congressional scholars have long asserted that who legislators see in their district affects how they represent their constituents on Capitol Hill (e.g., Dexter 1960; Fenno 1978; Kingdon 1968). However, the challenges of conceptualizing and measuring legislators' perceived districts have made it difficult to provide evidence that perceptions of constituents matter. In revisiting this central element of constituency representation in the wake of the growth of the cognitive psychology literature, this book sheds new light on how legislators represent their constituents by providing a theoretical foundation for legislative perceptions of constituents. This allows one to examine which constituents legislators see in their district as well as the mechanisms by which perceptions affect a wide range of legislative behavior. The resulting insights into constituency representation have implications not only for future congressional scholarship but also for the practice of congressional politics.

Which constituents are seen when legislators and their staff consider the relevance of policy to their district is important because our theories of legislative behavior implicitly assume that legislators are aware of all the relevant constituents in their district. However, if we reconsider whether this is a realistic assumption and investigate empirically its validity, it becomes apparent that legislative perceptions of the constituents in their district fall short of the assumed comprehensive, rationalistic view. The reality is that legislative enterprises do not see all relevant constituents in the district or even a representative subset. Instead, they see a truncated and unrepresentative version of their constituency. As a result, when legislators consider their constituency as they decide whether to introduce legislation or cast a vote, they consider their *perceived* constituency. Given the significant differences between the constituency in the legislator's mind and the constituency in the district, it is essential to take perceptions seriously when assessing congressional representation.

From a normative perspective, this divergence between the district in practice and the district in theory raises concerns that stem from the belief that a legislator should at least be aware of the citizens that he represents. As Pitkin (1967, 162) notes when discussing the relationship between a legislator and his constituents, "[the representative] need not always obey them, but he must consider them." But how does a legislator consider constituents that he does not even see? The fact that legislative perceptions are incomplete images of the constituency means that the representative relationships between legislative enterprises and subconstituencies often fail to meet this basic – yet fundamental – criterion. When relevant constituents go unseen by legislators and their staff, the scope of constituency representation in Congress is inherently limited (see Bachrach and Baratz 1962, 1963).

Perceptions of constituents also have implications for legislators' behavior. As Kingdon (1968, 7) observed, legislators' perceptions of the constituents in their district are "a variable intervening between the constituents and the behavior of the elected policy-maker." Whether sponsoring legislation, participating in congressional debate, or casting a vote, a legislator acts on behalf of the subconstituencies that he sees in his district, as compared to other, equally relevant subconstituencies in the district. Moreover, the impact of perceptions on legislative behavior is strong even when rationalist arguments about electoral, institutional, and partisan considerations are taken into account as alternate explanations for legislators' behavior. Put simply, on Capitol Hill a legislator represents the district as he sees it, not as it exists in reality.

Although legislators and their staff do not see all the relevant constituents in their district, it is not necessarily the case that Congress is populated with corrupt scoundrels. This type of caricature is common in the popular press and portrays Members of Congress as having little regard for constituency representation. But the reality is that the vast majority of legislators and their staff are committed to representing their constituents, even if they do not do it perfectly. Indeed, representing several hundred thousand people is not easy. Well-meaning legislators can fall short of accurately representing their constituents not because they are corrupt or deliberately choose to privilege some constituents, but rather because their reliance on cognitive heuristics brings inherent limitations. As a result, legislators work hard to represent the district as they see it, but the district they see is fundamentally flawed. Despite their best efforts, legislators are unlikely to represent all constituents in their district.

SUMMARY OF FINDINGS

The empirical examination of legislative perceptions of constituents presented here has produced a number of important findings that advance our understanding of congressional representation. A brief review of the main findings sets the stage for a discussion of their implications for political science scholarship and for politics more broadly.

The first key finding is that legislators see only a limited number of the subconstituencies in their district who are relevant to a specified policy. In fact, across health and natural resources policies, legislative offices see less than one-third of the policy-relevant subconstituencies in the district. The information-based theory of legislative perception identifies the mechanisms that explain why legislative enterprises see such a limited district, and in doing so, confirms the intuition that some constituents in the district are more visible to legislators than others.

Second, legislative perceptions of the constituents in their district are biased. The subset of constituents that legislators and their staff see when they look at the district is not a representative sample of the collection of relevant subconstituencies but instead systematically favors some constituents over others. Specifically, the district in the "mind's eye" of the legislative enterprise is dominated by constituents who contribute more money to the legislator and who frequently contact the legislative office. Other constituents – regardless of their relevance to the policy at hand or their objective presence in the district – are unlikely to be part of a legislator's image of this district. The resulting view of the district is what the legislative enterprise believes the district to be; it is *not* the result of conscious calculations or decisions. Taken together, these first two findings provide unique insight into legislators' view of the district from Capitol Hill, which is both limited and biased. Understanding which few subconstituencies legislators typically see when they look at their district – and which subconstituencies they frequently do not see – is an important step toward unpacking what common refrains such as "constituents matter," or legislators represent "the district," actually mean in practice.

The third major finding is that perceptions of constituents in the district affect legislators' participation in the day-to-day activities in the House. By examining the content of legislators' participation in committee hearings, markup sessions, and the floor debate, it is possible to trace the consequences of legislative perceptions of subconstituencies for legislators' actions. The evidence across health policy and natural resources policy is clear: Legislators are unlikely to participate on behalf of those subconstituencies that they do not see in their district. The subsequent concern is that if legislators are less likely to represent the perspectives of policy-relevant subconstituencies they do not see, the legislation that emerges from these debates is unlikely to reflect the concerns and interests of those constituents. Moreover, because the constituents who are off legislators' proverbial "radar screens" are those who did not contribute a lot of money or contact the legislative office frequently, their absence from the policy debate suggests that certain viewpoints will be systematically underrepresented in policy. John Stuart Mill highlights this fundamental connection between voice and representation in his essay on democratic representation, noting that "It is important that everyone of the governed have a voice in the government, because it can hardly be expected that those who have no voice will not be unjustly postponed to those who have."[1] In this case, if certain types of constituents are less likely to be seen by their representatives, it is only logical to expect that legislators and their staff will overlook their concerns and instead act in ways that advantage the constituents they see in the district. If legislative perceptions were comprehensive, or even representative, reflections of the actual district, then legislators' participation on behalf of their perceived district would not raise normative concerns. But the evidence presented here suggests that this is not the case. Consequently, the limited and biased nature of legislative perceptions of the district is troubling because of its impact on legislators' involvement in the policy-making process.

Lastly, legislative perceptions of the district *as a whole* also affect legislators' behavior, as shown in the domain of energy and environmental policy. When legislators and their staff perceive the overall district as consisting of a greater number of subconstituencies relevant to natural resources issues, legislators are more active in sponsoring legislation to address these issues. More surprising is the fact that rational, reelection-minded legislators, who are expected to be less active when they see

---

[1] Mill as quoted in Pitkin (1967, 202).

competing constituency interests in their district, are in fact more active in introducing legislation than their colleagues. Additionally, seeing competing subconstituencies in the district has a moderating effect on legislators' voting records. When a legislator sees constituents on both sides of an issue, he is significantly less likely to take extreme positions when casting votes on natural resources legislation. One implication of this finding is that unbalanced legislative perceptions may contribute to polarization in the modern House by fostering more extreme voting records. However, if more legislators see constituents in their district on both sides of an issue, their more moderate actions may help to reduce levels of polarization. The influence of overall district perceptions on legislative behavior provides further evidence that legislators are responsive to the district as they see it and that *perceived* constituents matter. In sum, these findings provide both good news and bad news for constituency representation in the U.S. House of Representatives: Legislators take actions to represent their district, but the district that they see lacks many of the relevant constituents in their district.

IMPLICATIONS FOR INSTITUTIONAL DESIGN: IS 435 THE MAGIC NUMBER?

In laying out the challenges of congressional representation – from the existence of multiple issue-specific subconstituencies in a district to the limitations of cognitive heuristics – this book asserts that the ideals of representative democracy are difficult to attain in the day-to-day world of Capitol Hill. As noted throughout the chapters, a signature characteristic of the modern congressional environment is the large and complex congressional district. The number of constituents in a congressional district makes representation more difficult, a point not lost on Members of Congress themselves. The theory of legislative perception put forth here identifies an important way in which legislators and their staff adapt to the difficulty of representing the approximately 700,000 constituents in their district – they employ cognitive heuristics that allow them to more efficiently gather and use information about their constituents when deciding what actions to take in Washington. However, the price for making the job of representing so many people more manageable is that legislative perceptions of their district are incomplete and biased in favor of certain constituents over other equally relevant constituents.

One approach to reducing the shortcomings and biases that characterize legislative perceptions and constituency representation is to focus on the conditions that lead individuals to rely more heavily on cognitive shortcuts, namely the complexity of the congressional district. If representing a constituency on Capitol Hill can be made less difficult, then legislators and their staff would be less reliant on the accessibility heuristic, and therefore less vulnerable to the flaws that cognitive shortcuts introduce. Consistent with this goal are proposals to expand the membership of the U.S. House of Representatives and decrease the size of each congressional district. Admittedly, such efforts would reduce the need for heuristics but would not fully eliminate their use. However, as former Representative Marty Russo (D-IL) asserts, "It's tough to do a great job for 625,000 constituents. It'd be a lot easier to do it for 275,000 or 300,000."[2]

The membership of the U.S. House of Representatives has been fixed at 435 since 1911, with the exception of a temporary increase in the late 1950s to accommodate the statehood of Alaska and Hawaii. When the House was first comprised of 435 legislators, the population of the United States was 91 million people and the average district size was 210,583.[3] In the nearly one hundred years since then, the size of the House has not changed, but the population has grown to nearly 305 million people.[4] Moreover, the average population per representative in the U.S. House of Representatives is now more than three times the size of a congressional district in 1911 (see Figure 8.1).[5] Recent projections by the U.S. Census department indicate that the population will continue to grow and is expected to hit 400 million in 2039, producing the most diverse population in American history.[6] If the size of the U.S. House of Representatives is not expanded, the size of congressional districts will continue to increase, and legislators will soon face the challenge of representing nearly one million constituents. A likely consequence of the increased complexity of the congressional district is that legislators will become more reliant on cognitive shortcuts (like the accessibility heuristic) that produce a limited and biased image of the constituents in their district.

Up until the early 1900s, however, the size of the House increased following every decennial census as a response to the growing population.

---

[2] Quoted in *The Hill*, June 17, 2004.
[3] U.S. Census Bureau, "Population Base for Apportionment and the Number of Representatives Apportioned: 1790 to 1990."
[4] U.S. Census Bureau.
[5] U.S. Census Bureau.
[6] Roberts (2008).

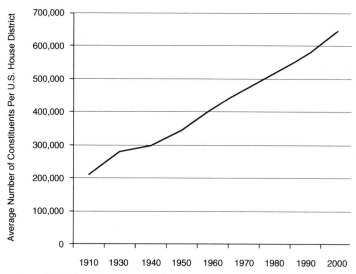

FIGURE 8.1. The Growing House District.

The current situation is the result of a statute passed by the House in 1911, not a constitutional mandate, that set the size of the U.S. House of Representatives at 435.[7] As a result, it only takes an act of Congress to return to a policy of having "the people's House" reflect the growing number of people. Toward this goal, a leading proponent of this reform, Democratic Representative Alcee Hastings of Florida, has repeatedly sponsored legislation to create a commission to study the issue of enlarging the U.S. House of Representatives. In 2001, Representative Hastings's proposal (H.R. 506) was cosponsored by only four colleagues and was referred to subcommittee, where no action was taken. Similarly, Representative Hastings sponsored nearly identical legislation in 2005 (H.R. 1989) that was also referred to subcommittee and was cosponsored by only one House colleague. Noting that "we're getting at the point where's there's just too many constituents in each district to serve them adequately," Representative Hastings most recently introduced H.R. 6396 in June 2008, but it had no cosponsors and did not move out of the House Judiciary Committee.[8]

[7] U.S. Census Bureau, "Congressional Apportionment – Historical Perspective."
[8] Quoted in "Would a Bigger Congress Be Better?" by Billy House. Media General News Service, June 8, 2008.

Beyond the halls of Congress, there is support for such reforms from both sides of the political spectrum. For instance, conservative columnists George Will and the late Robert Novak have expressed support for a larger House (and smaller congressional districts), as has the voting rights advocacy group, Fair Vote. In making their case for increasing the size of the House, some proponents argue that smaller congressional districts will make Congress more responsive to constituents, reduce the importance of money in congressional politics, and encourage political novices to run for office.[9] Proponents of reform are also quick to point out that the per capita representation rate for the U.S. House of Representatives (1 member to more than 645,000 people) compares unfavorably with other countries: the Russian State Duma has 450 members and a ratio of 1 member per 324,000 people, the British House of Commons has 659 members and a ratio of 1 member per 90,000 people, and the German Bundestag has 669 members and a ratio of 1 member per 124,000 people.[10]

Although there is no indication that calls to increase the membership of the U.S. House of Representatives will be heeded soon, it is a reform proposal that warrants closer examination by scholars, policy makers, and citizens alike. The research presented here suggests that there are significant costs to increasingly larger U.S. House districts. Constituency representation is not an easy task to begin with, but it becomes even more difficult as the size of congressional districts grows. Legislative enterprises looking for information about the relevance of policy issues to their district would face an ever greater volume of information about an ever larger number of constituents. Comprehensive information searches would be all but impossible given the time constraints and demands on legislators and their staff. Indeed, the conditions brought about by larger congressional districts would likely encourage legislators and their staff to rely more heavily on cognitive heuristics to make constituency representation manageable. Because perceptions of constituents in the district are the result of cognitive processes, not deliberate or conscious decisions, simply electing a new generation of legislators would not change these dynamics or improve legislative perceptions of the constituents in their district. As cognitive misers, all individuals rely on heuristics (Simon 1957), and new Members of Congress would be no different.

---

[9] See Will (2001) and Jacob (2000).
[10] "Dear Colleague" letter written by Representative Alcee Hastings (D-FL) May 21, 2001.

In light of the evidence that legislative perceptions affect constituency representation, an important question to ask when assessing this reform proposal is whether the benefits of smaller congressional districts outweigh the costs of significant institutional change. The answer to this question likely depends on whether one approaches it from the perspective of representation or lawmaking. If one considers the House to be first and foremost a representative body, then increasing the membership of the chamber – and thereby reducing the average size of a congressional district – would improve the representative relationship between legislators and their constituents. Smaller districts would reduce legislative enterprises' reliance on the information shortcuts that produce flawed perceptions by making it easier to gather information about constituents in the district. More complete and representative information about the constituency would, in turn, affect legislators' behavior such that more constituents' perspectives would be reflected in congressional debate and policy outcomes.

On the other hand, if one evaluates the proposed reform from the perspective of the House as a lawmaking body, then the costs of increasing membership could be quite high. The primary concern is that a larger membership would make the institution unwieldy, thus reducing the efficiency of an institution already derided by critics as ineffective. At its current size, the House of Representative relies on the division of labor through the committee system to promote efficiency and facilitate the lawmaking process. Although the current institutional arrangement might be able to absorb a modest increase in membership, it likely would not be able to accommodate the type of change that would bring the per capita representation rate in the U.S. House of Representatives in line with those in other advanced democracies.

As long as the size of the U.S. House of Representatives remains unchanged while the population increases, legislators will be forced to represent larger congressional districts. Increasingly large districts, however, present serious challenges for constituency representation. As this book demonstrates, the complexity of the constituency and the competing demands on legislators and their staff combine to produce widespread legislative reliance on cognitive shortcuts and pervasive legislative misperceptions of the constituents in the district. Although, these conditions will only intensify as the size of congressional districts grows, it is unclear that the call to reform the institution by increasing the number of House seats is a realistic solution, particularly as it brings significant trade-offs.

IMPLICATIONS FOR POLITICAL SCIENCE

The findings discussed earlier make the case for political scientists to reconsider constituency representation in Congress and to address the reality that legislators represent the constituency they see, which may or may not look like the constituency that scholars see. The most general implications of this research are that scholars should incorporate legislative perceptions and include issue-specific subconstituency measures in future studies of congressional representation. Perceptions are limited and biased, and exert an important, independent effect on the actions legislators take on Capitol Hill. As a result, if legislative perceptions of constituents are not taken into account, subsequent conclusions about legislators' activity and constituency representation are incomplete. Similarly, legislators see their district in terms of issue-specific subconstituencies, and models of representation that neglect this reality will likely provide only partial explanations of legislative behavior.

However, incorporating legislative perception and multiple relevant subconstituencies is not likely to be realistic for all research questions. In particular, the time- and labor-intensive measurement of legislative perceptions makes it unrealistic to call for its inclusion in all congressional research. Instead, the focus here is on more practical implications of this research for political scientists. There are numerous ways in which the insights into legislative perceptions and their effect on behavior can inform future research and promote greater recognition of what is – and is not – being explained in our models. More specifically, this research has important implications for how scholars define the congressional district, evaluate the influence of financial contributions, and assess the role of constituents as active partners in congressional representation.

A Dyadic Theory of Subconstituency Representation

Although this book is not the first to observe that the district is made up of multiple subgroups, the implications of the reality of many subconstituencies are often neglected. This research provides a new way to think about the complexity of the congressional district and the challenges of constituency representation. Within congressional scholarship, Fenno's (1978) concentric circles provide an influential departure point for many studies that have moved away from a uniform notion of "the district." Some scholars focus on the electoral, party, or race-based subgroups to whom legislators are believed to be responsive, but these approaches generally persist in dividing the district into only two groups (e.g., Canon 1999; Clinton 2006; Fiorina 1974; Griffin and Newman 2008; Hurley and Hill 2003; Hutchings 1998). In contrast, this book puts forth a dyadic theory of subconstituency representation that unpacks the district into multiple issue-specific subconstituencies defined by their common interests in a policy. In doing so, this conception of subconstituencies moves our concept of the district closer to the practice of congressional politics.

An important implication of issue-specific subconstituencies is that the representative relationship between a legislator and his district is more accurately described as a series of relationships between a legislator and each of the subconstituencies in his district. This notion of multiple representational relationships has consequences for the structure of empirical analysis and is the foundation of the dyadic theory of subconstituency representation advanced here. If "the district" is made up of subconstituencies, then it is necessary for scholars to be mindful of this structure when evaluating constituency representation in Congress. Research questions that focus on the match between the median voter and a legislator's behavior as a measure of representation do not hold up in light of dyadic representation. Additionally, just as there are varying extents to which legislators are deemed to represent their constituents (as opposed to concluding that legislators either do or do not represent their constituents), representation also varies across the subconstituencies in the district. Legislators behave in ways that are more representative of some constituents in their district and less representative of other constituents in their district. The dyadic theory of subconstituency representation pushes scholars to be more explicit in specifying who the relevant constituents are in the district as well as the standards for assessing constituency representation.

One practical implication of this dyadic theory of subconstituency representation is that representing the constituents in a district is a very difficult task, and this has implications for congressional scholars, not just legislators. Implicit in much of the political science literature on Congress are normative expectations of what constituency representation should entail, and many scholars conclude that Members of Congress fail to meet these standards. However, when congressional representation is reconceived of as a series of relationships between a legislative enterprise and the numerous subconstituencies in the district, it is not surprising that legislators and their staff fall short of democratic ideals about constituency representation. Pitkin (1967, 215) confronts this reality and notes that legislators have "a constituency rather than a single principal; and that raises problems about whether such an unorganized group can even have an interest for him to pursue, let alone a will to which he could be responsive." This is not to say that legislators do not want to fully represent their constituency, but rather that the challenges of doing so are significant and warrant further consideration in our theories of congressional behavior. In interviews with legislators and their staff members, it is apparent that legislators generally want to represent their constituents. As one Member of Congress said during the floor debate over the Patients' Bill of Rights, "Our job is to do what is in the best interests of the individuals we serve."[11] However, legislative enterprises' good faith efforts to provide constituency representation are limited by the fact that "the constituency" is actually a complex collection of subconstituencies and the legislative view of the district is imperfect. This reality suggests that it is time for congressional scholars to reengage normative questions about representation and the appropriate standards to which legislators are held in both our theoretical models and empirical assessments.

Mental Access

There is strong and unique evidence that financial contributions influence who legislators and their staff see when they look at their district. This research reveals that subconstituencies who contribute to legislative offices benefit from greater "mental access" to the legislative enterprise. Therefore, the impact of money is not that it buys votes directly, but that it shapes how legislators see their district, which in turn affects a wide range of legislative behavior.

The political science literature reaches mixed conclusions on the role of money in Congress, and the notion of mental access advanced here helps to bridge the belief that money plays a role in congressional politics with the difficulty of finding the smoking gun that provides proof of its influence. If the impact of money is felt, at least in part, on legislative perceptions of their constituents, then it is not surprising that evidence of its influence on legislative behavior has been inconsistent. Scholars have not looked to legislative perceptions of constituents in the district for evidence of the influence of money. Indeed, empirically pinpointing the mental access gained with campaign contributions requires a measure

[11] *Congressional Record*, August 2, 2001.

of legislative perceptions, which the literature previously lacked. As this book details, however, money does matter. Contributions affect which constituents legislators see in their district. Consequently, money permeates politics to a greater extent than previously thought, and its impact on representation is harder to trace.

The evidence that money buys mental access also has implications for campaign finance reform proposals. The evidence presented here indicates that the primary risk of financial contributions is not that legislators are corrupt and will parlay donations into legislative favors – although this certainly does occur – but rather that money sets the stage for representation in Congress. To carry out the theater metaphor, financial contributions effectively serve as spotlights on certain subconstituencies in the district, making it more likely that a legislative enterprise will see them while other relevant subconstituencies in the district remain in the dark and therefore less likely to be seen. Serious efforts to limit maximum financial contributions in hopes of equalizing contributions would reduce the salience of any one subconstituency's contributions, thus decreasing the likelihood that money would dramatically increase the accessibility of information about constituents. However, even strict limits would not completely eliminate the inequalities and inefficiencies that result when financial contributions shape legislators' images of their constituency because there would remain variation in constituents' ability to contribute. Only more dramatic reforms that replace the existing campaign finance system with public financing would eliminate the influence of money on legislative perceptions of constituents. Efforts to introduce full public financing of presidential elections are already part of the public conversation about campaign finance reform, and this research suggests that public financing of congressional elections warrants serious consideration as well.

An Active Role for Citizens

Similar to the way that financial contributions generate mental access, constituency-initiated contact also makes it more likely that a legislator sees a subconstituency in the district. As a result, the study of legislative perceptions of the district also has significant implications for the literature on citizen participation, as it identifies new evidence of the importance of constituents' contact with legislators and their staff on Capitol Hill. There is an extensive literature on citizen participation, including the biases that are manifest as some constituents are more (or less) likely to be politically active (e.g., Brady, Verba, and Schlozman 1994; Verba and Nie 1972). The majority of the literature approaches citizen participation from the citizens' perspective with an emphasis on understanding variation in their behavior, but here the focus is on the *impact* of that participation. When citizens contact their elected officials, they help to shape how legislators and their staff see the district that they represent. A legislative enterprise's image of the district is more likely to include subconstituencies that are active in contacting the legislative office, and this in turn means that the legislator is more likely to act on behalf of those constituents.

These findings highlight the importance of citizen participation in congressional politics. Contacting one's elected representative is not a naïve lesson from civics class, but it is a meaningful political tool. As such, concerns about the mobilization of bias remain. Significant disparities in political efficacy, political resources, and political information mean that those constituents who contact their legislator are unlikely to be a representative subset of the district population. The rise of electronic communication, which generally reduces the costs of communication and promotes individual participation, also raises concerns about the digital divide that leaves some constituents benefiting from improved online opportunities to contact their House member while other constituents fall further behind in their ability to take advantage of these online opportunities. However, given the variety of ways in which constituents can voice their preferences, there is also reason to be optimistic that a relatively wide range of constituents can take advantage of the opportunity to directly contact their legislator. As one Member of Congress said when describing hearing from his constituents, "People write longhand letters, real thoughtful letters … you'd be surprised."[12] As a result, every constituent should be encouraged to contact their legislator on issues that affect them because in doing so, they influence the legislative enterprise's image of the district and increase the likelihood that their legislator will act on their behalf on Capitol Hill. Efforts to increase citizen participation are consequential for constituency representation.

Returning to Core Questions

The study of Congress and legislative behavior is a dynamic endeavor with an extensive literature as evidence of the many questions examined

---

[12] Personal interview.

and approaches employed. There are, however, core questions that provide common touchstones for scholars, and how legislators see their constituents and the impact of these perceptions on their behavior is one such fundamental question for congressional scholars. This book takes up this question and approaches it in a way that reflects the intervening decades of research in both political science and cognitive social psychology. In doing so, a theory of legislative perception that is rooted in the broader psychology literature is established. This theoretical foundation makes it possible to examine both the nature of perceptions as well as the mechanism by which perception affects legislative behavior.

It is often (although not exclusively) the case that core questions originate in scholarship from decades past, and therefore can inadvertently get lost in the growing literature. However, there remains much value in returning to these questions that are at the heart of legislative studies. Approaching old questions in new ways means that scholars are likely to not only find new evidence to support (or disprove) long-held "truths" about Congress and congressional behavior, but they are also likely to raise new questions and shed light on previously unconsidered dynamics.

Appendix A

Sampling

Eighty-one offices were selected using purposive sampling designed to create a sample representative of the 435 Members of the U.S. House of Representatives on important dimensions such as party, seniority, region, and committee membership. The sampling process was conducted for health policy and natural resources policy separately to produce two independently chosen samples of forty legislative offices interviewed within each issue area.[1] In each issue area, legislators on the committee with primary jurisdiction were oversampled in order to create a sample with an equal number of committee members and non–committee members. Based on the composition of the full chamber and relevant committee, the forty health policy interviews and forty-one natural resources policy interviews were then allocated based on party, region, and seniority. Random sampling was used to select offices to be interviewed within the committee and non–committee groups. As a result, the sample is representative of the full committee or full House, respectively, in terms of party, seniority, and region (see Tables A1, A2, and A3). These dimensions are relevant to the sampling process because of the possibility that these features may affect the relationship between the legislative enterprise and constituents in the district. The overall effect of this process is that the sample of legislators closely mirrors the composition of the U.S. House of Representatives.

---

[1] In the case of natural resources policy, there are a total of forty-one offices sampled because one of the staff members interviewed was not active on both natural resources policies, so an additional office was sampled and interviewed.

TABLE A1. *Partisan Distribution in the U.S. House of Representatives, 107th Congress vs. Sample*

	Republicans	Democrats
Full House (n = 435)	51%	49%
Health Sample (n = 40)	50%	50%
Resources Sample (n = 41)	49%	51%
Energy and Commerce Committee (n = 57)	54%	46%
Energy and Commerce Sample (n = 19)	53%	47%
Resources Committee (n = 52)	54%	46%
Resources Sample (n = 21)	52%	48%

TABLE A2. *Average Career Tenure in the U.S. House of Representatives, 107th Congress vs. Sample*

	Republicans	Democrats
Full House (n = 435)	5.2 terms	5.8 terms
Health Sample (n = 40)	5.3 terms	6.8 terms
Resources Sample (n = 41)	5.4 terms	5.6 terms
Energy and Commerce Committee (n = 57)	4.8 terms	7.0 terms
Energy and Commerce Sample (n = 19)	5.1 terms	8.3 terms
Resources Committee (n = 52)	4.9 terms	5.8 terms
Resources Sample (n = 21)	5.4 terms	5.9 terms

TABLE A3. *Regional Distribution of House Members by Party, 107th Congress vs. Sample*

	East	South	Midwest	Southwest and West	California
Republican Full House (n = 222)	18%	29%	26%	19%	9%
Republican Health Sample (n = 20)	15%	40%	25%	10%	10%
Republican Resources Sample (n = 20)	15%	20%	20%	30%	15%
Democratic Full House (n = 213)	27%	18%	23%	17%	15%
Democratic Health Sample (n = 20)	25%	15%	35%	15%	10%
Democratic Resources Sample (n = 21)	33%	14%	29%	19%	14%

Appendix B

Interviews

Eighty-one structured, personal interviews were conducted with legislative staff members on health policy and natural resources policy. Legislative staff members play an integral role in congressional offices as both policy experts and constituent liaisons (e.g., Evans 2002; Salisbury and Shepsle 1981). Staff members are responsible for gathering information about policy issues, providing legislators with relevant information, and representing the legislative office in meetings and informal negotiations. Staff members regularly juggle numerous issues simultaneously in an environment with abundant information from multiple sources and significant time pressure. In the course of fulfilling these duties, staff members make judgments about the interests of the district every day. Additionally, it is the staff members who are most knowledgeable about which constituents write letters to the member and who meet with constituents and interest group representatives. For all of these reasons, scholars have turned to legislative staff members as an invaluable source of information about congressional decision making (e.g., Evans 1991a, 1991b; Hall 1996; Kingdon 1984, 1989). Additionally, a half dozen members of Congress were interviewed on these same policies. These interviews confirm the findings based on interviews with staff members, and provide additional insights into how the legislative enterprise views the district. This appendix provides further details of these interviews, including the measurement of legislative perceptions and constituency contact.

CONDUCTING THE INTERVIEWS

Having selected the legislative offices in the sample, the next step involved identifying the appropriate staff member responsible for health policy (or natural resources policy) and requesting an interview. Two strategies were relied upon to identify the staff members to interview. The first approach was to consult the Congressional Yellow Book and the legislator's Web site to determine the staff member responsible for the relevant issue. The second approach was to call the legislator's office to identify the staff member for the issue. The division of labor by policy area differs by legislative office such that the staff member responsible for natural resources policy in a given office does not necessarily hold the same formal title as the staff member responsible for natural resources policy in another office. Of the eighty-one offices interviewed, fifty-two respondents were senior legislative assistants or legislative assistants, eighteen respondents were legislative directors, three respondents were senior legislative counsel or legislative counsel, five respondents held other job titles (e.g., senior policy advisor), and three respondents were the chief of staff.

After the correct staff member was identified, he was contacted by phone to ask for a meeting. The response rate to requests for interviews was nearly 80%, as defined by the number of offices in which the correct staff member was contacted and granted an interview. This response rate is quite high for elite interviews.[1] As Appendix A illustrates, the sample of legislative offices interviewed is reflective of the U.S. House of Representatives, and the relatively few legislative offices that declined to be interviewed are also a cross section of the chamber as a whole. Of the twenty-two offices in which the staff member declined to be interviewed, ten were in the health policy sample, and twelve were in the natural resources policy sample. Sixteen staff members cited their office's blanket policy against participating in surveys or interviews, and six declined due to scheduling constraints. The party breakdown of this group reflects the small Republican majority in the House (thirteen Republican offices and nine Democratic offices), and the twenty-two offices are evenly divided (i.e., eleven and eleven) between members and nonmembers of the relevant committee. In short, the declined interviews do not exhibit any systematic patterns that might raise sampling concerns.

Although the appointments with staff members were made over the telephone, all interviews were face to face and took place "on location" on Capitol Hill in order to more accurately capture how legislative enterprises see constituents from their vantage point in Washington. Nearly

---

[1] In cases where a staff member declined to be interviewed, the random sampling process described in Appendix A was used to determine which office to contact next.

all interviews took place in the legislative office, and a small number of interviews were conducted in the other parts of the House office buildings (e.g., the House cafeteria). The interviews on health policy were conducted over eight weeks in the winter of 2002, and the interviews on natural resources policy were conducted over six weeks in the summer of 2002. All interviews were confidential, and each staff member interviewed was guaranteed that neither his identity nor that of his boss would be revealed. These guarantees were made verbally during the initial telephone conversation and reiterated at the beginning of the interview. After offering these assurances, staff members were asked for permission to tape-record the interview for note-taking purposes. In the case of health policy, 75% of staff members allowed the interview to be recorded, as did 77% of staff members asked in the case of resources policy.[2] Across the interviews, staff members were remarkably candid and forthcoming.

THE STRUCTURE OF THE INTERVIEWS

The interviews were carefully and deliberately designed. The interview protocol consisted of both open-ended and closed-ended questions, including the use of simple forms at the end of the interviews. The questions were pretested in House offices not included in the sample as well as with former congressional staff. During the pretests, close attention was paid to clarifying questions asked by respondents and any indications that the language used was unnatural or academic. After the pretests, the interview protocol was revised to more closely approximate the way that staff think about the relevance of policies to their constituents and to incorporate the realistic use of appropriate congressional jargon (e.g., acronyms, bill numbers) and other Hill-specific language. In addition, based on the survey research literature, particular attention was paid to question wording and question order.

In personal interviews, there often exists a tension between the use of structured questions, which facilitate the collection of comparable information, and a more open conversation, which provides for better rapport with the respondent (see Berry 2002). A researcher, obviously, would like to enjoy the benefits of both approaches, and the interview protocol here employs both. Open-ended questions dominate the early

---

[2] In cases where the interview was not conducted in the legislative office, permission to record the interview was not requested.

portions of the interviews while the closed-ended questions are reserved for later in the interview. Additionally, questions were constructed to focus on the perspective and experience of the staff members. This design serves to establish a good rapport and conversational style at the outset of the interviews, which is an essential foundation for asking more targeted questions, including the presentation of simple forms later in the interview.

The interview protocol was divided into four types of questions: general issue questions, perceptions of constituents in the district, context of subconstituency–legislative office relationships, and contact with constituents in the district. First, each interview began with a broad question about current health (or natural resources) issues and the health (or natural resources) needs and interests of the district, which served to focus the conversation on health policy (or natural resources policy). Included in this conversation were the two policies that served as the focus of the health policy interviews (i.e., the Patients' Bill of Rights and Medicare regulatory reform) and the natural resources policy interviews (i.e., the Securing America's Future Energy Act and wetlands conservation policy).

From this point, the interview focused on the two selected health policies (or natural resources policies). One policy was randomly selected to be discussed first, and a series of questions were asked regarding that legislation before the second policy was raised. The staff member was initially asked what the bill was about from the point of view of his office. This question was then followed by the primary question of interest: "who in the district is it [this bill] important to?" This basic question is a feature of daily life on Capitol Hill where staff members quickly call to mind information about constituents' interests on issues. In meetings and conversations, staff members regularly are asked by legislators, other legislative staff members, and policy makers to succinctly assess a policy's relevance to constituents in the district, and this question mirrors this common task. As discussed in Chapter 4, subconstituencies recalled in response to this open-ended question were recorded in the order recalled, and there was no limit to the number of subconstituencies that a staff member could recall. Staff members' responses to this question serve as the measure of whether or not a legislative enterprise perceived a given subconstituency in the district. Following this open-ended question, I asked the staff member to indicate the importance of the issue to the list of relevant subconstituencies using categories of "not important," "somewhat important," "important," and "very important." The list consists of those subconstituencies previously identified as relevant to the policy at hand by policy experts and media reports (see Chapter 4).

Following the questions designed to measure staff members' perceptions of their districts, the interviews turn to a series of questions about the context of these subconstituency–legislative office relationships. For each subconstituency recalled, the staff members were asked how they would characterize the relationship between that subconstituency and their respective offices, and they provided candid assessments and anecdotes. Staff were then asked whether the specific policy had come up during the legislator's campaign in the fall of 2000, and if so, whether it was a prominent issue. In their answers, staff members generally noted whether the issue was of interest to voters broadly, or only to a certain subconstituency. Staff members also noted whether the policy itself was raised (e.g., the Patients' Bill of Rights), or whether the policy was discussed as part of the broader issue (e.g., the North American Wetlands Conservation Act was not a campaign issue, but the environment was).

The fourth component of the interview focused on which subconstituencies were active in contacting the legislative office. This line of inquiry began with a relatively broad question about the overall amount of mail received on the issue: "Thinking about the amount of mail that comes into the office on health (or natural resources issues) in general, can you estimate what percentage of it is about the X bill?" Staff members' answers to this question used a range of metrics, from the percentage of mail, to the number of pieces of mail, to general amounts (i.e., "most," "a lot," "very little," etc.). Follow-up questions asked staffers to quantify the amount of mail in relative terms (e.g., one out of four letters on resources policy was about the energy bill).

Having introduced the subject of constituency contact, the focus shifted to *who* the staff member heard from on the issue. Staff members were asked to complete simple forms indicating how much contact they received from the list of relevant subconstituencies on the particular issue. There are no existing public data on contact between legislative offices and constituencies, so the interviews are an essential source of this unique information. Given the qualitative difference between mail contact (including email and fax) and personal contact (including phone calls and personal visits), two separate forms were used. Staff members were presented with a form and asked: "Here's a list of groups that have been involved in some districts. Could you think about how much mail you receive from these constituent groups on the energy bill and just check off the appropriate category?" After the staff member completed the form for mail context, this was followed by: "Now thinking about that same list, I have a similar form except that it focuses on how often you've heard from them here in the D.C. office by phone or in person. Again, could you just check off the appropriate category." Upon the completion of these questions, the interview moved to the second policy within the issue area and repeated the questions with reference to the new policy.

INTERVIEWING MEMBERS OF CONGRESS

As noted earlier, Members of the U.S. House of Representatives were interviewed in six offices in which I had previously interviewed the staff member. These interviews include an equal number of Democrats and Republicans and are also evenly divided between health policy and natural resources policy (i.e., three interviews focused on each issue area). Despite the number of staff members who were willing to help arrange interviews with their boss, scheduling these interviews proved to be quite difficult.[3] Although a small sample, these interviews provide valuable insight into the legislator's perceptions of the district. As with the staff interviews, I found House Members to be receptive to my questions and thoughtful in their responses. Again, considerable attention was paid to creating a good rapport during the interviews, and Members were quite candid in their comments.

Similar to the interviews with legislative staff members described previously, the interviews with members were conducted in person in Washington, D.C. As with staff members, the majority of the interviews were conducted in the legislator's office. The interviews with Members parallel those with staff members in terms of the content of the questions asked, with the exception that no forms were used during the interviews with legislators. The exclusive use of open-ended questions facilitated a conversational tone and allowed for more extensive probing of legislators' responses about representing his constituents.

As in the staff interviews, I began with a broad question about the needs and interests of the district in the area of health (or resources) policy. I then introduced the first of the two specific issues that were the focus of these interviews and asked to whom in the district was a

[3] In only seven of the forty cases in which I contacted the legislative office in which I had previously interviewed the legislative staff member was my request for a personal interview with the Member declined.

given issue important. This question captures legislative perceptions of constituents in the district, and these interviews illustrate that members and their staff see the district similarly. In offices in which both the staff member and legislator were interviewed, the Pearson correlation coefficient is .70 between all staff and Member responses when asked to whom in the district a policy is important. This suggests that legislators and their staff largely see – and do not see – the same subconstituencies when considering their district. This primary question of interest was followed by a series of open-ended questions concerning constituency contact and activity in the district on a given issue.

Appendix C

Measurement of Primary Independent Variables

MEASUREMENT OF CONSTITUENCY SIZE

Constituency size is measured by the number of individuals residing in the district who are identified as part of a given constituency.

Health Policy

Business: The number of individuals in the district employed in the business sector (firms of all sizes), excluding farms and nonemployer business. These data are obtained from the U.S. Census for the U.S. Small Business Association, Office of Advocacy. Note: The U.S. Small Business Association only provides these data at the state level, and therefore these data are converted to the district level based on the number of districts in a state.

Labor: The number of union members in the district. Data on "union affiliation of employed wage and salary workers by state" are taken from the Bureau of Labor Statistics, U.S. Department of Labor. Note: The U.S. Bureau of Labor Statistics only provides these data at the state level, and therefore these data are converted to the district level based on the number of districts in a state.

Physicians: The total number of individuals in the district employed in the "offices of physicians" in the district (North American Industry Classification System code 6211). These data are taken from the U.S. Census Bureau, 1997 Economic Census (NAICS). Note: The U.S. Census Bureau provides these data at the county level, and therefore these data are converted to district-level data based on county-to-congressional district maps.

Patients: The number of individuals enrolled in health maintenance organizations in the district. Data are taken from the Kaiser Family Foundation's 2001 study of HMO enrollment. Note: The Kaiser Family Foundation only provides these data at the state level, and the data are converted to the district level based on the number of districts in a state. For purposes of robustness, an alternate measure is used based on the number of district residents taken from *The Almanac of American Politics* (Barone and Cohen 2001).

Seniors: The number of district residents who are 65 years old or older. The source of these data is the U.S. Census Bureau, 2000 Census.

Insurers: The total number of individuals in the district employed in the insurance industry based on employment in "insurance carriers and related activities" (NAICS code 524). These data are taken from the U.S. Census Bureau, 2001 County Business Patterns (NAICS). Note: The U.S. Census Bureau only provides these data at the county level, and therefore these data are converted to district-level data based on county-to-congressional district maps.

Attorneys: The total number of individuals in the district employed in the "offices of lawyers" (NAICS code 54111). These data are taken from the U.S. Census Bureau, 2001 County Business Patterns (NAICS). Note: The U.S. Census Bureau only provides these data at the county level, and therefore these data are converted to district-level data based on county-to-congressional district maps.

Hospitals: The total number of individuals in the district employed by hospitals (NAICS code 622). These data are taken from the U.S. Census Bureau, 2001 County Business Patterns (NAICS). Note: The U.S. Census Bureau only provides these data at the county level, and therefore these data are converted to district-level data based on county-to-congressional district maps.

Medicare patients: The number of individuals in the district enrolled in Medicare. These data are taken from the Centers for Medicare and Medicaid Services. Note: The Center for Medicare and Medicaid Services provide these data at the county level, and therefore these data are converted to district-level data based on county-to-congressional district maps.

Pharmaceutical industry: The total number of individuals in the district employed in pharmaceutical and medical manufacturing (NAICS code 3254). The data come from the U.S. Census Bureau, 2001 County Business Patterns (NAICS). Note: The U.S. Census Bureau only provides these data at the county level, and therefore these data are converted to district-level data based on county-to-congressional district maps.

Natural Resources Policy

Consumers: The primary measure is the number of district residents in poverty (as defined by the U.S. Census Bureau), since lower income citizens are more vulnerable to changes in energy costs. These data are taken from the U.S. Census Bureau, 2000 Census and the Almanac of American Politics. For purposes of robustness, an alternate measure is used based on the district population.

Environmentalists: The number of Sierra Club members in each congressional district. The source of these data is membership records obtained from the Sierra Club headquarters.

Utility industry: The primary measure is the total number of individuals in the district employed by the utility industry based on employment in "fossil fuel electric power generation" (NAICS code 221112), and "electric power transmission, control, and distribution" (NAICS code 22112). These data are obtained from the U.S. Census Bureau, 2001 County Business Patterns (NAICS). For purposes of robustness, an alternate measure is used based on the number of individuals in the district employed in the broader utility industry (NAICS code 22). Note: The U.S. Census Bureau provides data on industry employment at the county level, and therefore these data are converted to district-level data based on county-to-congressional district maps.

Veterans: The number of veterans in each congressional district. The source of these data is the U.S. Census Bureau, 2000 Census.

Business: The number of individuals in the district employed in manufacturing industries (NAICS code 31). Source: U.S. Census Bureau, 2001 County Business Patterns (NAICS). Note: The U.S. Census Bureau provides data on industry employment at the county level, and therefore these data are converted to district-level data based on county-to-congressional district maps.

Labor: The number of union members in the district. Data on "union affiliation of employed wage and salary workers by state" are taken from the Bureau of Labor Statistics, U.S. Department of Labor. Note: The U.S. Bureau of Labor Statistics only provides these data at the state level, and therefore these data are converted to a district-level measure based on the number of districts in a state.

Oil and gas producers: The total number of individuals in the district employed in the oil and gas industry based on "oil and gas mining" (NAICS code 211), "drilling support employment" (NAICS code 213111), "oil and gas support employment" (NAICS code 213112), and "natural gas distribution" (NAICS code 2212). Source: U.S. Census Bureau, 2001 County Business Patterns (NAICS). Note: The U.S. Census Bureau provides data on industry employment at the county level, and therefore these data are converted to district-level data based on county-to-congressional district maps.

Mining industry: The total number of individuals in the district employed in the mining industry based on "coal mining" (NAICS code 2121), and "coal support employment" (NAICS code 213113). Source: U.S. Census Bureau, 2001 County Business Patterns (NAICS). Note: The U.S. Census Bureau provides data on industry employment at the county level, and therefore these data are converted to district-level data based on county-to-congressional district maps.

Native Americans: The number of Native Americans in each congressional district as reported by the U.S. Census Bureau's 2000 Census.

Renewable energy producers: The total number of individuals in the district employed in the renewable energy industry based on employment in "hydroelectric power generation" (NAICS code 221111), and "other electric power generation" (NAICS code 221119). Source: U.S. Census Bureau, 2001 County Business Patterns (NAICS). Note: The U.S. Census Bureau provides data on industry employment at the county level, and therefore these data are converted to district-level data based on county-to-congressional district maps.

Sportsmen: The number of Ducks Unlimited members in each congressional district. The source of these data is state membership records from the Ducks Unlimited organization, which are converted to district-level based on the number of districts in the state.

State and local government: The primary measure of this constituency is the number of state and local government employees in the district taken from the U.S. Census Bureau, 2001 Public Employee Data. For purposes of robustness, an alternate measure is used based on the number of parks and resources department employees in the state divided by the number of districts in the state. Source: U.S. Census Bureau, 2001 Public Employee Data.

Farmers: The number of individuals (16 and older) in the district employed in "farming, fishing, and forestry occupations" taken from the U.S. Census Bureau, 2000 Census.

Local residents: The population of the district. Source: Almanac of American Politics.

Developers: The number of individuals in the district employed in the construction sector (NAICS 23) taken from the U.S. Census Bureau, 2001 County Business Patterns (NAICS). Note: The U.S. Census Bureau provides data on industry employment at the county level, and therefore these data are converted to district-level data based on county-to-congressional district maps.

MEASUREMENT OF FINANCIAL CONTRIBUTIONS

Data on financial contributions from a constituency to a legislative office during the 1999–2000 election cycle are taken from the Center for Responsive Politics (www.opensecrets.org). The categories used in classifying contributors are those used by the Center for Responsive Politics (CRP), and noted here in quotation marks. In the few cases where the CRP did not provide an appropriate category, alternate classifications were used.

Health Policy

Business: Dollar amount of contributions from the "business" sector.

Labor: Dollar amount of contributions from "labor unions."

Physicians: Dollar amount of contributions from "health professionals."

Patients: Dollar amount of contributions over $200 from individuals in-state.

Seniors: Dollar amount of contributions from "retired."

Insurers: Dollar amount of contributions from the "insurance" sector.

Attorneys: Dollar amount of contributions from "lawyers/law firms." For purposes of robustness, the dollar amount of contributions from the American Trial Lawyers Association is used as an alternate measure of financial contributions from attorneys.

Hospitals: Dollar amount of contributions from "hospitals and nursing homes."

Medicare patients: Dollar amount of contributions over $200 from individuals in-state.

Pharmaceutical industry: Dollar amount of contributions from "pharmaceutical manufacturing."

Natural Resources Policy

Consumers: Dollar amount of contributions over $200 from individuals in-state.

Environmentalists: Dollar amount of contributions from the "environment" sector.

Utilities: Dollar amount of contributions from "electric utilities."

Veterans: Dollar amount of contributions from the Retired Enlisted Association and the Veterans of Foreign Wars.

Business: Dollar amount of contributions from the "business" sector.

Labor: Dollar amount of contributions from "labor unions."

Oil and gas producers: Dollar amount of contributions from the "oil and gas" industry.

Mining industries: Dollar amount of contributions from the "mining" industry and "coal mining" industry.

Native Americans: Dollar amount of contributions from individuals who are identified with the Native American community (as determined by keywords: Indian, Native, Tribe, and Tribal in the domain of donor name or donor's employer).

Renewable energy producers: Dollar amount of contributions from the "alternative energy production" sector.

Sportsmen: Dollar amount of contributions from the "gun rights" sector.

State and local government: Dollar amount of contributions from individuals who identified a city, county, or state government as their employer and the American Federation of State, County, and Municipal Employees (AFSCME).

Farmers: Dollar amount of contributions from the "crop production and basic processing" sector.

Local residents: Dollar amount of contributions over $200 from individuals in-state.

Developers: Dollar amount of contributions from the "construction" industry.

MEASUREMENT OF SHARED CAREER EXPERIENCE

Shared career experience is measured by a dichotomous variable, which is coded as "1" if either the legislator or staff member has relevant previous career experience with the specified subconstituency. Data on the previous careers of both legislators and staff members are taken from the *Congressional Yellow Book*. In addition, data on staff members' previous professional experience are supplemented by interview data.

MEASUREMENT OF CONTACT

Contact from subconstituencies to a legislative office is measured using pretested forms administered during the personal interviews with legislative staff. The first of these asked staff members to indicate how much mail they received on the issue from a list of policy-relevant subconstituencies. This form was then followed by a second form, on which staff members indicated the number of times the legislative office was contacted by phone or in person regarding the specified issue by the same list of policy-relevant subconstituencies. For mail contact, staff members were asked to indicate the amount of mail they received ("none," "a little," "some," or "a lot") from each subconstituency in the past year on the issue at hand. For personal contact, staff members were asked to indicate the number of times the staff member had contact with the constituency on the issue in the past year: never (0), once or twice (1–2 times), several times (3–5 times), many times (6–10 times), and repeated contact (more than 10 times). When a staff member indicated repeated contact with a subconstituency, a follow-up question was posed to clarify the number of contacts (and to distinguish situations in which a legislative enterprise was contacted eleven times from those in which they were contacted fifty times).

Health Policy

Business: Mail and personal contact from individuals identified with business at the local, state, or federal levels, including the Chamber of Commerce, National Federation of Independent Business, and the National Association of Manufacturers.

Labor: Mail and personal contact from individuals associated with organized labor, including the AFL-CIO.

Physicians: Mail and personal contact from health care professionals and individuals identified with the American Medical Association and medical specialty groups.

Patients: Mail and personal contact from consumers, women, working families, and the uninsured.

Seniors: Mail and personal contact from senior citizens and individuals associated with the AARP.

Insurers: Mail and personal contact from individuals associated with health insurers.

Attorneys: Mail and personal contact from attorneys and individuals associated with the American Trial Lawyers Association.

Hospitals: Mail and personal contact from individuals associated with hospitals and nursing homes and hospices.

Pharmaceutical industry: Mail and personal contact from individuals associated with individual pharmaceutical companies, generic pharmaceutical companies, and the Pharmaceutical Manufacturers and Researchers of America.

Natural Resources Policy

Consumers: Mail and personal contact from individuals, including working families, unemployed individuals, and individuals associated with consumer groups.

Environmentalists: Mail and personal contact from individuals associated with environmental advocacy groups, including national, state, and local conservation groups.

Utilities: Mail and personal contact from individuals associated with utility companies.

Veterans: Mail and personal contact with veterans and individuals associated with veterans' associations.

Business: Mail and personal contact with individuals associated with businesses (including small businesses, auto manufacturers, etc.), the Chamber of Commerce, and the National Association of Manufacturers.

Labor: Mail and personal contact with individuals from labor unions.

Oil and gas producers: Mail and personal contact with individuals from oil companies, natural gas companies, and the American Petroleum Institute.

Mining industries: Mail and personal contact from individuals associated with mining and coal companies.

Native Americans: Mail and personal contact from Native Americans and individuals associated with the Alaska Federation of Natives and other Native American organizations.

Renewable energy producers: Mail and personal contact from individuals associated with renewable energies and nuclear energy.

Sportsmen: Mail and personal contact from sportsmen and individuals associated with sporting organizations (e.g., Ducks Unlimited) and gun rights (e.g., the National Rifle Association).

State and local government: Mail and personal contact from employees and individuals associated with city, county, or state government.

Farmers: Mail and personal contact from farmers.

Local residents: Mail and personal contact from individual constituents, including working families.

Developers: Mail and personal contact from developers, builders, and property rights advocates.

MEASUREMENT OF TRADITIONAL PARTISAN TIES

Traditional partisan ties are measured by a dichotomous variable, which is coded as "1" if there exists a traditional tie between a legislative enterprise and a subconstituency.

Health Policy: The following subconstituencies are coded as having traditional partisan ties to the Democratic Party: labor, physicians, and attorneys. Business, insurers, hospitals, and the pharmaceutical industry are coded as traditionally tied to the Republican Party.

Natural Resources Policy: The following subconstituencies are coded as having a traditional partisan tie to the Democratic Party: environmentalists, consumers, labor unions, renewable energy producers, and state and local governments. Businesses, developers, sportsmen, agriculture, veterans, mining, utilities, and the oil and gas subconstituencies are all coded as traditionally tied to the Republican Party.

Appendix D

Measurement of Legislative Participation

In order to measure the quantity and content of legislators' participation in the policy debate on behalf of their constituents, the transcripts of committee (and subcommittee) hearings, committee markups, and the House floor debate were analyzed. Across the two policies examined in Chapter 6 (i.e., the Patients' Bill of Rights and the Securing America's Future Energy Act), fifteen committee (and subcommittee) hearings, six markups, and four floor debates were coded. In the case of hearings and floor debate, the official transcripts were obtained through the Government Printing Office, each transcript was coded independently by two coders, and reliability checks were conducted. Committee markup reports were not available publicly but were made available by the House committee by request in the committee office on Capitol Hill. Neither duplication nor removal of the material was possible, and as a result, the markup transcripts were coded only by the author.

The purpose of the content analysis is to determine how many times each legislator in the sample spoke on behalf of each subconstituency relevant to the policy at hand and to further categorize each comment as either supportive (positive or neutral in tone) or unsupportive (negative tone) of the subconstituency. Each sentence of a legislator's comments is coded, and a legislator can only participate on behalf of a given subconstituency once per sentence (even if the legislator invokes the subconstituency multiple times within the sentence). However, a legislator who invokes multiple subconstituencies within a single sentence is coded as participating on behalf of each of those subconstituencies.[1]

---

[1] Additionally, some sentences do not invoke a relevant subconstituency.

In advance of conducting the content analysis of these transcripts, a detailed coding scheme was developed that classified words and phrases according to the policy-relevant subconstituency that they invoked (see below). A research assistant was trained and familiarized with the coding scheme before analyzing the transcripts. All hearing and floor debate transcripts were independently coded by the research assistant and the author. The coded transcripts were then compared, resulting in an average intercoder reliability of 91%. Any discrepancies were resolved by the author.

PATIENTS' BILL OF RIGHTS

Business: Keywords include business, small business, employers, companies.

Physicians: Keywords include doctors, physicians, health care providers, health care professionals, nurses, specialists (e.g., pediatricians, surgeons).

Patients: Keywords include patients, managed care enrollees, people covered by a plan, member of an HMO. If clearly in context referring to a patient, also include terms like: individual, consumer (of health insurance), children, family, man, woman.

Labor: Keywords include labor, organized labor, unions, specific unions (e.g., AFL-CIO, UAW).

Seniors: Keywords include seniors, senior citizens, elderly, older population, retirees.

Insurers: Keywords include insurance industry, insurance companies, HMOs, specific insurance companies (e.g., Blue Cross Blue Shield, Aetna), managed care/managed care organization, health plan.

Attorneys: Keywords include attorneys, trial attorneys, lawyers.

SECURING AMERICA'S FUTURE ENERGY ACT

Consumers: Keywords include consumer(s), low-income citizens, working families, poor. Also include explicit references to impact of gas prices and electricity prices.

Environmentalists: Keywords include environmentalists, greens, conservationists, tree huggers, arctic refuge (or ANWR), pristine land/ wilderness, untouched lands/wilderness, environmental species, endangered species (ESA – Endangered Species Act).

Utilities: Keywords include utilities, electricity companies, electricity co-ops, regional transmission organizations (RTOs). Also include references to failures of utility companies like blackouts, brownouts, failed power grids, California electricity crisis.

Veterans: Keywords include veterans, military service, armed services, soldiers.

Business: Keywords include businesses, small business, small business owners, farmers, employers, manufacturers.

Labor: Keywords include labor, unions, workers, specific unions (e.g., Teamsters, AFL-CIO).

Oil and gas producers: Keywords include oil companies, natural gas, drilling, named companies (e.g., BP, Exxon), off-shore drilling, oil rigs, oil fields, pipeline(s).

Mining industries: Keywords include mines, coal, mining companies, uranium mining.

Native Americans: Keywords include Native people, Inuits, Eskimos, Indians.

Renewable energy producers: Keywords include hydro/hydroelectric power, solar, wind, geothermal, ethanol, biodiesel, alternative sources, nuclear power.

Appendix E

Instrumental Variables Model of Legislative Participation

Complete results of the estimated instrumental variables model of the probability of legislative participation on the Patients' Bill of Rights. As discussed in Chapter 6, the statistical analyses indicate that the possibility that perception might be endogenous to the model of legislative participation and needs to be accounted for in the choice of statistical estimator. The two models are estimated simultaneously using bivariate probit regression with standard errors clustered by legislative office.

TABLE A4. *Instrumental Variables Model of Probability of Legislative Participation, The Patients' Bill of Rights*

	Coefficient Robust S.E.
Probit Model of Legislative Participation	
Legislative Perception of Subconstituency	1.481 *(0.390)* ***
Subconstituency Size (in 1,000s)	−0.001 *(0.001)*
Financial Contributions (in $1,000s)	0.001 *(0.001)*
Contact from Subconstituency	
Mail Contact	0.053 *(0.151)*
Personal Contact	0.020 *(0.021)*
Electoral Safety (2000 Election)	0.027 *(0.008)* ***
Membership on Committee of Jurisdiction	0.869 *(0.277)* ***
Committee Leadership	−0.154 *(0.381)*
Minority Party	−0.140 *(0.248)*
Constant	0.184 *(1.271)*
Endogenous Regressor: Perception	
Membership on Committee	−0.248 *(0.181)*
Shared Professional Experience	0.130 *(0.223)*
Legislative Seniority	−0.019 *(0.014)*
Partisan Ties	−0.208 *(0.167)*
Mail Contact from Subconstituency	0.122 *(0.130)*
Personal Contact from Subconstituency	0.045 *(0.018)* ***
Subconstituency Size	−0.001 *(0.001)*
Financial Contributions	0.002 *(0.001)* ***
Constant	4.840 *(1.663)*
N	273
Wald Chi-Squared (17)	479.26 *(0.001)*
Wald Test $\rho = 0$	5.32 *(0.020)*

Two-tailed hypotheses tests: * $p < .10$, ** $p < .05$, *** $p < .01$.

Reported coefficients are for a probit model of legislative participation estimated using seemingly unrelated bivariate probit regression with standard errors clustered by legislative office.

References

Achen, Christopher H. 1978. Measuring Representation. *American Journal of Political Science* 22: 475–510.

Adler, E. Scott. 2000. Constituency Characteristics and the "Guardian" Model of Appropriations Subcommittees, 1959–1998. *American Journal of Political Science* 44(1): 104–114.

2002. *Why Congressional Reforms Fail: Reelection and the House Committee System*. Chicago: University of Chicago Press.

Adler, E. Scott, and John S. Lapinski. 1997. Demand-Side Theory and Congressional Committee Composition: A Constituency Characteristics Approach. *American Journal of Political Science* 41(3): 895–918.

Adler, E. Scott, and John S. Lapinski, eds. 2006. *The Macropolitics of Congress*. Princeton, NJ: Princeton University Press.

Ajzen, Icek. 1996. The Social Psychology of Decision Making. In *Social Psychology: Handbook of Basic Principles*, edited by E. Tory Higgins and Arie W. Kruglanski. New York: The Guilford Press. Pp. 297–328.

Akers, Mary Ann, and Paul Kane. 2007. Revolving Door Keeps Spinning Despite Lobbying Reforms. *Washington Post*, October 4, 2007. Page A23.

Allison, Graham T. 1971. *Essence of Decision: Explaining the Cuban Missile Crisis*. Boston: Little, Brown.

Arkes, Hal R., and Kenneth Hammond. 1986. *Judgment and Decision Making*. New York: Cambridge University Press.

Arnold, R. Douglas. 1990. *The Logic of Congressional Action*. London and New Haven, CT: Yale University Press.

2004. *Congress, the Press, and Political Accountability*. Princeton, NJ: Princeton University Press.

Austen-Smith, David. 1995. Campaign Contributions and Access. *American Political Science Review* 89: 566–581.

Axelrod, Robert, ed. 1976. *Structure of Decision: The Cognitive Maps of Political Elites*. Princeton, NJ: Princeton University Press.

Bachrach, Peter, and Morton S. Baratz. 1962. Two Faces of Power. *American Political Science Review* 56(4): 947–952.

1963. Decisions and Nondecisions: An Analytical Framework. *American Political Science Review* 57(3): 632–642.

Bailey, Michael, and David W. Brady. 1998. Heterogeneity and Representation: The Senate and Free Trade. *American Journal of Political Science* 42(2): 524–544.

Barone, Michael, and Richard E. Cohen. 2001. *The Almanac of American Politics 2002.* Washington, D.C.: National Journal.

Barrett, Edith, and Fay Lomax Cook. 1991. Congressional Attitudes and Voting Behavior: An Examination of Support for Social Welfare. *Legislative Studies Quarterly* 16(3): 375–391.

Bartels, Larry M. 1991. Constituency Opinion and Congressional Policy Making: The Reagan Defense Build Up. *American Political Science Review* 85 (2): 457–474.

1996. Uninformed Votes: Information Effects in Presidential Elections. *American Journal of Political Science* 40(1): 194–230.

2005. Economic Inequality and Political Representation. Working Paper. Princeton, NJ.

2008. *Unequal Democracy: The Political Economy of the New Gilded Age.* Princeton, NJ: Princeton University Press.

Bassili, John N. 1995. On the Psychological Reality of Party Identification: Evidence from the Accessibility of Voting Intentions and of Partisan Feelings. *Political Behavior* 17: 339–358.

Bauer, Raymond, Ithiel de Sola Pool, and Lewis Anthony Dexter. 1963. *American Business and Public Policy: The Politics of Foreign Trade.* New York: Atherton Press.

Baumgartner, Frank, Jeffrey Berry, Marie Hojnacki, David Kimball, and Beth Leech. 2004. *Advocacy and Public Policymaking Web Site.* State College: Pennsylvania State College.

Berry, Jeffrey M. 2002. Validity and Reliability Issues in Elite Interviewing. *PS: Political Science and Politics* 35(4): 679–682.

Bianco, William T. 1994. *Trust: Representatives and Constituents.* Ann Arbor: University of Michigan Press.

1997. Reliable Source or Usual Suspects? Cue-taking, Information Transmission, and Legislative Committees. *Journal of Politics* 59(3): 913–924.

1998. Different Paths to the Same Results: Rational Choice, Political Psychology, and Impression Formation in Campaigns. *American Journal of Political Science* 42(4): 1061–1081.

Binder, Sarah A. 1997. *Minority Rights, Majority Rule: Partisanship and the Development of Congress.* New York: Cambridge University Press.

Birnbaum, Jeffrey H. 2007. The Hill's Revolving-Door Rules Don't Work in Both Directions. *Washington Post.* January 16, 2007. Page A17.

Bishin, Benjamin G. 2000. Constituency Influence in Congress: Does Subconstituency Matter? *Legislative Studies Quarterly* 25: 389–413.

Black, Duncan. 1958. *Theory of Committees and Elections.* New York: Cambridge University Press.

Bodenhausen, Galen V., and Robert S. Wyer. 1987. Social Cognition and Social Reality: Information Acquisition and Use in the Laboratory and the

Real World. In *Social Information Processing and Survey Methodology*, edited by Hans J. Hippler, Norbert Schwarz, and Seymour Sudman. New York: Springer Verlag. Pp. 6–41.

Brady, David, and Edward P. Schwartz. 1995. Ideology and Interests in Congressional Voting: The Politics of Abortion in the U.S. Senate. *Public Choice* 84: 25–48.

Brady, Henry, Sidney Verba, and Kay Lehman Schlozman. 1994. Beyond SES: A Resource Model of Political Participation. *American Political Science Review* 89: 829–838.

Bruner, Jerome S. 1957. On Perceptual Readiness. *Psychological Review* 64: 123–152.

Burgin, Eileen. 1991. Representatives' Decisions on Participation in Foreign Policy Issues. *Legislative Studies Quarterly* 16: 521–546.

Burrell, Barbara. 1994. *A Woman's Place Is in the House: Campaigning for Congress in the Feminist Era*. Ann Arbor: University of Michigan Press.

Cain, Bruce E., John Ferejohn, and Morris Fiorina. 1987. *The Personal Vote: Constituency Service and Electoral Independence*. Cambridge, MA: Harvard University Press.

Canon, David T. 1999. *Race, Redistricting, and Representation: The Unintended Consequences of Black Majority Districts*. Chicago: University of Chicago Press.

Carlston, Donal E., and Eliot R. Smith. 1996. Principles of Mental Representation. In *Social Psychology Handbook of Basic Principles*, edited by E. Tory Higgins and Arie W. Kruglanski. New York: The Guilford Press. Pp. 184–210.

Carmines, Edward G., and James H. Kuklinski. 1990. Incentives, Opportunities, and the Logic of Public Opinion in American Political Representation. In *Information and Democratic Processes*, edited by John A. Ferejohn, and James H. Kuklinski. Urbana and Chicago: University of Illinois Press.

Carmines, Edward G., and James A. Stimson. 1989. *Issue Evolution: Race and the Transformation of American Politics*. Princeton, NJ: Princeton University Press.

Carpenter, Daniel, Kevin Esterling, and David Lazer. 2004. Friends, Brokers, and Transitivity: Who Talks with Whom in Washington Lobbying? *Journal of Politics* 66(1): 224–246.

Chong, Dennis. 1993. How People Think, Reason, and Feel About Rights and Liberties. *American Journal of Political Science* 37:867–899.

Clapp, Charles L. 1963. *The Congressman: His Work as He Sees It*. Washington, D.C.: Brookings Institution.

Clausen, Aage R. 1973. *How Congressmen Decide: A Policy Focus*. New York: St. Martin's Press.

1977. The Accuracy of Leader Perceptions of Constituency Views. *Legislative Studies Quarterly* 2: 361–384.

Clausen, Aage R., Soren Holmberg, and Lance deHaven-Smith. 1983. Contextual Factors in the Accuracy of Leaders' Perceptions of Constituents' Views. *Journal of Politics* 45: 449–472.

Clinton, Joshua. 2006. Representation in Congress; Constituents and Roll Calls in the 106th House. *Journal of Politics* 68(2): 397–409.

Cobb, Michael D., and Jeffrey A. Jenkins. 2001. Race and the Representation of Blacks' Interests During Reconstruction. *Political Research Quarterly* 54(1): 181–204.

Conover, Pamela Johnston, and Stanley Feldman. 1986. The Role of Inference in the Perception of Political Candidates. In *Political Cognition*, edited by Richard R. Lau and David O. Sears. Hillsdale, NJ: Lawrence Erlbaum Associates. Pp. 127–158.

1989. Candidate Perception in an Ambiguous World: Campaigns, Cues, and Inference Processes. *American Journal of Political Science* 33(4): 912–940.

Converse, Jean M., and Stanley Presser. 1986. *Survey Questions: Handcrafting the Standardized Questionnaire.* Beverly Hills, CA: Sage Publications.

Converse, Phillip E., and Roy Pierce. 1986. *Political Representation in France.* Cambridge, MA: Harvard University Press.

Cox, Gary, and Mathew McCubbins. 1993. *Legislative Leviathan: Party Government in the House.* Berkeley: University of California Press.

2005. *Setting the Agenda: Responsible Party Government in the U.S. House of Representatives.* New York: Cambridge University Press.

Davidson, Roger H., and Walter J. Oleszek. 2000. *Congress and Its Members.* Washington, D.C.: CQ Press.

DeGregorio, Christine. 1995. Patterns of Senior Staff Use in Congressional Committees. *Polity* 32: 261–275.

Denzau, Arthur T., William Riker, and Kenneth Shepsle. 1985. Farquharson and Fenno: Sophisticated Voting and Home Style. *American Political Science Review* 79(4): 1117–1134.

DeSart, Jay A. 1995. Information Processing and Partisan Neutrality: A Reexamination of the Party Decline Thesis. *Journal of Politics* 57: 776–795.

Dexter, Lewis Anthony. 1956. What Do Congressmen Hear? The Mail. *Public Opinion* 20: 16–27.

1957. The Representative and His District. *Human Organization* 16: 2–14.

Druckman, James N. 2001. The Implications of Framing Effects for Citizen Competence. *Political Behavior* 23: 225–256.

Eagly, Alice, and Shelly Chaiken. 1993. *The Psychology of Attitudes.* New York: Harcourt Brace Jovanovich College Publishers.

Eagly, Alice H., and Shelly Chaiken. 1998. Attitude Structure and Function. In *Handbook of Social Psychology*, edited by Daniel T. Gilbert, Susan T. Fiske, and Gardner Lindzey. New York: McGraw-Hill.

Erikson, Robert S. 1978. Constituency Opinion and Congressional Behavior: A Reexamination of the Miller-Stokes Representation Data. *American Journal of Political Science* 22(3): 511–535.

1990. Roll Calls, Reputations, and Representation in the U.S. Senate. *Legislative Studies Quarterly* 15(4): 623–642.

Erikson, Robert S., Norman R. Luttbeg, and William B. Holloway. 1975. Knowing One's District: How Legislators Predict Referendum Voting. *American Journal of Political Science* 19(2): 231–246.

Erikson, Robert S., Michael MacKuen, and James A. Stimson. 2002. *The Macro Polity.* New York: Cambridge University Press.

Erikson, Robert S., and Gerald C. Wright. 2000. Representation of Constituency Ideology in Congress. In *Continuity and Change in Congressional Elections*, edited by David Brady and John Cogan. Stanford: Stanford University Press. Pp. 149–177.

Esaiasson, Peter, and Soren Holmberg. 1996. *Representation from Above: Members of Parliament and Representative Democracy in Sweden*. Aldershot, UK: Dartmouth Publishing Company.

Esterling, Kevin M. 2007. Buying Expertise: Campaign Contributions and Attention to Policy Analysis in Congressional Committees. *American Political Science Review* 101(1): 93–109.

Eulau, Heinz. 1987. The Congruence Model Revisited. *Legislative Studies Quarterly* 12: 171–214.

Eulau, Heinz, and Alan Abramowitz. 1978. Recent Research on Congress in a Democratic Perspective. In *The Politics of Representation: Continuities in Theory and Research*, edited by Heinz Eulau and John C. Wahlke with others. Beverly Hills: Sage Publications. Pp. 253–279.

Eulau, Heinz, and Paul D. Karps. 1977. The Puzzle of Representation: Specifying Components of Responsiveness. *Legislative Studies Quarterly* 2: 233–254.

Evans, C. Lawrence. 1991a. *Leadership in Committee*. Ann Arbor: University of Michigan Press.

1991b. Participation and Policy Making in the Senate Committees. *Political Science Quarterly* 106(3): 479–498.

2001. Senators, Drug Imports, and Representation. Paper read at Annual Meeting of the American Political Science Association, August 2001, at San Francisco, CA.

2002. How Senators Decide: An Exploration. In *U.S. Senate Exceptionalism*, edited by Bruce I. Oppenheimer. Columbus: The Ohio State University Press.

Evans, Diana. 1996. Before the Roll Call: Interest Group Lobbying and Public Policy Outcomes in House Committees. *Political Research Quarterly* 49(2): 287–304.

2004. *Greasing the Wheels: Using Pork Barrel Projects to Build Majority Coalitions in Congress*. New York: Cambridge University Press.

Fazio, Russell H. 1990. A Practical Guide to the Use of Response Latency in Social Psychological Research. *Review of Personality and Social Psychology* 11: 74–97.

Fazio, Russell H., and C. J. Williams. 1986. Attitude Accessibility as a Moderator of the Attitude-Perception and Attitude-Behavior Relation: An Investigation of the 1984 Presidential Election. *Journal of Personality and Social Psychology* 51: 505–514.

Fenno, Richard F., Jr. 1973. *Congressmen in Committees*. Boston: Little, Brown.

1978. *Home Style: House Members in Their Districts*. Boston: Little, Brown.

1986. Observation, Context, and Sequence in the Study of Politics. *American Political Science Review* 80: 3–16.

1996. *Senators on the Campaign Trail*. Norman: University of Oklahoma Press.

2006. *Congressional Travels: Places, Connections, and Authenticity*. New York: Pearson/Longman.

Festinger, Leon. 1957. *A Theory of Cognitive Dissonance*. Stanford, CA: Stanford University Press.

Fiedler, Klaus, and Jeanette Schmidt. 1995. Heuristics. In *The Blackwell Encyclopedia of Social Psychology*, edited by Anthony S. R. Manstead and Miles Hewstone. Oxford: Blackwell Press. Pp. 296–300.

Fiorina, Morris P. 1974. *Representatives, Roll Calls, and Constituencies*. Boston: D. C. Heath.

1989. *Congress: Keystone of the Washington Establishment*. 2nd ed. New Haven, CT: Yale University Press.

Fleisher, Richard. 1993. PAC Contributions and Congressional Voting on National Defense. *Legislative Studies Quarterly* 18(3): 391–409.

Foerstel, Karen, and Herbert N. Foerstel. 1996. *Climbing the Hill: Gender Conflict in Congress*. New York: Praeger.

Fox, Harrison W., Jr., and Susan Webb Hammond. 1977. *Congressional Staffs: The Invisible Force in American Lawmaking*. New York: Free Press.

Freedman, Jonathan L., and David O. Sears. 1965. Selective exposure. In *Advances in Experimental Social Psychology*, Vol. II, edited by Leonard Berkowitz. New York: Academic Press. Pp. 58–97.

Friedman, Sally. 1993. Committee Advancement of Women and Blacks in Congress: A Test of the Responsible Legislator Thesis. *Women and Politics* 13: 27–52.

Fulton, Sarah A., Cherie D. Maestas, Sandy Maisel, and Walter J. Stone. 1996. The Sense of a Woman: Gender, Ambition, and the Decision to Run for Congress. *Political Research Quarterly* 59(2): 235–248.

Gamble, Katrina L. 2007. Black Political Representation: An Examination of Legislative Activity within U.S. House Committees. *Legislative Studies Quarterly* 32: 421–448.

George, Alexander L. 1969. The "Operational Code": A Neglected Approach to the Study of Political Leaders and Decisionmaking. *International Studies Quarterly* 13: 190–222.

Gerber, Michael S. 2002. Healthcare Unlikely to Dominate the Fall Elections. *The Hill*, September 18.

Gertzog, Irwin N. 1995. *Congressional Women: Their Recruitment, Integration, and Behavior*. New York: Praeger.

Gettleman, Jeffrey. 2005. A Swift Climb Up the Ladder for an Ex-Aide to Menendez. *New York Times*, July 17. Page 30.

Gilliam, Franklin D., Jr., and Shanto Iyengar. 2000. Prime Suspects: The Influence of Local Television News on the Viewing Public. *American Journal of Political Science* 44(3): 560–573.

Goff, Brian L., and Kevin B. Grier. 1993. On the (Mis)measurement of Legislator Ideology and Shirking. *Public Choice* 76: 5–20.

Goldstein, Amy. 2001. The Patients' Rights Fight, Round 2; Bills Have Passed House and Senate. Now It Gets Rough. *The Washington Post*, August 5, 2001. Page A5.

Goren, Paul. 1997. Political Expertise and Issue Voting in Presidential Elections. *Political Research Quarterly* 50: 387–412.

Grenzke, Janet M. 1989. Shopping in the Congressional Supermarket: The Currency is Complex. *American Journal of Political Science* 33: 1–24.

Griffin, John D., and Brian Newman. 2005. Are Voters Better Represented? *Journal of Politics* 67(4): 1206–1227.

2008. *Minority Report: Evaluating Political Equality in America.* Chicago: University of Chicago Press.

Hagen, Michael G. 1995. References to Racial Issues. *Political Behavior* 17: 49–88.

Hall, Richard L. 1987. Participation and Purpose in Committee Decision Making. *American Political Science Review* 81: 105–127.

1992. Measuring Legislative Influence. *Legislative Studies Quarterly* 17(2): 205–231.

1996. *Participation in Congress.* New Haven, CT: Yale University Press.

Hall, Richard L., and C. Lawrence Evans. 1990. The Power of Subcommittees. *Journal of Politics* 52: 335–354.

Hall, Richard L., and Bernard Grofman. 1990. The Committee Assignment Process and the Conditional Nature of Committee Bias. *American Political Science Review* 84: 1149–1166.

Hall, Richard L., and Kristina C. Miler. 2008. Lobbying as Subsidy to Legislative Agents. *Journal of Politics* 70: 1–16.

Hall, Richard L., and Frank W. Wayman. 1990. Buying Time: Moneyed Interests and the Mobilization of Bias in Congressional Committees. *American Political Science Review* 84: 797–820.

Hansen, John Mark. 1991. *Gaining Access.* Chicago: University of Chicago Press.

Hansen, Orval. 2001. The Role of Mail in Decisions in Congress. In *Inside the House: Former Members Reveal How Congress Really Works*, edited by Lou Frey, Jr. and Michael T. Hayes. Lanham, MD: University Press of America.

Hardin, John W. 1998. Advocacy versus Certainty: The Dynamics of Committee Jurisdiction Concentration. *The Journal of Politics* 60(2): 374–397.

Hastie, Reid. 1986. A Primer of Information-Processing Theory for the Political Scientist. In *Political Cognition*, edited by Richard R. Lau and David O. Sears. Hillsdale, NJ: Lawrence Erlbaum Associates.

Hastie, Reid, and A. P. Kumar. 1979. Person Memory: Personality Traits as Organizing Principles in Memory for Behaviors. *Journal of Personality and Social Psychology* 37: 25–34.

Hedlund, Ronald D., and H. Paul Friesema. 1972. Representatives' Perceptions of Constituency Opinion. *Journal of Politics* 34(3): 730–752.

Heider, Fritz. 1944. Social perception and phenomenal causality. *Psychological Review* 51: 358–374.

1958. *The Psychology of Interpersonal Relations.* New York: Wiley.

Herbst, Susan. 1998. *Reading Public Opinion: How Political Actors View the Democratic Process.* Chicago: University of Chicago Press.

Hermann, Richard. 1985. *Perception and Behavior in Soviet Foreign Policy.* Pittsburgh: Pittsburgh University Press.

Herstein, John A. 1981. Keeping the Voter's Limits in Mind: A Cognitive Process Analysis of Decision Making in Voting. *Journal of Personality and Social Psychology* 40: 843–861.

Higgins, E. Tory, and John A. Bargh. 1987. Social Cognition and Social Perception. *Annual Review of Psychology* 38: 369–425.

Higgins, E. Tory, William S. Rholes, and Carl R. Jones. 1977. Category Accessibility and Impression Formation. *Journal of Experimental Social Psychology* 13: 141–154.

Hill, Kim Quaile, and Patricia A. Hurley. 1999. Dyadic Representation Reappraised. *American Journal of Political Science* 43(1): 109–137.

2002. Symbolic Speeches in the U.S. Senate and Their Representational Implications. *Journal of Politics* 64(1): 219–231.

Hojnacki, Marie, and David C. Kimball. 1998. Organized Interests and the Decision of Whom to Lobby in Congress. *American Political Science Review* 92: 775–790.

1999. The Who and How of Organizations' Lobbying Strategies in Committee. *Journal of Politics* 61: 999–1024.

Holian, David, Timothy Krebs, and Michael Walsh. 1997. Constituency Opinion, Ross Perot, and Roll-Call Behavior in the U.S. House: The Case of NAFTA. *Legislative Studies Quarterly* 12(3): 369–392.

Houston, David A., and Russell H. Fazio. 1989. Biased Processing as a Function of Attitude Accessibility: Making Objective Judgments Subjectively. *Social Cognition* 7(1): 51–66.

Huckfeldt, Robert, Jeffrey Levine, William Morgan, and John Sprague. 1999. Accessibility and the Political Utility of Partisan and Ideological Orientations. *American Journal of Political Science* 43(3): 888–911.

Huckfeldt, Robert, Jeffrey Mondak, M. Craw, and J. Mendez. 2005. Making Sense of Candidates: Partisanship, Ideology, and Issues as Guides to Judgment. *Cognitive Brain Research* 23: 11–23.

Huckfeldt, Robert, John Sprague, and Jeffrey Levine. 2000. The Dynamics of Collective Deliberation in the 1996 Election: Campaign Effects on Accessibility, Certainty, and Accuracy. *American Political Science Review* 94: 641–651.

Huddy, Leonie, and Nayda Terkildsen. 1993. The Consequences of Gender Stereotypes of Women Candidates at Different Levels and Types of Offices. *Political Research Quarterly* 46(3): 503–525.

Hurley, Patricia A. 1982. Collective Representation Reappraised. *Legislative Studies Quarterly* 7: 119–136.

Hurley, Patricia A., and Kim Quaile Hill. 2003. Beyond the Demand-Input Model: A Theory of Representational Linkages. *Journal of Politics* 65(2): 304–326.

Hurwitz, Mark S., David W. Rohde, and Roger J. Moiles. 2001. Distributive and Partisan Issues in Agriculture Policy in the 104th House. *American Political Science Review* 95: 911–922.

Hutchings, Vincent L. 1998. Issue Salience and Support for Civil Rights Legislation Among Southern Democrats. *Legislative Studies Quarterly* 23(4): 521–544.

Iyengar, Shanto. 1990. Framing Responsibility for Political Issues: The Case of Poverty. *Political Behavior* 12: 19–40.

Iyengar, Shanto, and Donald R. Kinder. 1987. *News That Matters: Television and American Public Opinion*. Chicago: University of Chicago Press.

Jackson, Brooks. 1988. *Honest Graft*. New York: Knopf.

Jackson, John E. 1974. *Constituency and Leaders in Congress: Their Effects on Senate Voting Behavior*. Cambridge, MA: Harvard University Press.

Jackson, John E., and David C. King. 1989. Public Goods, Private Interests, and Representation. *American Political Science Review* 83: 1143–1164.

Jackson, John E., and John W. Kingdon. 1992. Ideology, Interest Group Scores, and Legislative Votes. *American Journal of Political Science* 36(3): 805–823.

Jacob, Paul. 2000. More Politicians? U.S. Term Limits Weekly Commentary #174. May 8.

Jacobs, Lawrence R., Eric Lawrence, Robert Shapiro, and Steven Smith. 1998. Congressional Leadership of Public Opinion. *Political Science Quarterly* 113: 21–41.

Jacobs, Lawrence R., and Robert Y. Shapiro. 2000. *Politicians Don't Pander: Political Manipulation and the Loss of Democratic Responsiveness*. Chicago: University of Chicago Press.

Jacoby, William G. 2000. Issue Framing and Public Opinion on Government Spending. *American Journal of Political Science* 44(4): 750–767.

Janis, Irving L. 1982. *Groupthink: Psychological Studies of Policy Decisions and Fiascoes*. Boston: Houghton Mifflin.

Jervis, Robert. 1976. *Perception and Misperception in International Politics*. Princeton, NJ: Princeton University Press.

1986. Cognition and Political Behavior. In *Political Cognition*, edited by Richard R. Lau and David O. Sears. Hillsdale, NJ: Lawrence Erlbaum Associates.

Jewell, Malcolm. 1983. Legislator-Constituency Relations and the Representative Process. *Legislative Studies Quarterly* 8(3): 303–337.

Jones, Bryan D. 1994. *Reconceiving Decision-Making in Democratic Politics: Attention, Choice, and Public Policy*. Chicago: University of Chicago Press.

2001. *Politics and the Architecture of Choice: Bounded Rationality and Governance*. Chicago: University of Chicago Press.

Jones, Bryan D., and Frank R. Baumgartner. 2005. *The Politics of Attention: How Government Prioritizes Problems*. Chicago: University of Chicago Press.

Jones, Edward E. 1998. Major Developments in Five Decades of Social Psychology. In *The Handbook of Social Psychology*, edited by Daniel T. Gilbert, Susan T. Fiske, and Gardner Lindzey. Boston: McGraw-Hill.

Kahneman, Daniel, and Amos Tversky. 1973. On the psychology of prediction. *Psychological Review* 80: 237–251.

Kalt, Joseph P., and Mark A. Zupan. 1984. Capture and Ideology in the Economic Theory of Politics. *American Economic Review* 74: 279–300.

Kantin, Kerry L. 2001. GOP Divided over Alaska Oil. *The Hill*. March 7.

Kanwisher, Nancy. 1989. Cognitive Heuristics and American Security Policy. *Journal of Conflict Resolution* 33: 652–675.

Kathlene, Lyn. 1994. Power and Influence in State Legislative Policymaking: The Interaction of Gender and Position in Committee Hearing Debates. *American Political Science Review* 88: 560–576.

Kau, James B., and Paul H. Rubin. 1978. Voting on Minimum Wages: A Time-Series Analysis. *Journal of Political Economy* 86(2): 337–342.

1982. *Congressmen, Constituents, and Contributors: Determinants of Roll Call Voting in the House of Representatives*. Boston: Martinus Nijhoff Publishing.

Kinder, Donald R. 1993. Rational and Not-So-Rational Processes of Judgment and Decision. In *Experimental Foundations of Political Science*, edited by Donald R. Kinder and Thomas R. Palfrey. Ann Arbor: University of Michigan Press.

King, David C. 1997. *Turf Wars: How Congressional Committees Claim Jurisdiction*. Chicago: University of Chicago Press.

Kingdon, John W. 1967. Politicians' Beliefs About Voters. *American Political Science Review* 61(1): 137–145.

1968. *Candidates for Office: Beliefs and Strategies*. New York: Random House.

1977. Models of Legislative Voting. *Journal of Politics* 39(3): 563–595.

1984. *Agendas, Alternatives, and Public Policies*. Boston: Little, Brown.

1989. *Congressmen's Voting Decisions*. 3rd ed. New York: Harper & Row.

Kirkpatrick, David D. 2006. Panel Approves a Revolving Door. *New York Times*, September 21.

Koch, Jeffrey W. 2002. Gender Stereotypes and Citizens' Impressions of House Candidates' Ideological Orientations. *American Journal of Political Science* 46(2): 453–462.

Koger, Gregory. 2003. Position-Taking and Cosponsorship in the U.S. House. *Legislative Studies Quarterly* 28(2): 225–246.

Kollman, Ken. 1997. Inviting Friends to Lobby: Interest Groups, Ideological Bias, and Congressional Committees. *American Journal of Political Science* 41: 519–544.

1998. *Outside Lobbying: Public Opinion and Interest Group Strategies*. Princeton, NJ: Princeton University Press.

Kornberg, Allan. 1966. Perception and Constituency Influence on Legislative Behavior. *Western Political Quarterly* 19(2): 285–292.

Kornblut, Anne E. 2006. Once Just an Aide, Now a King of K Street. *New York Times*, February 5.

Krehbiel, Keith. 1990. Are Congressional Committees Composed of Preference Outliers? *American Political Science Review* 84:149–163.

1991. *Information and Legislative Organization*. Ann Arbor: University of Michigan Press.

1993. Constituency Characteristics and Legislative Preferences. *Public Choice* 76: 21–37.

Krosnick, Jon A. 1989. Attitude Importance and Attitude Accessibility. *Personality and Social Psychology Bulletin* 15: 297–308.

Kuklinski, James H. 1977. District Competitiveness and Legislative Roll Call Behavior: A Reassessment of the Marginality Hypothesis. *American Journal of Political Science* 20(3): 627–638.

1978. Representativeness and Elections: A Policy Analysis. *American Political Science Review* 72(1): 165–77.

ed. 2001. *Citizens and Politics*. Cambridge: Cambridge University Press.

2002. *Thinking About Political Psychology*. Cambridge: Cambridge University Press.

Kuklinski, James H., and Richard Elling. 1977. Representational Role, Constituency Opinion, and Legislative Roll Call Behavior. *American Journal of Political Science* 21(1): 135–147.

Kuklinski, James H., and Norman L. Hurley. 1994. On Hearing and Interpreting Political Messages: A Cautionary Tale of Citizen Cue-Taking. *Journal of Politics* 56: 729–751.

Kuklinski, James H., and Donald J. McCrone. 1980. Policy Salience and the Causal Structure of Representation. *American Politics Quarterly* 8(2): 139–164.

Kuklinski, James H., and Paul Quirk. 2000. Reconsidering the Rational Public: Cognition, Heuristics, and Mass Opinion. In *Elements of Reason: Cognition, Choice, and the Bounds of Rationality*, edited by Arthur Lupia, Mathew D. McCubbins, and Samuel L. Popkin. Cambridge: Cambridge University Press.

Kuklinski, James H., Paul J. Quirk, Jennifer Jerit, David Schwieder, and Robert F. Rich. 2001. The Political Environment and Citizen Competence. *American Journal of Political Science* 45(2): 410–424.

Lakoff, George. 2008. *The Political Mind: Why You Can't Understand 21st Century American Politics with an 18th Century Brain*. New York: Viking.

Langbein, Laura I. 1986. Money and Access: Some Empirical Evidence. *Journal of Politics* 48(4): 1052–1062.

Larson, Deborah Welch. 1985. *Origins of Containment: A Psychological Explanation*. Princeton, NJ: Princeton University Press.

Lascher, Edward L., Jr., Steven Kelman, and Thomas J. Kane. 1993. Policy Views, Constituency Pressure, and Congressional Action on Flag Burning. *Public Choice* 76: 79–102.

Lau, Richard R. 1989. Construct Accessibility and Electoral Choice. *Political Behavior* 11(1): 5–32.

Lau, Richard R., and David P. Redlawsk. 2001. Advantages and Disadvantages of Using Cognitive Heuristics in Political Decision Making. *American Journal of Political Science* 45 (4): 951–971.

2006. *How Voters Decide: Information Processing in Election Campaigns*. New York: Cambridge University Press.

Lau, Richard R., Richard A. Smith, and Susan T. Fiske. 1991. Political Beliefs, Policy Interpretations, and Political Persuasion. *Journal of Politics* 53: 644–675.

Lavine, H., Eugene Borgida, John L. Sullivan, and C. J. Thomsen. 1996. The Relationship of National and Personal Issue Salience to Attitude Accessibility on Foreign and Domestic Policy Issues. *Political Psychology* 17: 293–316.

Lebow, Richard N. 1981. *Between Peace and War*. Baltimore: Johns Hopkins University Press.

Levy, Jack S. 1983. Misperception and the Causes of War. *World Politics* 36: 76–99.

　2003. Political Psychology and Foreign Policy. In *Oxford Handbook of Political Psychology*, edited by David O. Sears, Leonie Huddy, and Robert Jervis. New York: Oxford University Press.

Lewis, Charles. 1998. *The Buying of Congress: How Special Interests Have Stolen Your Right to Life, Liberty, and the Pursuit of Happiness*. New York: Avon Books.

Lindsay, James M. 1990. Parochialism, Policy, and Constituency Constraints: Congressional Voting on Strategic Weapons Systems. *American Journal of Political Science* 34(4): 936–960.

Lindzey, Gardner, and Elliot Aronson. 1985. Major Developments in Social Psychology During the Past Five Decades. In *Handbook of Social Psychology*, edited by Gardner Lindzey and Elliot Aronson. New York: Random House.

Lippman, Walter. 1922. *Public Opinion*. New York: Free Press.

Lodge, Milton, Kathleen M. McGraw, and Patrick Stroh. 1989. An Impression-Driven Model of Candidate Evaluation. *American Political Science Review* 83(2): 399–420.

Lodge, Milton, Kathleen McGraw, Pamela Johnston Conover, Stanley Feldman, and Arthur Miller. 1991. Where is the Schema?: Critiques. *American Political Science Review* 85: 1341–1380.

Lodge, Milton, Patrick Stroh, and John Wahlke. 1990. Black-Box Models of Candidate Evaluation. *Political Behavior* 12(1): 5–18.

Long, J. Scott. 1997. *Regressional Models for Categorical and Limited Dependent Variables*. Thousand Oaks, CA: Sage Publications.

Lord, Charles. G., Lee Ross, and Mark R. Lepper. 1979. Biased assimilation and attitude polarization: The effects of prior theories on subsequently considered evidence. *Journal of Personality and Social Psychology* 37: 2098–2109.

Lupia, Arthur. 1994. Shortcuts Versus Encyclopedias: Information and Voting Behavior in California Insurance Reform Elections. *American Political Science Review* 88(1): 63–76.

Maltzman, Forrest, and Lee Siegelman. 1996. The Politics of Talk: Unconstrained Floor Time in the U.S. House of Representatives. *Journal of Politics* 58: 810–821.

Markus, Hazel, and R. B. Zajonc. 1985. The Cognitive Perspective in Social Psychology. In *Handbook of Social Psychology*, edited by Gardner Lindzey and Elliot Aronson. New York: Random House.

Martin, Paul S. 2003. Voting's Rewards: Voter Turnout, Attentive Publics, and Congressional Allocation of Federal Money. *American Journal of Political Science* 47(1): 110–127.

Matthews, Donald R. 1959. The Folkways of the United States Senate: Conformity to Group Norms and Legislative Effectiveness. *American Political Science Review* 53: 1064–1089.

1960. *U.S. Senators and Their World*. Chapel Hill: University of North Carolina Press.

Matthews, Donald R., and James A. Stimson. 1975. *Yeas and Nays: Normal Decision-Making in the U.S. House of Representatives*. New York: John Wiley and Sons.

Mayhew, David. 1974. *Congress: The Electoral Connection*. New Haven, CT: Yale University Press.

McCarty, Nolan, Keith T. Poole, and Howard Rosenthal. 2006. *Polarized America: The Dance of Ideology and Unequal Riches*. Cambridge, MA: MIT Press.

McCrone, Donald J., and James H. Kuklinski. 1979. The Delegate Theory of Representation. *American Journal of Political Science* 23(2): 278–300.

McCrone, Donald, and Walter J. Stone. 1986. The Structure of Constituency Representation: On Theory and Method. *Journal of Politics* 48(4): 956–975.

McGraw, Kathleen M. 2000. Contributions of the Cognitive Approach to Political Psychology. *Political Psychology* 21(4): 805–832.

McGraw, Kathleen M., Edward Hasecke, and Kimberly Conger. 2003. Ambivalence, Uncertainty, and Processes of Candidate Evaluation. *Political Psychology* 24(3): 421–448.

McIntire, Mike. 2006. New House Majority Leader Keeps Old Ties to Lobbyists. *New York Times*, July 15.

McKissick, Gary. 1995. Policy Entrepreneurs and Recurring Issues in Congress. Typescript.

Mercer, Jonathan. 1996. *Reputation and International Politics*. Ithaca, NY: Cornell University Press.

Miler, Kristina C. 2007. The View from the Hill: Legislative Perceptions of Constituents. *Legislative Studies Quarterly* 32(4): 597–628.

2009. The Limitations of Heuristics for Political Elites. *Political Psychology* 30(6): 863–894.

Mill, John Stuart. 1975 [1861]. Considerations on Representation Government. In *Three Essays*. Oxford: Oxford University Press.

Miller, Warren E., and Donald E. Stokes. 1963. Constituency Influence in Congress. *American Political Science Review* 57(1): 45–56.

Mondak, Jeffrey J. 1993. Public Opinion and Heuristic Processing of Source Cues. *Political Behavior* 15: 167–192.

Mondak, Jeffrey J., and Robert Huckfeldt. 2006. The Accessibility and Utility of Candidate Character in Electoral Decision Making. *Electoral Studies* 25: 20–34.

Morris, Jonathan S. 2001. Reexamining the Politics of Talk: Partisan Rhetoric in the 104th House. *Legislative Studies Quarterly* 26(1): 101–121.

Nelson, Thomas E., Rosalee A. Clawson, and Zoe M. Oxley. 1997. Media Framing of a Civil Liberties Conflict and Its Effect on Tolerance. *American Political Science Review* 91(3): 567–583.

Nisbett, Richard, and Lee Ross. 1980. *Human Inference: Strategies and Shortcomings of Social Judgment*. Englewood Cliffs, NJ: Prentice-Hall.

Oleszek, Walter J. 2004. *Congressional Procedures and the Policy Process*. Washington, D.C.: CQ Press.

Olson, Mancur, Jr. 1965. *The Logic of Collective Action*. Cambridge, MA: Harvard University Press.

Overby, L. Marvin. 1991. Assessing Constituency Influence: Congressional Voting on the Nuclear Freeze, 1982–83. *Legislative Studies Quarterly* 16(2): 297–312.

Page, Benjamin, and Robert Shapiro. 1983. Effects of Public Opinion on Policy. *American Political Science Review* 77(1): 175–190.

1992. *The Rational Public*. Chicago: University of Chicago Press.

Page, Benjamin L., Robert Y. Shapiro, Paul W. Gronke, and Robert M. Rosenberg. 1984. Constituency, Party, and Representation in Congress. *Public Opinion Quarterly* 48(4): 741–756.

Payne, James L. 1980. Show Horses and Work Horses in the United States House of Representatives. *Polity* 12(30): 428–456.

Peffley, Mark, Jon Hurwitz, and Paul M. Sniderman. 1997. Racial Stereotypes and Whites' Political Views of Blacks in the Context of Welfare and Crime. *American Journal of Political Science* 41(1): 30–60.

Peltzman, Samuel. 1984. Constituent Interest and Congressional Voting. *Journal of Law and Economics* 27: 181–210.

Pitkin, Hannah F. 1967. *The Concept of Representation*. Berkeley: University of California Press.

Poole, Keith T. 1981. Dimensions of Interest Group Evaluation of the U.S. Senate, 1969–1978. *American Journal of Political Science* 25: 49–67.

Poole, Keith T., and Howard Rosenthal. 1985. A Spatial Model for Legislative Roll Call Analysis. *American Journal of Political Science* 29: 357–384.

1991. On Dimensionalizing Roll Call Votes in the U.S. Congress. *American Political Science Review* 85: 955–975.

Popkin, Samuel. 1991. *The Reasoning Voter: Communication and Persuasion in Presidential Campaigns*. Chicago: University of Chicago Press.

Quattrone, George A., and Amos Tversky. 1988. Contrasting Rational and Psychological Analyses of Political Choice. *American Political Science Review* 82(3): 720–736.

Rabe-Hesketh, Sophia, and Anders Skrondal. 2005. *Multilevel and Longitudinal Modeling Using Stata*. College Station, TX: Stata Press.

Rahn, Wendy M. 1993. The Role of Partisan Stereotypes in Information Processing about Political Candidates. *American Journal of Political Science* 37: 472–496.

Rahn, Wendy M., John L. Sullivan, and Thomas J. Rudolph. 2002. Political Psychology and Political Science. In *Thinking About Political Psychology*, edited by J. H. Kuklinski. Cambridge: Cambridge University Press.

Reingold, Beth. 1992. Concepts of Representation among Female and Male Legislators. *Legislative Studies Quarterly* 17(4): 509–537.

Reyes, R., W. Thompson, and Gordon H. Bower. 1980. Delayed Effects of Availability on Judgment. *Journal of Personality and Social Psychology* 39: 2–12.

Ripley, Randall B. 1969. *Power in the Senate*. New York: St. Martin's Press.

Roberts, Sam. 2008. "In a Generation, Minorities May Be the U.S. Majority." *New York Times*. August 13.

Romzek, Barbara S., and Jennifer A. Utter. 1997. Congressional Legislative Staff: Political Professionals or Clerks? *American Journal of Political Science* 41(4): 1251–1279.

Rosenstone, Steven, and John Mark Hansen. 1993. *Mobilization, Participation, and Democracy in America*. Chicago: University of Chicago Press.

Ross, Lee. 1977. The Intuitive Psychologist and His Shortcomings: Distortions in the Attribution Process. In *Advances in Experimental Social Psychology*, edited by L. Berkowitz. New York: Academic Press.

Salisbury, Robert H., and Kenneth A. Shepsle. 1981. Congressman as Enterprise. *Legislative Studies Quarterly* 6: 559–576.

Sanbonmatsu, Kira. 2002. Gender Stereotypes and Vote Choice. *American Journal of Political Science* 46(1): 20–34.

Schattschneider, E. E. 1960. *The Semisovereign People*. Hinsdale, IL: Dryden.

Schiller, Wendy. 1995. Senators as Political Entrepreneurs: Using Bill Sponsorship to Shape Legislative Agendas. *American Journal of Political Science* 39: 186–203.

2000. *Partners and Rivals: Representation in U.S. Senate Delegations*. Princeton, NJ: Princeton University Press.

Schwarz, Norbert. 1998. Accessible Content and Accessibility Experiences: The Interplay of Declarative and Experiential Information in Judgment. *Personality and Social Psychology Review* 2(2): 87–99.

Schwarz, Norbert, Herbert Bless, Fritz Strack, Gisela Klumpp, Helga Rittenauer-Schatka, and Annette Simons. 1991. Ease of Retrieval as Information: Another Look at the Availability Heuristic. *Journal of Personality and Social Psychology* 61(2): 195–202.

Schwarz, Norbert, Herbert Bless, Michaela Wänke, and Piotr Winkielman. 2003. Accessibility Revisited. In *Foundations of Social Cognition: A Festschrift in Honor of Robert S. Wyer, Jr.*, edited by Galen V. Bodenhausen and Alan J. Lambert. Mahwah, NJ: Lawrence Erlbaum Associates.

Schwarz, Norbert, and Leigh Ann Vaughn. 2002. The Availability Heuristic Revisited: Ease of Recall and Content of Recall as Distinct Sources of Information. In *Heuristics and Biases: The Psychology of Intuitive Judgment*, edited by Thomas Gilovich, Dale Griffin, and Daniel Kahneman. New York: Cambridge University Press. Pp. 103–118.

Shapiro, Catherine, David W. Brady, Richard Brody, and John Ferejohn. 1990. Linking Constituency Opinion and Senate Voting Scores: A Hybrid Explanation. *Legislative Studies Quarterly* 15(4): 599–622.

Shaw, Marvin E., and Philip R. Costanzo. 1970. *Theories of Social Psychology*. New York: McGraw-Hill.

Shepsle, Kenneth A. 1978. *The Giant Jigsaw Puzzle: Democratic Committee Assignments in the Modern House*. Chicago: University of Chicago Press.

Shepsle, Kenneth A., and Barry R. Weingast. 1987. The Institutional Foundations of Committee Power. *American Political Science Review* 81: 85–104.

Sherif, M., and C. I. Hovland. 1961. *Social Judgment*. New Haven, CT: Yale University Press.

Shotts, Kenneth W. 2002. Gerrymandering, Legislative Composition, and National Policy Outcomes. *American Journal of Political Science* 46(2): 398–414.

Simon, Herbert A. 1957. *Models of Man*. New York: John Wiley & Sons.

Sinclair, Barbara. 1989. *The Transformation of the U.S. Senate*. Baltimore: Johns Hopkins Press.

Smith, Eliot R. 1984. Attributions and Other Inferences: Processing Information about the Self versus Other. *Journal of Experimental Social Psychology* 20: 97–115.

1998. Mental Representation and Memory. In *The Handbook of Social Psychology*, edited by Daniel T. Gilbert, Susan T. Fiske, and Gardner Lindzey. New York: McGraw-Hill.

Smith, Richard A. 1984. Advocacy, Interpretation, and Influence in the U.S. Congress. *American Political Science Review* 78: 44–63.

Sniderman, Paul M., Richard A. Brody, and Philip E. Tetlock. 1991. *Reasoning and Choice: Explorations in Political Psychology*. Cambridge: Cambridge University Press.

Snijders, Tom, and Roel Bosker. 1999. *Multilevel Analysis: An Introduction to Basic and Advanced Multilevel Modeling*. London: Sage Publications.

Stein, Janice Gross. 1985. Calculation, Miscalculation, and Conventional Deterrence II: The View from Jerusalem. In *Psychology and Deterrence*, edited by Robert Jervis, Richard N. Lebow, and Janice Gross Stein. Baltimore: Johns Hopkins University Press.

1993. Building Politics Into Psychology: The Misperception of Threat. In *Political Psychology*, edited by Neil Kressel. New York: Paragon.

Stern, Philip M. 1988. *The Best Congress Money Can Buy*. New York: Pantheon Press.

Stimson, James A., Michael B. MacKuen, and Robert S. Erikson. 1995. Dynamic Representation. *American Political Science Review* 89(3): 543–565.

Stolberg, Sheryl Gay. 2006. Lobbyist Turns Senator but Twists Same Arms. *New York Times*, February 28.

Stone, Walter J. 1979. Measuring Constituency-Representative Linkages: Problems and Prospects. *Legislative Studies Quarterly* 4(4): 623–639.

Strattman, Thomas. 2002. Can Special Interests Buy Congressional Votes? Evidence from Financial Services Legislation. *Journal of Law and Economics* 45(2): 345–373.

Sulkin, Tracy E. 2005. *Issue Politics in Congress*. New York: Cambridge University Press.

2009. *Congressional Bill Sponsorship Data*. Urbana: University of Illinois.

Sullivan, John L., L. Earl Shaw, Gregory E. McAvoy, and David G. Barnum. 1993. The Dimensions of Cue-Taking in the House of Representatives: Variation By Issue Area. *Journal of Politics* 55(4): 975–997.

Sullivan, John L., and Eric M. Uslaner. 1978. Congressional Behavior and Electoral Marginality. *American Journal of Political Science* 22(3): 536–553.

Taber, Charles S. 1998. The Interpretation of Foreign Policy Events: A Cognitive Process Theory. In *Problem Representation in Foreign Policy Decision Making*, edited by Donald A. Sylvan and James F. Voss. New York: Cambridge University Press.

Tate, Katherine. 2003. *Black Faces in the Mirror: African Americans and Their Representatives in the U.S. Congress.* Princeton, NJ: Princeton University Press.

Taylor, Shelley E., and Susan T. Fiske. 1978. Salience, Attention, and Attribution: Top of the Head Phenomena. In *Advances in Experimental Social Psychology*, edited by L. Berkowitz. New York: Academic Press.

Tetlock, Philip E. 2005. *Expert Political Judgment: How Good Is It? How Can We Know?* Princeton, NJ: Princeton University Press.

Theriault, Sean. 2005. *Power of the People: Congressional Competition, Public Attention, and Voter Retribution.* Columbus: Ohio State University Press.

Thomas, Sue. 1994. *How Women Legislate.* New York: Oxford University Press.

Turner, Mark. 2000. Backstage Cognition in Reason and Choice. In *Elements of Reason: Cognition, Choice, and the Bounds of Rationality*, edited by Arthur Lupia, Matthew McCubbins, and Samuel Popkin. Cambridge: Cambridge University Press.

Tversky, Amos, and Daniel Kahneman. 1973. Availability: A Heuristic for Judging Frequency and Probability. *Cognitive Psychology* 5: 207–232.

1974. Judgment Under Uncertainty: Heuristics and Biases. *Science* 185: 1124–1131.

1982a. Availability: A Heuristics for Judging Frequency and Probability. In *Judgment Under Uncertainty: Heuristics and Biases*, edited by Daniel Kahneman, Paul Slovic, and Amos Tversky. Cambridge, UK: Cambridge University Press.

1982b. Judgments of and by Representativeness. In *Judgment Under Uncertainty: Heuristics and Biases*, edited by Daniel Kahneman, Paul Slovic, and Amos Tversky. Cambridge: Cambridge University Press.

1983. Extensional versus Intensional Reasoning: The Conjunction Fallacy in Probability Judgment. *Psychology Review* 90: 293–315.

Valentino, Nicholas, Vincent Hutchings, and Ismail White. 2002. Cues That Matter: How Political Ads Prime Racial Attitudes During Campaigns. *American Political Science Review* 96: 75–90.

Verba, Sidney, and Norman Nie. 1972. *Participation in America.* New York: Harper & Row.

Verba, Sidney, Kay Lehman Schlozman, and Henry E. Brady. 1995. *Voice and Equality: Civic Voluntarism in American Politics.* Cambridge, MA: Harvard University Press.

Verba, Sidney, Kay Lehman Schlozman, Henry Brady, and Norman H. Nie. 1993. Citizen Activity: Who Participates? What Do They Say? *American Political Science Review* 87(2): 825–840.

Wawro, Gregory. 2000. *Legislative Entrepreneurship in the U.S. House of Representatives.* Ann Arbor: University of Michigan Press.

2001. A Panel Probit Analysis of Campaign Contributions and Roll-Call Votes. *American Journal of Political Science* 45(3): 563–579.

Weisberg, Herbert F., Jon A. Krosnick, and Bruce D. Bowen. 1989. *Introduction to Survey Research and Data Analysis*. Chicago: Scott, Foresman.

Weissberg, Robert. 1978. Collective v. Dyadic Representation in Congress. *American Political Science Review* 72(2): 535–547.

Welch, Susan, and John G. Peters. 1983. Private Interests and Public Interests: An Analysis of the Impact of Personal Finance on Congressional Voting on Agriculture Issues. *Journal of Politics* 45(2): 378–396.

Welch, W. P. 1982. Campaign Contributions and Legislative Voting: Milk Money and Dairy Price Supports. *Western Political Science Quarterly* 35: 478–495.

Westen, Drew. 2007. *The Political Brain: The Role of Emotion in Deciding the Fate of the Nation*. New York: Public Affairs.

Whitby, Kenny J. 1997. *The Color of Representation: Congressional Behavior and Black Interests*. Ann Arbor: University of Michigan Press.

Whiteman, David. 1995. *Communication in Congress: Members, Staff, and the Search for Information*. Lawrence: University of Kansas Press.

Wilcox, Clyde, and Aage Clausen. 1991. The Dimensionality of Roll-Call Voting Reconsidered. *Legislative Studies Quarterly* 16: 393–406.

Will, George F. 2001. "Congress Just Isn't Big Enough." *The Washington Post*, January 14.

Williams, Melissa S. 1998. *Voice, Trust, and Memory: Marginalized Groups and the Failings of Liberal Representation*. Princeton, NJ: Princeton University Press.

Witko, Christopher. 2006. PACs, Issue Context, and Congressional Decisionmaking. *Political Research Quarterly* 59(2): 283–295.

Wleizen, Christopher. 2004. Patterns of Representation: Dynamics of Public Preferences and Policy. *Journal of Politics* 66(1): 1–24.

Wolman, Harold L., and Dianna M. Wolman. 1977. The Role of the U.S. Senate Staff in the Opinion Linkage Process: Population Policy. *Legislative Studies Quarterly* 2(3): 281–293.

Wright, Gerald C. 1989. Policy Positions in the Senate: Who Is Represented? *Legislative Studies Quarterly* 14(2): 465–486.

Wright, John R. 1985. PACs, Contributions, and Roll Calls: An Organizational Perspective. *American Political Science Review* 79: 400–414.

1990. Contributions, Lobbying, and Committee Voting in the U.S. House of Representatives. *American Political Science Review* 84: 417–438.

1996. *Interest Groups and Congress: Lobbying, Contributions, and Influence*. Needham Heights, MA: Allyn and Bacon.

Wyer, Robert S., and Thomas K. Srull. 1989. *Memory and Cognition in its Social Context*. Hillsdale, NJ: Lawrence Erlbaum Associates.

Zaller, John R. 1992. *The Nature and Origins of Mass Opinion*. Cambridge: Cambridge University Press.

Index

CPSIA information can be obtained at www.ICGtesting.com
Printed in the USA
BVOW07s1033060214

344148BV00001B/76/P

9 781107 677005